FREEDOM AND THE LAW

D0208345

Bruno Leoni

BRUNO LEONI

FREEDOM
AND
THE LAW

EXPANDED THIRD EDITION

FOREWORD BY ARTHUR KEMP

Liberty Fund

Indianapolis

LibertyPress is a publishing imprint of Liberty Fund, Inc., a foundation established to encourage study of the ideal of a society of free and responsible individuals.

The cuneiform inscription that serves as the design motif for our endpapers is the earliest-known written appearance of the word "freedom" (*ama-gi*), or "liberty." It is taken from a clay document written about 2300 B.C. in the Sumerian city-state of Lagash.

Freedom and the Law © 1961 by William Volker Fund. Reprinted 1972 under the sponsorship of the Institute for Humane Studies, Inc., Fairfax, VA. Reprinted 1991 by Liberty Fund, Inc. All rights reserved. All inquiries should be addressed to Liberty Fund, Inc., 7440 North Shadeland Avenue, Indianapolis, IN 46250-2028. This book was manufactured in the United States of America.

The Law and Politics © 1991 by Silvana Leoni. Printed by permission of Silvana Leoni.

Foreword © 1991 by Arthur Kemp.

Frontispiece courtesy of Silvana Leoni.

Library of Congress Cataloging-in-Publication Data

Leoni, Bruno.
    Freedom and the law / Bruno Leoni : foreword by Arthur Kemp. —
Expanded 3rd ed.
        p.   cm.
    Includes bibliographical references and index.
    ISBN 0-86597-096-3 (hardcover). — ISBN 0-86597-097-1 (paperback)
    1. Liberty.   2. Law—Philosophy.   I. Title.
K487.L5L46   1991
340′.1—dc20   91-3283
                                      CIP

10 9 8 7 6 5 4 3 2 1

922151

CONTENTS

FOREWORD
TO THE THIRD
EDITION

Bruno Leoni was a devoted proponent, in virtually all his activities, of those ideals we call liberal. He was a remarkably talented, intelligent, able, persuasive, multifaceted individual who might well have deserved the description Renaissance man, if it were not for the fact that the words have been so frequently misapplied.

Born April 26, 1913, Bruno Leoni lived a dynamic, intense, vigorous, and complex life as a scholar, lawyer, merchant, amateur architect, musician, art connoisseur, linguist, and—above all else—as a defender of the principles of individual freedom in which he so passionately believed. He was Professor of Legal Theory and the Theory of the State at the University of Pavia, where he also served as Chairman of the Faculty of Political Science, as Director of the Institute of Political Science, and as founder-editor of the quarterly journal, *Il Politico*. As a distinguished visiting scholar, he traveled all over the world, delivering lectures at the Universities of Oxford and Manchester (in England), and Virginia and Yale (in the United States), to mention only a few. As a practicing attorney, he maintained both his law office and his residence in Turin where he was also active in the Center for Methodological Studies. He found time, on occasion, to contribute columns to the economic and financial newspaper of Milan, *24 ore*. His successful efforts in saving the lives of many allied military personnel during the German occupation of northern Italy gained him not only a gold watch inscribed "To Bruno Leoni for Gallant Service to the Allies, 1945," but also the eternal gratitude of too many persons to mention. In September 1967, he was elected President of the Mont Pelerin Society at the Congress of the Society held in Vichy, France. This was the culmination of long years of service as Secretary of the Society to which he devoted a major portion of his time and energies.

Bruno Leoni died tragically on the night of November 21, 1967, at the height of his career, at the peak of his powers, and in the prime of his life. The community of scholars all over the world is poorer without him because it has been denied those promised accomplishments and achievements he could not live to finish.

For anyone interested in knowing something of the depth and breadth of his interests, there is no better place to start than a perusal of two sources. A compilation of the works of Bruno Leoni, together with poignant testimonials by his friends and colleagues, may be found in the volume entitled, *Omaggio a Bruno Leoni,* collected and edited by Dr. Pasquale Scaramozzino (Ed. A. Giuffre, Milan, 1969). A casual reading will convince even the most skeptical of his wide-ranging interests and scholarly erudition. There is also the cumulative index to *Il Politico,* the multidisciplinary quarterly he founded in 1950, prepared so ably by Professor Scaramozzino.

* * *

From 1954 through 1959, I had the pleasure, the duty, and the honor to administer six Institutes on Freedom and Competitive Enterprise held at Claremont Men's College (now Claremont McKenna College) in Claremont, California. The Institutes were designed to present a program of graduate lectures in economics and political science of special interest to those teaching related subjects as members of the faculties of American colleges and universities. At each of these Institutes three distinguished scholars were invited to present individually an analysis of freedom as the source of economic and political principles; an analysis of the development of the free market mechanism and its operation; and a study of the philosophical bases, characteristics, virtues, and defects of the private enterprise system.

Approximately thirty Fellows participated in each of these Institutes, selected from a long list of applicants and nominees—most were professors or instructors in economics, political science, business administration, sociology, and history. A few were research scholars or writers and, here and there, even an academic dean or two. In all, about 190 Fellows participated in the six Institutes, drawn from ninety different colleges and universities located in forty different states, Canada, and Mexico.

The distinguished lecturers, in addition to Professor Bruno Leoni, included Professor Armen A. Alchian, Professor Goetz A. Briefs, Professor Ronald H. Coase, Professor Herrell F. De Graff, Professor Aaron Director, Professor Milton Friedman, Professor F. A. Hayek, Professor Herbert Heaton, Professor John Jewkes, Professor Frank H. Knight, Dr. Felix Morley, Jacques L. Rueff, and Professor David McCord Wright.

In an effort to increase both the quality and quantity of international intellectual communication, so far as possible at least one lecturer at each Institute represented the European scholarly tradition.

* * *

I first met Bruno Leoni in September 1957 at the Mont Pelerin Society meeting in St. Moritz, Switzerland. We were both relatively new members of the Society, and both of us were presenting formal papers at one of the sessions. Following my return to the United States, I convinced my colleagues of the desirability of inviting Leoni as one of the lecturers for the upcoming Institute. Leoni eagerly accepted. In 1958, Leoni joined Milton Friedman and Friedrich Hayek (the latter two each doing a second stint) as lecturers at the Fifth Institute on Freedom and Competitive Enterprise that was held from June 15 to June 28. It was an impressive faculty. Professor Hayek's lectures ultimately became a part of his *Constitution of Liberty*, Professor Friedman's his volume on *Capitalism and Freedom*. Professor Leoni's lectures were to become *Freedom and the Law*.

Few who attended those sessions have forgotten them. The intellectual stimulation, the discussions lasting far into the night, the camaraderie—all these combined into a nearly perfect whole. Leoni, a superb linguist fluent in English, French, and German as well as his native tongue, delivered his lectures in English from handwritten notes. I suspect they were written at odd times and, certainly, on odd pieces of paper. They were constantly being amended as he became more accustomed to the group. He even brought with him a small book that had belonged to his father—a dictionary of American slang of the twenties. The lectures as well as some of the discussions were recorded on tape.

I prepared the first draft of *Freedom and the Law* from these notes and tapes at the strong urging of F. A. (Baldy) Harper and with financial assistance from the William Volker Fund. Later a professional editor added the finishing touches. This work was done with the author's express approval and retained the order and form of delivery as far as possible. This volume is as close to the original series of lectures as the constraints of the written word permit.

The original notes, manuscript, and tapes were deposited at the Institute for Humane Studies, Inc., in Menlo Park, California. When they moved to George Mason University, this material was deposited at the Hoover Institution of War, Revolution and Peace at Stanford University.

The first edition of *Freedom and the Law* was published by D. Van Nostrand Company of Princeton, New Jersey, in 1961 as part of the William Volker Fund Series in the Humane Studies. A second edition, virtually unchanged except for my new Foreword, was sponsored by the Institute for Humane Studies and published by Nash Publishing Company of Los Angeles in 1972. For this new edition, I have incorporated into the Foreword some of the remarks I made at the Mont Pelerin Society General Meeting in St. Vincent, Italy, on September 1, 1986, on "The Legacy of Bruno Leoni."

Although most of Leoni's works are in Italian, *Freedom and the Law* is not. At one of the Mont Pelerin Society meetings, an Italian gentleman asked if permission could be obtained to undertake an Italian translation. I replied affirmatively and enthusiastically, but nothing, so far as I know, has come of it. There have been two translations into Spanish; one published by the Centro de Estudios Sobre La Libertad in Buenos Aires (1961), and one by the Biblioteca de la Libertad, Union Editorial in Madrid (1974). Both translate the title as *La Libertad y La Ley*.

Since its first publication, *Freedom and the Law* has enjoyed, I am told, considerable attention by students of law and economics. For example, in 1986, two conferences on the book were held under the direction of Liberty Fund, Inc. One was held in Atlanta in May and the other in Turin, Italy, in September. The major new paper prepared for the former—"Bruno Leoni in Retrospect," by Peter H. Aranson—was subsequently published in the Summer 1988 issue of the *Harvard Journal of Law and Public Policy* along with *"Freedom and the Law:* A Comment on Professor Aranson's Article," by Leonard P. Liggio and Thomas G. Palmer.

In the opinion of many, *Freedom and the Law* is the least conventional and most challenging of all Leoni's works, promising to bridge, as Professor F. A. Hayek has written, "the gulf which has come to separate the study of law from that of the theoretical social sciences. . . . Perhaps the richness of suggestions which this book contains will be fully apparent only to those who have already been working on similar lines. Bruno Leoni would have been the last to deny that it merely points a way and that much work still lay ahead before the seeds of new ideas which it so richly contains could blossom forth in all their splendor."

That promised bridge, unfortunately, was never completed. It is our fond hope in publishing this third edition of *Freedom and the Law*, together with some related lectures given in 1963, that the many students and colleagues, friends and admirers of Bruno Leoni will expand and develop the ideas and suggestions contained herein beyond the point where his efforts so abruptly ceased.

Bruno Leoni was a remarkable student of law and political science and had a substantial understanding of economics as well. I recall with a mixture of sorrow and joy the many facets of a Bruno Leoni I admired, loved, and enjoyed being with.

June 1990
Arthur Kemp
Professor Emeritus, Economics,
Claremont McKenna College,
Claremont, California

FREEDOM

AND

THE LAW

INTRODUCTION

It seems to be the destiny of individual freedom at the present time to be defended mainly by economists rather than by lawyers or political scientists.

As far as lawyers are concerned, perhaps the reason is that they are in some way forced to speak on the basis of their professional knowledge and therefore in terms of contemporary systems of law. As Lord Bacon would have said, "They speak as if they were bound." The contemporary legal systems to which they are bound seem to leave an ever-shrinking area to individual freedom.

Political scientists, on the other hand, often appear to be inclined to think of politics as a sort of technique, comparable, say, to engineering, which involves the idea that people should be dealt with by political scientists approximately in the same way as machines or factories are dealt with by engineers. The engineering idea of political science has, in fact, little, if anything, in common with the cause of individual freedom.

Of course, this is not the only way to conceive of political science as a technique. Political science can also be considered (although this happens less and less frequently today) as a means of enabling people to behave as much as possible as they like, instead of behaving in the ways deemed suitable by certain technocrats.

Knowledge of the law, in its turn, may be viewed in a perspective other than that of the lawyer who must speak as if he were bound whenever he has to defend a case in court. If he is sufficiently well versed in the law, a lawyer knows very well how the legal system of his country works (and also sometimes how it does

3

not work). Moreover, if he has some historical knowledge, he may easily compare different ways in which successive legal systems have worked within the same country. Finally, if he has some knowledge of the way in which other legal systems work or have worked in other countries, he can make many valuable comparisons that usually lie beyond the horizon of both the economist and the political scientist.

In fact, freedom is not only an economic or a political concept, but also, and probably above all, a legal concept, as it necessarily involves a whole complex of legal consequences.

While the political approach, in the sense I have tried to outline above, is complementary to the economic one in any attempt to redefine freedom, the legal approach is complementary to both.

However, there is still something lacking if this attempt is to succeed. During the course of the centuries many definitions of freedom have been given, some of which could be considered incompatible with others. The result is that a univocal sense could be given to the word only with some reservation and after previous enquiries of a linguistic nature.

Everyone can define what he thinks freedom to be, but as soon as he wants us to accept his formulation as our own, he has to produce some truly convincing argument. However, this problem is not peculiar to statements about freedom; it is one that is connected with every kind of definition, and it is, I think, an undoubted merit of the contemporary analytical school of philosophy to have pointed out the importance of the problem. A philosophical approach must therefore be combined with the economic, the political, and the legal approaches in order to analyze freedom.

This is not in itself an easy combination to achieve. Further difficulties are connected with the peculiar nature of the social sciences and with the fact that their data are not so univocally ascertainable as those of the so-called natural sciences.

In spite of this, in analyzing freedom, I have tried, as far as possible, to consider it first as a datum, namely, a psychological attitude. I have done the same with constraint, which is, in a sense, the opposite of freedom, but which is also a psychological attitude on the part of both those who try to do the constraining and those who feel that they are being constrained.

One could hardly deny that the study of psychological attitudes reveals differences and variations among them, so that a univocal theory of freedom, and consequently also of constraint, with reference to the ascertainable facts is difficult to formulate.

This means that people belonging to a political system in which freedom is defended and preserved for each and all against constraint cannot help being constrained at least to the extent that their own interpretation of freedom, and consequently also of constraint, does not coincide with the interpretation prevailing in that system.

However, it seems reasonable to think that these interpretations on the part of people generally do not differ so much as to foredoom to failure any attempt to arrive at a theory of political freedom. It is permissible to assume that at least within the same society the people who try to constrain others and those who try to avoid being constrained by others have approximately the same idea of what constraint is. It can therefore be inferred that they have approximately the same idea of what the absence of constraint is, and this is a very important assumption for a theory of freedom envisaged as the absence of constraint, such as is suggested in this book.

To avoid misunderstandings, it must be added that a theory of freedom as the absence of constraint, paradoxical as it may appear, does not preach absence of constraint in all cases. There are cases in which people have to be constrained if one wants to preserve the freedom of other people. This is only too obvious when people have to be protected against murderers or robbers, although it is not so obvious when this protection relates to constraints and, concomitantly, freedoms that are not so easy to define.

However, a dispassionate study of what is going on in contemporary society not only reveals that constraint is inextricably intertwined with freedom in the very attempt to protect the latter, but also, unfortunately, that according to several doctrines, the more one increases constraint, the more one increases freedom. Unless I am wrong this is not only an evident misunderstanding, but also an ominous circumstance for the fate of individual freedom in our time.

People often mean by "freedom" (or "liberty") both the absence of constraint *and something else as well*—for instance, as a distinguished American judge would have said, "enough economic security to allow its possessor the enjoyment of a satisfactory life." The same people very often fail to realize the possible contradictions between these two different meanings of freedom and the unpleasant fact that you cannot adopt the latter without sacrificing to a certain extent the former, and vice versa. Their syncretistic view of freedom is simply based on a semantic confusion.

Other people, while contending that constraint is to be increased in their society in order to increase "freedom," merely pass over in silence the fact that the "freedom" they mean is only their own, while the constraint they want to increase is to be applied exclusively to other people. The final result is that the "freedom" they preach is only the freedom to constrain other people to do what they would never do if they were free to choose for themselves.

Today freedom and constraint pivot more and more on legislation. People generally realize fully the extraordinary importance of technology in the changes that are taking place in contemporary society. On the other hand, they do not seem to realize to the same extent the parallel changes brought about by legislation, often without any necessary connection with technology. What they appear to realize even less is that the importance of the latter changes in contemporary society depends in its turn on a silent revolution in present-day ideas about the actual function of legislation. In fact, the increasing significance of legislation in almost all the legal systems of the world is probably the most striking feature of our era, besides technological and scientific progress. While in the Anglo-Saxon countries common law and ordinary courts of judicature are constantly losing ground to statutory law and administrative authorities, in the Continental countries civil law is undergoing a parallel process of submersion as a result of the thousands of laws that fill the statute books each year. Only sixty years after the introduction of the German Civil Code and a little more than a century and a half after the introduction of the Code Napoléon the very idea that the law might not be identical with legislation seems odd both to students of law and to laymen.

Legislation appears today to be a quick, rational, and far-reaching remedy against every kind of evil or inconvenience, as compared with, say, judicial decisions, the settlement of disputes by private arbiters, conventions, customs, and similar kinds of spontaneous adjustments on the part of individuals. A fact that almost always goes unnoticed is that a remedy by way of legislation may be too quick to be efficacious, too unpredictably far-reaching to be wholly beneficial, and too directly connected with the contingent views and interests of a handful of people (the legislators), whoever they may be, to be, in fact, a remedy for all concerned. Even when all this is noticed, the criticism is usually directed against particular statutes rather than against legislation as such, and a new remedy is always looked for in "better" statutes instead of in something altogether different from legislation.

The advocates of legislation—or rather, of the notion of legislation as a panacea—justify this way of fully identifying it with law in contemporary society by pointing to the changes continually being brought about by technology. Industrial development, so we are told, brings with it a great many problems that older societies were not equipped to solve with their ideas of law.

I submit that we still lack proof that the many new problems referred to by these advocates of inflated legislation are really brought about by technology[1] or that contemporary society, with its notion of legislation as a panacea, is better equipped to solve them than older societies that never so blatantly identified law with legislation.

The attention of all the advocates of inflated legislation as an allegedly necessary counterpart of scientific and technological progress in contemporary society needs to be drawn to the fact that the development of science and technology, on the one hand, and that of legislation, on the other, are based respectively on *two completely different* and even contradictory ideas. In fact, the development of science and technology at the beginning of our modern era was made possible precisely because procedures

---

[1] It seems reasonable to believe that universal suffrage, for instance, has given rise to as many problems as technology, if not more, although it may well be conceded that there are many connections between the development of technology and universal suffrage.

had been adopted that were in full contrast to those that usually result in legislation. Scientific and technical research needed and still needs individual initiative and individual freedom to allow the conclusions and results reached by individuals, possibly against contrary authority, to prevail. Legislation, on the other hand, is the terminal point of a process in which authority always prevails, possibly against individual initiative and freedom. Whereas scientific and technological results are always due to relatively small minorities or particular individuals, often, if not always, in opposition to ignorant or indifferent majorities, legislation, especially today, always reflects the will of a contingent majority within a committee of legislators who are not necessarily more learned or enlightened than the dissenters. Where authorities and majorities prevail, as in legislation, individuals must yield, regardless of whether they are right or wrong.

Another characteristic feature of legislation in contemporary society (apart from a few instances of direct democracy in small political communities like the Swiss *Landsgemeinde*) is that the legislators are assumed to *represent* their citizens in the legislative process. Whatever this may mean—and this is what we shall try to discover in the following pages—it is obvious that representation, like legislation, is something altogether extraneous to the procedures adopted for scientific and technological progress. The very idea that a scientist or a technician should be "represented" by other people in the carrying on of scientific or technical research appears as ridiculous as the idea that scientific research should be entrusted, not to particular individuals acting as such even when they collaborate in a team, but to some kind of legislative committee empowered to reach a decision by majority vote.

Nonetheless, a way of reaching decisions that would be rejected out of hand in scientific and technological fields is coming to be adopted more and more as far as law is concerned.

The resulting situation in contemporary society is a kind of schizophrenia, which, far from being denounced, has been hardly noticed so far.

People behave as if their need for individual initiative and individual decision were almost completely satisfied by the fact of their personal access to the benefits of scientific and technological achievements. Strangely enough, their corresponding needs for individual initiative and individual decision in the political and legal spheres seem to be met by ceremonial and almost magical procedures such as elections of "representatives" who are supposed to know by some mysterious inspiration what their constituents really want and to be able to decide accordingly. True, individuals still have, at least in the Western world, the possibility of deciding and acting as individuals in many respects: in trading (at least to a great extent), in speaking, in personal relations, and in many other kinds of social intercourse. However, they seem also to have accepted in principle once and for all a system whereby a handful of people whom they rarely know personally are able to decide what everybody must do, and this within very vaguely defined limits or practically without limits at all.

That the legislators, at least in the West, still refrain from interfering in such fields of individual activity as speaking or choosing one's marriage partner or wearing a particular style of clothing or traveling usually conceals the raw fact that they actually do have the power to interfere in every one of these fields. But other countries, while already offering a completely different kind of picture, reveal at the same time how much farther the legislators can go in this respect. On the other hand, fewer and fewer people now seem to realize that just as language and fashion are the products of the convergence of spontaneous actions and decisions on the part of a vast number of individuals, so the law too can, in theory, just as well be a product of a similar convergence in other fields.

Today the fact that we do not need to entrust to other people the task of deciding, for instance, how we have to speak or how we should spend our leisure time fails to make us realize that the same should be true of a great many other actions and decisions that we take in the sphere of law. Our present notion of the law is definitely affected by the overwhelming importance that we attach to the function of legislation, that is, to *the will of other people* (whoever they may be) *relating to our daily behavior*. I try to make clear in the following pages one of the chief consequences of our ideas in this respect. We are actually far from attaining through legislation the ideal certainty of the law, in the practical sense that this ideal should have for anybody who must plan for

the future and who has to know, therefore, what the legal consequences of his decisions will be. While legislation is almost always
certain, that is, precise and recognizable, as long as it is "in
force," people can never be certain that the legislation in force
today will be in force tomorrow or even tomorrow morning. The
legal system centered on legislation, while involving the possibility that other people (the legislators) may interfere with our actions every day, also involves the possibility that they may change
their way of interfering every day. As a result, people are prevented not only from freely deciding what to do, but from fore-
seeing the legal effects of their daily behavior.

It is undeniable that today this result is due both to inflated
legislation and to the enormous increase of a quasi-legislative or
pseudo-legislative activity on the part of the government, and
one cannot help agreeing with writers and scholars like James
Burnham in the United States, Professor G. W. Keeton in England, and Professor F. A. Hayek, who, in recent years, have
bitterly complained about the weakening of the traditional legislative powers of Congress in the United States or the "passing"
of the British Parliament as a consequence of a corresponding
enlargement of the quasi-legislative activities of the executive.
However, one cannot lose sight of the fact that the ever-growing
power of governmental officials may always be referred to some
statutory enactment enabling them to behave, in their turn, as
legislators and to interfere in that way, almost at will, with every
kind of private interest and activity. The paradoxical situation of
our times is that we are governed by men, not, as the classical
Aristotelian theory would contend, because we are not governed
by laws, but because we *are*. In this situation it would be of very
little use to invoke the law against such men. Machiavelli himself
would not have been able to contrive a more ingenious device to
dignify the will of a tyrant who pretends to be a simple official
acting within the framework of a perfectly legal system.

If one values individual freedom of action and decision, one
cannot avoid the conclusion that there must be something wrong
with the whole system.

I do not maintain that legislation should be entirely discarded.
Probably this has never happened in any country at any time. I
do maintain, however, that legislation is actually incompatible

with individual initiative and decision when it reaches a limit that contemporary society seems already to have gone far beyond.

My earnest suggestion is that *those who value individual freedom should reassess the place of the individual within the legal system as a whole.* It is no longer a question of defending this or that particular freedom—to trade, to speak, to associate with other people, etc.; nor is it a question of deciding what special "good" kind of legislation we should adopt instead of a "bad" one. It is a question of deciding whether individual freedom is compatible in principle with the present system centered on and almost completely identified with legislation. This may seem like a radical view. I do not deny that it is. But radical views are sometimes more fruitful than syncretistic theories that serve to conceal the problems more than they solve them.

Fortunately we do not need to take refuge in Utopia in order to find legal systems different from the present ones. Both Roman and English history teach us, for instance, a completely different lesson from that of the advocates of inflated legislation in the present age. Everybody today pays lip service to the Romans no less than to the English for their legal wisdom. Very few realize, however, what this wisdom consisted in, that is, how independent of legislation those systems were in so far as the ordinary life of the people was concerned, and consequently how great the sphere of individual freedom was both in Rome and in England during the very centuries when their respective legal systems were most flourishing and successful. One even wonders why anyone still studies the history of Roman or of English law if this essential fact about both is to remain largely forgotten or simply ignored.

Both the Romans and the English shared the idea that the law is something to be *discovered* more than to be *enacted* and that nobody is so powerful in his society as to be in a position to identify his own will with the law of the land. The task of "discovering" the law was entrusted in their countries to the jurisconsults and to the judges, respectively—two categories of people who are comparable, at least to a certain extent, to the scientific experts of today. This fact appears the more striking when we consider that Roman magistrates, on the one hand, and the British Parliament, on the other, had, and the latter still has, in principle, almost despotic powers over the citizens.

For centuries, even on the Continent, legal tradition was far from gravitating around legislation. The adoption of Justinian's *Corpus Juris* in the Continental countries resulted in a peculiar activity on the part of the jurists, whose task it was once again to find out what the law was, and this, to a great extent, independently of the will of the rulers of each country. Thus, Continental law was called, quite appropriately, "lawyers' law" (*Juristenrecht*) and never lost this character, not even under the absolutist regimes preceding the French Revolution. Even the new era of legislation at the beginning of the nineteenth century began with the very modest idea of reassessing and restating lawyers' law by *rewriting* it afresh in the codes, but not in the least by *subverting* it through them. Legislation was intended chiefly as a compilation of past rulings, and its advocates used to stress precisely its advantages as an unequivocal and clear-cut abridgment as compared with the rather chaotic mass of individual legal works on the part of the lawyers. As a parallel phenomenon, written constitutions were adopted on the Continent primarily as a way of putting into black and white the series of principles already laid down piecemeal by English judges as far as the English constitution had been concerned. In the nineteenth-century Continental countries both codes and constitutions were conceived as means of expressing the law as something that was by no means identical with the contingent will of the people who were enacting these codes and constitutions.

In the meanwhile, the increasing importance of legislation in the Anglo-Saxon countries had chiefly the same function and corresponded to the same idea, namely, that of restating and epitomizing the existing law as it had been elaborated by the courts down through the centuries.

Today, both in the Anglo-Saxon and in the Continental countries, the picture has almost completely changed. Ordinary legislation and even constitutions and codes are more and more presented as the direct expression of the contingent will of the people who enact them, while often the underlying idea is that their function is to state, not what the law is as a result of a secular process, but what the law *should be* as a result of a completely new approach and of unprecedented decisions.

While the man on the street is becoming accustomed to this

new meaning of legislation, he is adapting himself more and more to the notion of it as corresponding, not to a "common" will, that is, a will that may be presumed as existent in all citizens, but to the expression of the particular will of certain individuals and groups who were lucky enough to have a contingent majority of legislators on their side at a given moment.

In this way, legislation has undergone a very peculiar development. It has come to resemble more and more a sort of *diktat* that the winning majorities in the legislative assemblies impose upon the minorities, often with the result of overturning long-established individual expectations and creating completely unprecedented ones. The succumbing minorities, in their turn, adjust themselves to their defeat only because they hope to become sooner or later a winning majority and be in the position of treating in a similar way the people belonging to the contingent majority of today. In fact, majorities may be built and pulled down within legislatures according to a regular procedure that is now being methodically analyzed by certain American scholars—a procedure that American politicians call "log-rolling" and that we should call "vote-trading." Whenever groups are insufficiently represented in the legislature to impose their own will on some other dissenting group, they resort to vote-trading with as many neutral groups as possible within the legislature in order to place their intended "victim" in a minority position. Each of the "neutral" groups bribed today is in its turn prepared to bribe other groups in order to impose its own will on other intended "victims" tomorrow. In this way, majorities change within the legislature, but there are always "victims," as there are always beneficiaries of the sacrifice of these "victims."

Unfortunately, this is not the only grave disadvantage of the inflation of the legislative process today. Legislation always involves a kind of coercion and unavoidable constraint of the individuals who are subject to it. The attempt made in recent times by some scholars to consider the choices made by individuals in their capacity as members of a decision-making group (such as a constituency or a legislature) as equivalent to choices made in other fields of human action (e.g., in the market) fail to observe a fundamental difference between these two types of choice.

True enough, both the individual choice in the market and the

choices made by individuals as members of a group are dependent for their success on the behavior of other people. For instance, nobody can buy if there is nobody to sell. Individuals
making choices in the market, however, are always free to repu-
diate their choice, in part or as a whole, whenever they do not
like the possible results of it. Poor as it may seem, even this
possibility is denied to individuals trying to make their choices as
members of a group, whether a constituency or a legislature or
other. What the winning part of the group decides is deemed to
be decided by the group itself; and unless they leave the group,
the losing members are not even free to reject the result of a
choice when they do not like it.

It may be held by the advocates of inflated legislation that
this is an unavoidable evil if groups are to decide at all and
their decisions are to be effective. The alternative would be to
split the groups into an increasing number of smaller factions
and finally into individuals. In that event the groups could no
longer work as units. Thus, loss of individual freedom is the
price paid for the alleged benefits received from the groups'
working as units.

I do not deny that group decisions may often be reached only
at the cost of the loss of the individual's freedom to choose and,
concomitantly, to refuse to make a choice. What I wish to point
out is that group decisions actually are worth that cost *much less
frequently* than it would appear to a superficial observer.

Substituting legislation for the spontaneous application of
nonlegislated rules of behavior is indefensible unless it is proved
that the latter are uncertain or insufficient or that they generate
some evil that legislation could avoid while maintaining the advantages of the previous system. This preliminary assessment is
simply unthought of by contemporary legislators. On the contrary, they seem to think that legislation is always good in itself
and that the burden of the proof is upon the people who do not
agree. My humble suggestion is that their implication that a law
(even a bad law) is better than nothing should be much more
supported by evidence than it is.

On the other hand, only if we fully realize how much constraint is implied by the very process of legislation are we in a
position to decide how far we should go in introducing any legis-

lative process whatsoever while trying at the same time to preserve individual freedom.

It seems to be unquestionable that we should, on this basis, reject the resort to legislation *whenever it is used merely as a means of subjecting minorities in order to treat them as losers in the field.* It seems also unquestionable that we should reject the legislative process *whenever it is possible for the individuals involved to attain their objectives without depending upon the decision of a group and without actually constraining any other people to do what they would never do without constraint.* Finally, it seems simply obvious that *whenever any doubt arises about the advisability of the legislative process as compared with some other kind of process having for its object the determination of the rules of our behavior, the adoption of the legislative process ought to be the result of a very accurate assessment.*

If we were to submit existing legislation to the kind of trial I am here proposing, I wonder how much of it would survive.

A completely different question is to ascertain how such a trial could be carried out. I do not contend that it could be easily accomplished. Too many vested interests and too many prejudices are obviously ready to defend the inflation of the legislative process in contemporary society. However, unless I am wrong, everybody will be confronted sooner or later with the problem of a resulting situation that seems to promise nothing but perpetual unrest and general oppression.

A very old principle appears to have been violated in contemporary society—a principle already enunciated in the Gospel and, much earlier, in the Confucian philosophy: "Do not do unto others what you would not wish others to do unto you." I do not know of any other statement in the modern philosophy of freedom that sounds so strikingly concise as this. It may seem dull in comparison with the sophisticated formulae sometimes clothed in obscure mathematical symbols that people seem to like so much today in economics as well as in political science. Nevertheless, the Confucian principle would appear to be still applicable for the restoration and the preservation of individual freedom at the present time.

To be sure, the task of finding out what people would not want others to do to them is not easy. However, it seems to be comparatively easier than the task of determining what people would like to do by themselves or in collaboration with others. The common will, conceived as the will common to each and every member of a society, is much more easily ascertainable, as far as its content is concerned, in the "negative" way already evidenced by the Confucian principle than in any other "positive" way. Nobody would contest the fact that an inquiry among any group whatsoever conducted with the object of ascertaining what its members do *not* want to suffer as a result of the direct action of other people on them would give clearer and more precise results than any inquiry relating to their wishes in other respects. Indeed, the celebrated rule of "self-protection" propounded by John Stuart Mill not only can be reduced to the Confucian principle but becomes actually applicable only if so reduced, for nobody could effectively decide what is and what is not harmful to any particular individual in a given society without relying in the end upon the judgment of each member of that society. It is for all of them to define what is harmful, and this is, in fact, what any one of them would not want others to do to him.

Now experience shows that, in a sense, there are no minorities in any group relating to a whole series of things that "should not be done." Even people who are possibly ready to do these things to others admit that they do not want others to do these same things to them.

Pointing out this simple truth is not the same as saying that there is no difference between one group or one society and another in this respect, still less that any group or society always retains the same feelings and convictions throughout its history. But no historism and no relativism could prevent us from recognizing that in any society feelings and convictions relating to actions that should *not* be done are much more homogeneous and easily identifiable than any other kind of feelings and convictions. Legislation protecting people against what they do not want other people to do to them is likely to be more easily determinable and more generally successful than any kind of legislation based on other "positive" desires of the same individuals. In fact, such desires are not only usually much less homogeneous and compatible with one another than the "negative" ones, but are also often very difficult to ascertain.

To be sure, as some theorists emphasize, "there is always some

interrelation between the state machinery which produces legislative changes and the social opinion of the community in which
they are intended to operate."[2] The only trouble is that this interrelation may mean very little in disclosing the "social opinion
of the community" (whatever this may mean) and even less in
expressing the actual opinions of the people concerned. There is
no such thing as "social opinion" in many cases, nor is there any
convincing reason to dignify as "social opinion" the private opinions of groups and individuals who happen to be in a position to
enact the law in those cases, often at the expense of other groups
and individuals.

To contend that legislation is "necessary" whenever other
means fail to "discover" the opinion of the people concerned
would only be another way of evading the solution of the problem. If other means fail, this is no reason to infer that legislation
does not. Either we assume that a "social opinion" on the matter
concerned does not exist or that it exists but is very difficult to
discover. In the first case, introducing legislation implies that this
is a good alternative to the lack of a "social opinion"; in the
latter case, introducing legislation implies that the legislators
know how to discover the otherwise undiscoverable "social opinion." In either case one or the other of these assumptions should
be carefully proved before legislation is introduced, but it is only
too obvious that nobody attempts to do so, least of all the legislators. The suitability or even the necessity of the alternative (i.e.,
legislation) appears to be simply taken for granted even by theorists who should know better. They like to state that "what could
once be regarded as more or less technical lawyers' law may today be a matter of urgent economic and social policies," that is,
of statutory regulations.[3] However, both the way of ascertaining
what is "urgent" and the criteria required to decide its urgency,
including the reference to "social opinion" in this respect, remain in the dark, while the possibility of reaching a satisfactory
conclusion by way of a statute is simply taken for granted. It
seems to be only a question of enacting a statute—and that is all.

The advocates of inflated legislation at the present time have

---

[2] W. Friedmann, *Law in a Changing Society* (London: Stevens & Sons, 1959), p. 7.
[3] Ibid., p. 30.

drawn from the reasonable assumption that no society is centered on exactly the same convictions as other societies and that,
moreover, many convictions and feelings are not easily identifiable within the same society the very peculiar conclusion that
therefore what real people decide or do not decide within a society
should be neglected altogether and replaced by what any handful
of legislators may happen to decide for them at any time.

In this way, legislation is conceived as an assured means of
introducing homogeneity where there was none and rules where
there were none. Thus, legislation appears to be "rational," or,
as Max Weber would have said, "one of the characteristic com-
ponents of a process of rationalization. . . . penetrating into all
spheres of communal action." But, as Weber himself took care to
emphasize, only a limited measure of success can be attained
through the extension of legislation and the threat of coercion
that supports it. This is due not only to the fact that, as Weber
again pointed out, "the most drastic means of coercion and punishment are bound to fail where the subjects remain recalci-
trant" and that "the power of law over economic conduct has in
many respects grown weaker rather than stronger as compared
with earlier conditions." Legislation may have and actually has in
many cases today a negative effect on the very efficacy of the
rules and on the homogeneity of the feelings and convictions
already prevailing in a given society. For legislation may also deliberately or accidentally disrupt homogeneity by destroying established rules and by nullifying existing conventions and
agreements that have hitherto been voluntarily accepted and
kept. Even more disruptive is the fact that the very possibility of
nullifying agreements and conventions through supervening legislation tends in the long run to induce people to fail to rely on
any existing conventions or to keep any accepted agreements.
On the other hand, the continual change of rules brought about
by inflated legislation prevents it from replacing successfully and
enduringly the set of nonlegislative rules (usages, conventions,
agreements) that happen to be destroyed in the process. What
could have been deemed a "rational" process then proves in the
end to be self-defeating.

This fact cannot be ignored simply by saying that the idea of a
"limited" sphere of state norms "has now lost its validity and

meaning in the increasingly industrialized and articulated society of our time."[4]

One may well say that von Savigny's deprecation, at the beginning of the last century, of the trend toward codification and written legislation in general seems to have faded among the clouds of history. One may also observe that at the beginning of the present century a similar fate appears to have befallen the reliance placed by Eugen Ehrlich on the "living law of the people" as against legislation enacted by the "representatives" of the people. However, not only do Savigny's and Ehrlich's criticisms of legislation remain unrefuted today, but the serious problems they raised in their own times, far from having been eliminated, are proving more and more difficult to solve or even to ignore in the present age.

This is certainly due, among other things, to the conventional faith of our time in the virtues of "representative" democracy, notwithstanding the fact that "representation" appears to be a very dubious process even to those experts on politics who would not go so far as to say with Schumpeter that representative democracy today is a "sham." This faith may prevent one from recognizing that the more numerous the people are whom one tries to "represent" through the legislative process and the more numerous the matters in which one tries to represent them, the less the word "representation" has a meaning referable to the actual will of actual people other than that of the persons named as their "representatives."

The demonstration—already adduced in the early twenties by economists like Max Weber, B. Brutzkus, and, more completely, Professor Ludwig von Mises—that a centralized economy run by a committee of directors suppressing market prices and proceeding without them does not work because the directors cannot know, without the continuous revelation of the market, what the demand or the supply would be has remained so far unchallenged by any acceptable argument advanced by its adversaries, such as Oskar Lange, Fred M. Taylor, H. D. Dickinson, and other supporters of a pseudo-competitive solution of the problem. Indeed, this demonstration may be deemed the most important

---

[4] Ibid., p. 4.

and lasting contribution made by the economists to the cause of individual freedom in our time. *However, its conclusions may be considered only as a special case of a more general realization that no legislator would be able to establish by himself, without some kind of continuous collaboration on the part of all the people concerned, the rules governing the actual behavior of everybody in the endless relationships that each has with everybody else.* No public opinion polls, no referenda, no consultations would really put the legislators in a position to determine these rules, any more than a similar procedure could put the directors of a planned economy in a position to discover the total demand and supply of all commodities and services. The actual behavior of people is continuously adapting itself to changing conditions. Moreover, actual behavior is not to be confused with the expression of opinions like those emerging from public opinion polls and similar enquiries, any more than the verbal expression of wishes and desires is to be confused with "effective" demand in the market.

The inescapable conclusion is that in order to restore to the word "representation" its original, reasonable meaning, there should be a drastic reduction either in the number of those "represented" or in the number of matters in regard to which they are allegedly represented, or in both.

It is difficult to admit, however, that a reduction in the number of those represented would be compatible with individual freedom if we assume that they are entitled to express their own will at least as electors. On the other hand, a reduction in the number of matters in regard to which people are to be represented does definitely result in a corresponding increase in the number of matters in regard to which people can make free decisions as individuals without being "represented" at all. *The latter reduction thus seems to be the only path left for individual freedom to take at the present time.* I do not deny that those who are accustomed to taking advantage of the process of representation, either as representatives or as members of represented groups, have something to lose by such a reduction. However, it is obvious that they also have much to gain from it in all those cases in which they would have been the intended "victims" of an unrestricted legislative process. The result should be, in the end, as favorable for the cause of individual freedom as, according to

Hobbes, it is for all human beings to be ultimately restrained from interfering with one another's lives and property so that they may emerge from the pitiful stage which he describes as "the war of all against all."

In fact, what we are often confronted with today is nothing less than a potential *legal war of all against all,* carried on by way of legislation and representation. The alternative can only be a state of affairs in which such a legal war cannot any longer take place, or at least not so widely or so dangerously as it now threatens to do.

Of course, a mere reduction in the area covered by legislation today could not completely solve the problem of the legal organization of our society for the preservation of individual freedom, any more than legislation now solves that problem by actually suppressing that freedom step by step.

Usages, tacit rules, the implications of conventions, general criteria relating to the suitable solutions of particular legal problems also with reference to possible changes in the opinions of people at any given time and in the material background of those opinions—all these are yet to be discovered. One may well say that this is an undeniably difficult, sometimes painful, and very often long process. It always was. According to the experience of our ancestors, the usual way of meeting this difficulty— as we have already pointed out—not only in Anglo-Saxon countries but everywhere in the West, was to entrust the process to specially trained persons like lawyers or judges. The very nature of the activity of such people and the extent of their personal initiative in finding legal solutions are still open questions. It cannot be denied that lawyers and judges are men like any others and that their resources are limited; neither can it be denied that they may be subject to the temptation to substitute their own personal will for the impartial attitude of a scientist whenever the case is obscure and their own deeply rooted convictions are concerned. Moreover, one could contend that the activity of such types of *honoratiores* in contemporary society seems to be as devoid of real sanction as that of the legislators, as far as a true interpretation of the people's will is concerned.

However, the position of lawyers and judges in the countries of the West as well as that of other *honoratiores* in similar societies in the past is fundamentally different from that of legislators, at least in three very important respects. First, judges or lawyers or others in a similar position are to intervene only when they are asked to do so by the people concerned, and their decision is to be reached and become effective, at least in civil matters, only through a continuous collaboration of the parties themselves and within its limits. Second, the decision of judges is to be effective mainly in regard to the parties to the dispute, only occasionally in regard to third persons, and practically never in regard to people who have no connection with the parties concerned. Third, such decisions on the part of judges and lawyers are very rarely to be reached without reference to the decisions of other judges and lawyers in similar cases and are therefore to be in indirect collaboration with all other parties concerned, both past and present.

All this means that the authors of these decisions have no real power over other citizens beyond what those citizens themselves are prepared to give them by virtue of requesting a decision in a particular case.

It means also that this very power is further limited by the unavoidable reference of every decision to decisions issued in similar cases by other judges.[5] Finally, it means that the whole process can be described as a sort of vast, continuous, and chiefly spontaneous collaboration between the judges and the judged in order to discover what the people's will is in a series of definite instances—a collaboration that in many respects may be compared to that existing among all the participants in a free market.

If we contrast the position of judges and lawyers with the position of legislators in contemporary society, we can easily realize how much more power the latter have over the citizens and how much less accurate, impartial, and reliable is their attempt, if any, to "interpret" the people's will.

In these respects a legal system centered on legislation resembles in its turn—as we have already noticed—*a centralized economy in which all the relevant decisions are made by a handful of directors, whose knowledge of the whole situation is fatally limited and whose respect, if any, for the people's wishes is subject to that limitation.*

---

[5] The special position of supreme courts in this last respect is only a qualification of the general principle underlined above, and we shall revert to it later.

No solemn titles, no pompous ceremonies, no enthusiasm on the part of applauding masses can conceal the crude fact that both the legislators and the directors of a centralized economy are only particular individuals like you and me, ignorant of 99 percent of what is going on around them as far as the real transactions, agreements, attitudes, feelings, and convictions of people are concerned. One of the paradoxes of our era is the continual retreat of traditional religious faith before the advance of science and technology, under the implied exigency of a cool and matter-of-fact attitude and dispassionate reasoning, accompanied by a *no less continual retreat from the same attitude and reasoning in regard to legal and political questions.* The mythology of our age is not religious, but political, and its chief myths seem to be "representation" of the people, on the one hand, and the charismatic pretension of political leaders to be in possession of the truth and to act accordingly, on the other.

It is also paradoxical that the very economists who support the free market at the present time do not seem to care to consider whether a free market could really last within a legal system centered on legislation. The fact is that economists are very rarely lawyers, and vice versa, and this probably explains why economic systems, on the one hand, and legal systems, on the other, are usually analyzed separately and seldom put into relation to each other. This is probably the reason why the strict relationship between the market economy and a legal system centered on judges and/or lawyers instead of on legislation is much less clearly realized than it should be, although the equally strict relationship between a planned economy and legislation is too obvious to be ignored in its turn by scholars and people at large.

Unless I am wrong, *there is more than an analogy between the market economy and a judiciary or lawyers' law, just as there is much more than an analogy between a planned economy and legislation.* If one considers that the market economy was most successful both in Rome and in the Anglo-Saxon countries within the framework of, respectively, a lawyers' and a judiciary law, the conclusion seems to be reasonable that this was not a mere coincidence.

All this does not mean, of course, that legislation is not useful—besides those instances in which it is a question of determining what "should not be done" according to the commonly shared feelings and convictions of people—in cases where there may be widespread interest in having some definite rules of behavior even when the people concerned have not yet come to any conclusions about what the content of such rules should be. It is well known that people sometimes prefer to have any rule whatsoever rather than none at all. This may happen in several contingent cases. The very need of some definite rule was probably the reason why, as Karl Hildebrand said of the archaic Roman legal rules, or as Eugen Ehrlich said of Justinian's *Corpus Juris* in the Middle Ages, people seem inclined to accept sometimes a rather rigid or obsolete or otherwise unsatisfactory rule before they find a more suitable one.

The problem of our time, however, seems to be just the contrary: not that of being content with unsuitable rules because of a fundamental scarcity and "hunger for rules," but that of getting rid of a host of harmful or at least useless rules because of a tremendous glut and, so to say, an indigestible surfeit of them.

On the other hand, it cannot be denied that the lawyers' law or the judiciary law may tend to acquire the characteristics of legislation, including its undesirable ones, whenever jurists or judges are entitled to decide ultimately on a case. Something of this kind seems to have occurred during the postclassical period of the Roman law when the emperors conferred on certain jurisconsults the power to issue legal opinions (*jus respondendi*) which became ultimately binding on judges in given circumstances. In our time the mechanism of the judiciary in certain countries where "supreme courts" are established results in the imposition of the personal views of the members of these courts, or of a majority of them, on all the other people concerned whenever there is a great deal of disagreement between the opinion of the former and the convictions of the latter. But, as I try to stress in Chapter 8 of this book, this possibility, far from being necessarily implied in the nature of lawyers' law or of judiciary law, is rather a deviation from it and a somewhat contradictory introduction of the legislative process under the deceptive label of lawyers' or judiciary law at its highest stage. But this deviation can be avoided and is therefore not an insurmountable obstacle to the satisfactory performance of the judicial function of determining what the will of the people is. After all, checks and balances may well be applied within the sphere assigned to the exercise of the judiciary function, namely, in the highest stages of it, just as they are applied among the various functions and powers of our political society.

One final remark needs to be made. What I am dealing with here are mainly *general* principles. I do not offer particular solutions for particular problems. I am convinced, however, that such solutions can be found much more easily in accordance with the general principles I have proposed than by applying others.

On the other hand, no abstract principle will work effectively by itself; people must always do something to make it work. This applies to the principles that I have advanced in this book no less than it does to any others. I do not seek to change the world, but merely to submit some modest ideas that should be, unless I am wrong, carefully and fairly considered before concluding, as do the advocates of inflated legislation, that things are unchangeable and, although not the best, are the inevitable response to our needs in contemporary society.

1

WHICH FREEDOM?

Abraham Lincoln, in a speech at Baltimore in 1864, recognized both the difficulty of defining "freedom" and the fact that the Civil War between the North and the South was based, in a way, on a misunderstanding related to that word. "The world," he said, "has never had a good definition of the word 'liberty.' . . . In using the same word, we do not mean the same thing."[1]

In fact, it is not easy to define "freedom" or to be aware completely of what we are doing when we define it. If we want to define "freedom," we must first decide the purpose of our definition. A "realistic" approach removes the preliminary problem: "freedom" is something that is simply "there," and the only question is to find the proper words to describe it.

An example of a "realistic" definition of freedom is that given by Lord Acton at the beginning of his *History of Freedom*: "By liberty I mean assurance that every man shall be protected in doing what he believes to be his duty against the influence of authority and majorities, custom and opinion." Many critics would say that there is no reason to call "freedom" only the assurance that every man shall be protected in doing what he believes to be his *duty,* and not, for example, his *right* or his *pleasure*; nor is there any reason to say that this protection ought to be assured only against majorities or authority, and not against minorities and individual citizens.

As a matter of fact, when Lord Acton, at Bridgenorth in 1877, delivered his famous lectures on the history of freedom, the respect accorded to religious minorities by the English authorities

---

[1] Quoted in Maurice Cranston, *Freedom* (London: Longmans, Green & Co., 1953), p. 13.

and the English majority was still one of the big issues of the political life of the Victorian age in the United Kingdom. With the abrogation of such discriminatory laws as the Corporation Act of 1661 and the Test Act of 1673, and with the admission, in 1870, of the Protestant Dissenters and of the Catholics (the Papists, as they were called) to the universities of Oxford and Cambridge, the so-called Free Churches had just won a battle that had lasted two centuries. Previously these universities had been open only to students belonging to the Reformed Church of England. Lord Acton, as is known, was himself a Catholic and for this reason had been prevented, much against his will, from attending Cambridge. The "freedom" he had in mind was the freedom that Franklin Delano Roosevelt, in the most famous of his slogans, called "freedom of religion." Lord Acton, as a Catholic, belonged to a religious minority at a time when respect for religious minorities in England was beginning to prevail against the hostility of the Anglican majorities and against such acts of the legal authority as, say, the Corporation Act. Thus, what he meant by "freedom" was religious freedom. Most probably this was also what the members of the Free Churches in the United Kingdom and many other people in the Victorian age meant by "freedom"—a term that was then obviously connected, among other things, with legal technicalities like the Corporation Act or the Test Act. But what Lord Acton did in his lectures was to present his idea of "freedom" as freedom *tout court*.

This happens quite frequently. The history of political ideas evinces a series of definitions such as the one given by Lord Acton.

A more careful approach to the problem of defining "freedom" would involve a preliminary inquiry. "Freedom" is first of all a word. I would not go so far as to say that it is *only* a word, as several representatives of the contemporary analytical school, in their self-styled philosophical revolution, might maintain. Thinkers who begin by asserting that something is simply a word and conclude that it is nothing but a word remind me of the saying that one must not throw the baby out with the bath water.

But the very fact that "freedom" is first of all a word calls, I think, for some preliminary linguistic remarks.

Linguistic analysis has received increasing attention in certain quarters, especially after the Second World War, but it is not yet very popular. Many people do not like it or do not bother about it. Learned men not devoted to philosophical or philological matters are more or less inclined to think of it as an idle occupation. Neither can we receive much encouragement from the example of the contemporary analytical school of philosophers. After having focused their attention on linguistic problems and made the latter the center of their research, they seem more inclined, instead of analyzing, to destroy altogether the very meaning of the words belonging to the vocabulary of politics. Moreover, linguistic analysis is not easy. But I would suggest that it is particularly necessary in these times of semantic confusion.

When we try to define or simply to name what is generally called a "material" thing, we find it rather easy to be understood by our listeners. Should uncertainty arise about the meaning of our words, it would be sufficient, in order to eliminate the misunderstanding, simply to point to the thing we are naming or defining. Thus, two different words referring to the same thing and used respectively by us and by our listener would prove equivalent. We could substitute one word for the other, whether we speak the same language as our listener (as we do in the case of synonyms) or different languages (as we do in the case of translations).

This simple method of pointing out material things is the basis of all conversation among people who speak different languages or among people who speak a language and those who do not yet speak it—e.g., children. It was this that made it possible for early European explorers to make themselves understood by the inhabitants of other parts of the world and that still makes it possible for thousands of contemporary American tourists to spend their holidays, say, in Italy without knowing a word of Italian. In spite of this ignorance on their part they are understood perfectly for many practical purposes by Italian waiters, taxi drivers, and porters. The common factor in conversation is the possibility of pointing to material things like food, luggage, and so on. Of course, it is not always possible to point out the material things we refer to by our words. But whenever two different words refer to material things, they prove easily interchangeable. Natural scientists agree quite easily about the use of words designating newly discovered phenomena. Usually they choose Greek or Latin words, and their method is successful, since uncertainty can be avoided by pointing out which phenomena are designated by these words.

This calls to mind the wisdom of the reply made by an old Confucian pedagogue to his heavenly disciple, a very young Chinese emperor who had been asked by his teacher the name of some animals they met while taking a walk through the countryside. The young emperor replied, "They are sheep."

"The Son of Heaven is perfectly right," the pedagogue said politely. "I must add only that these kinds of sheep are usually called pigs."

Unfortunately, much greater difficulty arises if we try to define things that are not material and if our listener does not know the meaning of the word we are using. In such a case we cannot point out to him any material object. Our way of understanding each other is completely different and it is necessary to resort to altogether different ways of discovering a common factor, if any, between our language and his. Banal and self-evident as it appears, this fact is probably not noticed, or at least it is not emphasized sufficiently, when we consider the use of our language. We are so accustomed to our vocabularies that we forget the importance we attached to pointing out things at the beginning of our learning process. We are inclined to think of our linguistic achievements mainly in terms of definitions simply read in a book. On the other hand, as many of these definitions refer to material things, we often behave as if nonmaterial things were simply "there" and as if it were only a question of attaching to them a verbal definition.

This explains certain metaphysical trends among those ancient Greek philosophers who treated nonmaterial things—justice, for example—as if they were similar to visible, material things. It also explains more recent attempts to define the "law" or the "state" as if they were entities like the sun or the moon. As Professor Glanville Williams points out in his recent essay (1945) on the controversy concerning the word "law," the English jurist John Austin, the celebrated founder of jurisprudence, maintained that his definition of "law" corresponded to "law properly defined," without having the least doubt that there exists such a thing as "the law properly defined." In our day a view rather similar to that of Austin has been advanced by the well-known Professor Hans Kelsen, who boasted in his *General Theory of Law and the State* (1947) and still boasts of discovering that what is "properly called" the "State" is nothing but the legal order.

The naive belief that nonmaterial things can easily be defined comes to an abrupt end as soon as we try to translate, for instance into Italian or French, *legal* terms like "trust," "equity," or "common law." In all these cases not only are we unable to point to any material thing that would permit an Italian or a Frenchman or a German to understand what we mean, but we can find no Italian, French, or German dictionary that will give us the corresponding words in these languages. Thus, we feel that something has been lost in passing from one language to the other. As a matter of fact, nothing has been lost. The problem is that neither the French nor the Italians nor the Germans have exactly such concepts as those denoted by the English words "trust," "equity," and "common law." In a certain sense, "trust," "equity," and "common law" are *entities*, but as neither the Americans nor the English can simply point them out to the French or to the Italians, it is difficult for the former to be understood by the latter in this respect.

It is this fact that still renders it practically impossible to translate an English or American legal book into German or Italian. Many words could not be translated into corresponding words because the latter are simply nonexistent. Instead of a translation, it would be necessary to supply a long, cumbrous, and complicated *explanation* of the historical origin of many institutions, their present way of working in Anglo-Saxon countries, and the analogous working of similar institutions, if any, in Continental Europe. In turn, the Europeans could not point out to the Americans or to the English anything material to indicate a *conseil d'état*, a *préfecture*, a *cour de cassation*, a *corte costituzionale*, or the like.

These words are often so firmly rooted in one definite historical environment that we cannot find corresponding words in the language of other environments.

Of course, students of comparative law have attempted on several occasions to bridge the gap between the European and the Anglo-Saxon legal traditions. For instance, there is the very recent essay included in the *Bibliographical Guide to the Law of the United Kingdom*, published by the London Institute of Advanced Legal Studies and devoted mainly to foreign scholars, that is, to the students of "civil law." But an essay is not a dictionary, and this is precisely the point I am making.

Thus, reciprocal ignorance is the result of different institutions in different countries, and historical ignorance is the result of changing institutions within the same country. As Sir Carleton Kemp Allen reminds us in his recent book, *Aspects of Justice* (1958), most English reports of medieval cases are now simply unreadable, not only because they are written—as he so wittily puts it—in "dog Latin" and "bitch French," but also because the English (and everybody else) lack the corresponding institutions.

Unfortunately, this is not the only difficulty of being unable to point to material things in the definition of legal concepts. Words that have apparently the same sound may have completely different meanings relating to different times and places.

This is often the case with nontechnical words or with words originally having a technical use, but which were introduced into everyday language rather carelessly without paying heed to their technical sense or without even recognizing it. If it is unfortunate that strictly technical words, such as those belonging, for instance, to legal language, cannot be translated at all into corresponding words in other languages, it is even more unfortunate that nontechnical or half-technical words can be translated only too easily into other words in the same language or into cognate words of other languages that have a similar sound. In the first case a confusion is created between words that actually are not synonyms, while in the latter case people speaking a different language think that the meaning they attach to a word in their language corresponds to the different meaning you attach to an apparently similar word in yours.

Many terms belonging both to the language of economics and to the language of politics are typical in this respect. The German philosopher Hegel once said that anyone can determine the suitability of a legal institution without being a lawyer, just as

anyone, without being a shoemaker, can decide whether a pair of
shoes is suitable for his feet or not. This does not seem to apply
to *all* legal institutions. Few people actually are suspicious and
inquisitive about the framework of such legal institutions as contracts, evidence, etc. But many people think that political and
economic institutions are just their business. They suggest, for
instance, that governments must adopt or reject this or that policy in order to redress, say, the economic situation of a country
or to modify the terms of international trade or both.

All these people use what we call "ordinary language," which
includes many words that belonged originally to such technical
vocabularies as the language of law or of economics. These languages use terms in a definite and unambiguous way. But as soon
as such technical words are introduced into ordinary language,
they quickly become *nontechnical* or *half-technical* words (I use the
word "half" as in the expression "half-baked"), because no one
bothers to recognize their original meaning in the technical languages or to fix upon a new meaning for them in ordinary
language.

When, for instance, people speak of "inflation" in America,
they usually mean an increase in prices. Yet until quite recently
people usually meant by "inflation" (and they still mean this in
Italy) an increase in the quantity of money circulating in a country. Thus, the semantic confusion that can arise from the ambig-
uous use of this originally technical word is bitterly regretted by
those economists who, like Professor Ludwig von Mises, hold
that the increase in prices is the consequence of the increase in
the quantity of money circulating in the country. The use of the
same word, "inflation," to mean different things is considered by
these economists as an inducement to confuse a cause with its
effects and to adopt an incorrect remedy.

Another striking instance of a similar confusion is offered by
the contemporary use of the word "democracy" in several countries and by different people. This word belongs to the language
of politics and of the history of political institutions. Now it belongs also to ordinary language, and this is the reason why a great
deal of misunderstanding arises at present among people using
the same word with completely different meanings—say, the man
in the street in America and the political rulers in Russia.

I would suggest that a special reason why the meanings of half-technical words tend to be confused is that within technical languages (such as that of politics) the meaning of these words was originally connected with other technical words that often have not been introduced into ordinary language for the simple reason that they could not be translated easily or at all. Thus, applications that gave an unequivocal meaning to the original use of a word have been lost.

"Democracy," for instance, was a term belonging to the language of politics in Greece at the time of Pericles. We cannot understand its meaning without referring to such technical terms as *polis, demos, ecclesia, isonomia,* and so on, just as we cannot understand the meaning of contemporary Swiss "democracy" without referring to such technical terms as *Landsgemeinde, referendum,* etc. We notice that words like *ecclesia, polis, Landsgemeinde,* and *referendum* are usually quoted in other languages without being translated because there are no satisfactory words for that purpose.

Lacking their original connection with technical words, half-technical or nontechnical terms often go adrift in ordinary language. Their meaning can change according to the people using them, although their sound is always the same. To make matters worse, several meanings of the same word may prove mutually incompatible in some respects, and this is a continual source not only of misunderstandings, but also of verbal disputes or worse.

Political and economic affairs are the main victims of this semantic confusion, when, for instance, several types of behavior implied by different meanings of the same word prove to be mutually incompatible and attempts are made to grant them all a place in the same legal and political system.

I do not say that this confusion, which is one of the most obvious characteristics of the history of the countries of the West at the present time, is semantic only, but it is *also* semantic. Men such as Ludwig von Mises and F. A. Hayek have pointed out on several occasions the necessity of removing semantic confusions, not only for economists but for political scientists as well. It is a very important task for learned people to collaborate in the elimination of semantic confusion in the language of politics no less than in that of economics. Of course, this confusion, as Professor Mises frankly recognizes, is not always fortuitous, but corresponds in several instances to certain mischievous plans on the part of those who try to exploit the familiar sound of favorite words like "democracy" in order to convince others to adopt new forms of behavior.[2] But this is probably not the only explanation of a complex phenomenon that manifests itself all over the world.

I am reminded of what Leibniz once said about the way our civilization is threatened by the fact that after the invention of the printing press too many books might be written and diffused and too few would be actually read by each individual, with the probable result that the world could be plunged into a new era of barbarism.

As a matter of fact, many writers, chiefly philosophers, have contributed much to semantic confusion. Some of them have used words taken from ordinary language and given them odd meanings. In many cases they never bothered to state what they actually meant by using a word, or they gave rather arbitrary definitions that were at variance with those in the dictionaries, but that were accepted by readers and disciples. This practice has contributed, at least to some extent, to the confusion of the meanings accepted in ordinary language.

In many cases these definitions, purportedly more accurate and profound than the usual ones, were simply presented as the result of an inquiry about the nature of the mysterious "thing" that the writers wanted to define. Because of the connections between ethical and political subjects, on the one hand, and between economic and ethical subjects, on the other, some philosophers contributed, consciously or not, to an increase in the huge stock of semantic confusion and to the contradictions between the meanings of words in the ordinary language of today.

All that I have said on this topic applies as well to the word "freedom" and to its Latin synonym "liberty," and to certain derivative terms such as "liberal" and "liberalism."

It is not possible to point to a material "thing" when we refer to "freedom" in ordinary language or in the technical languages

---

[2] Evidence of planned semantic confusion of this kind may be found in the *Guide to Communist Jargon* by R. N. Carew-Hunt (London: Geoffrey Bles, 1957).

of economics and of politics to which this word belongs. Moreover, this word has different meanings according to the historical environments in which it has been used in both ordinary language and the technical languages of politics and of economics. We cannot understand, for example, the meaning of the Latin term *libertas* without making reference to such technical terms of the Roman language of politics as *res publica* or *jus civitatis* or to some other technical terms like *manus* (which designated the power of the *patres familias* over their wives, children, slaves, land, chattels, and so on) or *manumissio*, which designated the legal act—or rather the legal ceremony—by which a slave changed his status and became *libertus*. On the other hand, we cannot understand the meaning of "freedom" in the language of politics of modern England without referring to such other technical terms as *habeas corpus* or the *rule of law*, which have never been translated, so far as I know, into exactly corresponding words in other languages.

Regardless of its technical implications, the word "freedom" entered very early into the ordinary languages of Western countries. This implied sooner or later a disconnection of the word itself from several technical terms belonging to the legal or to the political language of these countries. Finally, in the past hundred years the word "freedom" seems to have begun to float unanchored (as a contemporary author might say). Semantic changes have been introduced at will by a number of different people in different places. Many new meanings have been proposed by philosophers that are at variance with the meanings already accepted in the ordinary languages of the West. Shrewd people have tried to exploit the favorable connotations of this word in order to persuade others to change their corresponding ways of behaving into new and even contrary ones. Confusions arose whose number and gravity have increased as the various uses of the word "freedom" in philosophy, economics, politics, morality, and so on, have become more numerous and serious.

The very word *free*, to take a trivial example, in its use in ordinary English, may or may not correspond to the French word *libre* or to the Italian *libero*. Of course, the Italians and the French attach to this word several meanings that correspond to the English and the American ones, such as when it is said that the American Negro became "free"—that is, was no longer in bondage—after the Civil War. However, neither the French nor the Italians ever use *libre* or *libero* in the same way as the English and the Americans use "free" to mean, for instance, that something is gratuitous.

It has become usual, especially in modern times, to speak of freedom as one of the basic principles of good political systems. The meaning of "freedom" as it is used to define or simply to name that principle is not at all the same in the ordinary language of each country. When, for instance, Colonel Nasser or the Algerian *fellagha* speak today of their "freedoms" or of the "freedom" of their countries, they are referring only, or also, to something that is completely different from what the Founding Fathers meant in the Declaration of Independence and in the first ten amendments to the American Constitution. Not all Americans are inclined to recognize this fact. I cannot agree with writers like Chester Bowles, who apparently maintains in his recent book, *New Dimensions of Peace* (London, 1956), that there is little or no difference in this respect between the political attitude of the English settlers in the American colonies of the British Crown and that of such people as the Africans, the Indians, or the Chinese, who are now praising "freedom" in their respective countries.

The English and American political systems have been imitated to a certain extent, and are imitated still in many respects, by all the peoples of the world. European nations have contrived some very good-looking imitations of these systems, and this is also due to the fact that their history and their civilization were somewhat similar to those of the English-speaking peoples. Many European countries, imitated now in their turn by their former colonies all over the world, have introduced into their political systems something similar to the English Parliament or to the American Constitution and thus flatter themselves that they have political "freedom" of the kind presently enjoyed by the English or the Americans or which these countries once enjoyed in the past. Unfortunately, even in countries which have, as Italy does, for example, the oldest European civilization, "freedom" as a political principle means something different from what it would mean if it were actually connected, as it is in both England and the United States, with the institution of *habeas corpus* or with the first ten amendments to the American Constitution. The rules may seem to be almost the same, but they do not work in the same way. Neither the citizens nor the officials interpret them as the English or the Americans do, the resulting practice being rather different in many respects.

I can find no better example of what I mean here than the fact that in England and the United States criminal cases must be settled—and are actually settled—by "a speedy and public trial" (as called for in the Sixth Amendment to the American Constitution). In other countries, including Italy, notwithstanding laws such as certain special articles (e.g., 272) of the Italian *Codice di Procedura Penale* that contain several provisions relating to persons suspected of a crime and kept in prison awaiting trial, a man who has been held to answer for a crime may stay in prison for as much as one or two years. When at last he is found guilty and condemned, he perhaps must be set free immediately since he has already spent in prison all the time of his sentence. Of course, if he is proved not guilty, no one can restore to him the years lost in jail. One is sometimes told that in Italy the judges are not sufficiently numerous and that the organization of the trials probably is not so efficient as it could be, but public opinion is obviously not alert or active enough to denounce these defects of the judiciary system, which do not appear so clearly incompatible with the principle of political freedom as they would to public opinion in England or the United States.

"Freedom," then, as a term designating a general political principle, may have only apparently similar meanings for different political systems. It must be pointed out also that this word may have different meanings and different implications at different times in the history of the same legal system, and, what is even more striking, it may have different meanings at the same time in the same system under different circumstances and for different people.

An example of the first case is provided by the history of military conscription in the Anglo-Saxon countries. Until comparatively recent times, military conscription, at least in time of peace, was considered both by the English and by the American people as incompatible with political freedom. On the other

hand, Continental Europeans such as the French or the Germans
(or the Italians since the second half of the nineteenth century)
considered it almost self-evident that they had to accept military
conscription as a necessary feature of their political systems without even wondering whether the latter could still therefore be
called "free." My father—who was Italian—used to tell me that
when he went to England for the first time in 1912, he asked his
English friends why they had no military conscription, confronted as they were with the fact that Germany had become a
redoubtable military power. He always received the same proud
reply: "Because we are a free people." If my father could visit
the English or the Americans again, the man in the street would
not say to him that because there is military conscription these
countries are no longer "free." The meaning of political freedom in these nations has simply changed in the meantime. Because of these changes, connections which were taken for
granted before are now lost, and contradictions appear which
are strange enough to the technicians, but which other people
accept unconsciously or even willingly as natural ingredients of
their political or economic system.

Unprecedented legal powers conferred upon trade unions
both in the United States and in the United Kingdom today are a
good example of what I mean by "contradictions" in this respect. In the language employed by the Chief Justice of Northern Ireland, Lord MacDermott, in his recent *Hamlin Lectures*
(1957), the Trade Disputes Act of 1906 "put trade unionism in
the same privileged position which the British Crown enjoyed
until ten years ago in respect to wrongful acts committed in its
behalf." This law accorded protection to a series of acts committed in pursuance of an agreement or combination by two or
more people in contemplation or furtherance of a trade dispute
which had been always actionable before—for example, acts inducing the breach of a contract of service or interfering with the
trade, business, or employment of some other person or with the
right of some other person to dispose of his capital or of his
labor as he wishes. As Lord MacDermott points out, this is a
broad provision and can be used to cover acts which are done
outside the trade or employment involved and which must inevitably cause loss or hardship to interests having no part in the

dispute. Another statute, the Trade Union Act of 1913, repealed by another Trade Disputes and Trade Union Act in 1927, but fully restored by the Trade Disputes and Trade Union Act of 1946 when the Labour Party had returned to office, gave British trade unions an enormous political power over their members and also over the whole political life of that country by authorizing the unions to spend the money of their members for purposes not directly related to trade and without even consulting the members themselves about what they actually wanted done with their money.

Before the passage of these Trade Union Acts there was no doubt that the meaning of political "freedom" in England was connected with the equal protection of the law, accorded, against the constraint of anyone, to everyone to dispose of his capital or of his labor as he pleased. Since the enactment of these statutes in Great Britain there is no longer protection against everyone in this respect, and there is no doubt that this fact has introduced a striking contradiction in the system so far as freedom and its meaning are concerned. If you are now a citizen of the British Isles, you are "free" to dispose of your capital and of your labor in dealing with individuals, but you are no longer free to do so in dealing with people who belong to trade unions or who act in behalf of trade unions.

In the United States, by virtue of the Adamson Act of 1916, as Orval Watts writes in his brilliant study of *Union Monopoly,* the Federal government for the first time used its police power to do what the unions probably "could not have accomplished without a long and costly struggle." The subsequent Norris-LaGuardia Act of 1932, in a certain sense the American counterpart of the English Trade Union Act of 1906, restricted federal judges in their use of injunctions in labor disputes. Injunctions in American and English law are court orders that certain people shall not do certain things which would cause a loss that could not be remedied later by a damage suit. As Watts pointed out, "injunctions do not make the law. They merely apply principles of laws already on the statute books, and labor unions often use them for this purpose against employers and against rival unions." Originally, injunctions were usually issued by federal judges in favor of employers whenever a large number of people with small means could cause damage with an unlawful purpose and by unlawful acts, such as the destruction of property. American courts used to behave in a way similar to that of the English courts before 1906. The English Act of 1906 was conceived as a "remedy" on behalf of labor unions against the decisions of the English courts, just as the Norris-LaGuardia Act of 1932 was intended to defend the unions from the orders of American courts. At first sight one might think that both the American and the English courts were prejudiced against the unions. Many people said so both in the United States and in England. As a matter of fact, the courts adopted against the unions only the same principles that they still apply against all other people who conspire, for instance, to damage property. Judges could not admit that the same principles that worked to protect people from constraint by others could be disregarded when those others were union officials or union members. The term "freedom from constraint," for the judges, had an obvious technical meaning that explained the issuing of injunctions to protect employers as well as everyone else from other people's constraint.

Nevertheless, after the passage of the Norris-La Guardia Act everyone became "free" in this country from the constraint of everyone else except in cases where union officials or union members wanted to constrain employers to accept their demands by threatening or actually causing damages to the employers themselves. Thus, the expression "freedom from constraint" in the particular case of injunctions has changed its meaning in America not less than in England since the passage of the American Norris-LaGuardia Act of 1932 and the English Trade Disputes Act of 1906. The American Wagner Labor Relations Act made things even worse in 1935, not only by limiting further the meaning of "freedom" on the part of the citizens who were employers, but also by openly changing the meaning of the word "interference" and therefore introducing a semantic confusion that deserves to be quoted in a linguistic survey of "freedom." As Watts has pointed out, "No one should *interfere* with the legitimate activities of anyone else if to *interfere* means the use of coercion, fraud, intimidation, restraint, or verbal abuse." Thus, a wage earner does not interfere with the owners of General Motors when he goes to work for Chrysler. But, as Watts points out in his essay, we could not say that he does not interfere if we had to apply to his behavior the criteria used by the Wagner Act to establish when an employer "interferes" with the union activities of the employees whenever he hires, for instance, nonunion employees in preference to union members. Thus, of this use of the word "interference," the extraordinary semantic result is that while union people do not interfere when they constrain employers to accept their demands by unlawful acts, employers do interfere when they do not constrain anyone else to do anything whatever.[3]

We are reminded of some strange definitions, such as the one given by Proudhon ("Property is theft"), or of the story of Akaki Akakievitch in Gogol's famous tale *The Overcoat*, in which a robber deprives a poor man of his overcoat, saying, "You have stolen my overcoat!" If we consider the connections that the word "freedom" has in ordinary language with the word "interference," we can have a fair idea of the extent to which a change such as the one we have seen may now affect the very meaning of "freedom."

If we ask what is actually the meaning of "freedom from constraint" in such present-day political and legal systems as the American or the English, we are confronted with tremendous difficulties. We must say, to be honest, that there is more than one legal meaning of "freedom from constraint," depending on the people who are constrained.

Most probably this situation is connected with a semantic change that huge pressure and propaganda groups have promoted in recent times and are still promoting all over the world in the sense given to the word "freedom" in ordinary language. Professor Mises is accurate when he says that the advocates of contemporary totalitarianism have tried to reverse the meaning of the word "freedom" (as it was previously more or less commonly accepted in Western civilization) by applying the word "liberty" to the condition of individuals under a system in which they have no right other than that of obeying orders.

[3] A recent essay by Roscoe Pound, former Dean of the Harvard Law School, entitled "Legal Immunities of Labor Unions," provides a detailed description of the immunities these organizations currently enjoy in American law. The essay is printed in *Labor Unions and Public Policy* (Washington, D.C.: American Enterprise Association, 1958).

This semantic revolution is probably connected in its turn with the speculations of certain philosophers who enjoy defining "freedom," in opposition to all the usual meanings of the word in ordinary language, as something that implies coercion. Thus, Bosanquet, the English disciple of Hegel, could state in his *Philosophical Theory of the State* that "we can speak, without a contradiction, of being forced to be free." I agree with Maurice Cranston when he suggests, in his recent essay on this subject, that such definitions of freedom are based mainly on a theory of the "bifurcated man," that is, of man as a "mind-body unit" that is at the same time rational and "irrational." Freedom thus would imply a sort of coercion by the rational part of man over the irrational part. But these theories often are strictly connected with the notion of a coercion that can be physically applied by self-styled "rational" people on behalf of, but also eventually against the will of, allegedly "irrational" people. Plato's theories seem to me the most notorious example in this respect. His philosophical notion of a bifurcated man is strictly connected with his political notion of a society in which rational men ought to rule the others, if necessary without regard to the latter's consent—like surgeons, he says, that cut and burn without bothering about the cries of their patients.

All the difficulties to which I have referred warn us that we cannot use the word "freedom" and be rightly understood without first defining clearly the meaning we attach to that word. The realistic approach to defining "freedom" cannot be successful. There is no such thing as "freedom" independent of the people who speak of it. In other words, we cannot define "freedom" in the same manner as we define a material object that everyone can point to.

2

"FREEDOM" AND "CONSTRAINT"

A more careful approach to the problem of defining "freedom" than the realistic one that we have here rejected would involve a preliminary inquiry concerning the nature and purpose of such a definition. It is customary to distinguish "stipulative" from "lexicographic" definitions. Both are descriptive of the meaning attached to a word; but the former refers to a meaning that the author of the definition proposes to adopt for the word in question, whereas the latter refers to the meaning that ordinary people give to the word in common usage.

Since the Second World War a new trend in linguistic philosophy has emerged. It recognizes the existence of languages whose purpose is not only descriptive or even not descriptive at all—languages that the school of the so-called Vienna Circle would have condemned as altogether wrong or useless. The adherents of this new movement grant recognition also to nondescriptive (sometimes called "persuasive") languages. The aim of persuasive definitions is not to describe things, but to modify the traditional meaning of words with favorable connotations in order to induce people to adopt certain beliefs or certain forms of behavior. It is obvious that several definitions of "freedom" may be and have been contrived in this way with the object of inducing people, for instance, to obey the orders of some ruler. The formulation of such persuasive definitions would not be a proper task for the scholar. On the other hand, the scholar is entitled to make stipulative definitions of "freedom." By doing so, a student may at the same time escape the charge of using equivocal defini-

43

tions for purposes of deception and relieve himself of the necessity of elaborating a lexicographic definition, the difficulties of
which are obvious because of the already mentioned multiplicity
of meanings actually given to the word "freedom."

Stipulative definitions may appear to be, on the surface, a solution to the problem. Stipulating seems to depend entirely on us
or at most also on a partner who agrees with us about what we
want to define. When the adherents of the linguistic school speak
of stipulative definitions, they emphasize the arbitrariness of
such formulations. This is evidenced, for instance, by the enthusiasm with which the advocates of stipulative definitions quote an
authority who is not properly a philosopher—at least not an
official one. This oft-quoted gentleman is Lewis Carroll, the brilliant author of *Alice in Wonderland* and *Through the Looking-Glass,*
who describes the impossible and sophisticated characters met by
Alice during her travels. One of these, Humpty Dumpty, made
words say what he wanted them to say and also paid them a sort
of salary for their service.

> "When *I* use a word," Humpty Dumpty said in a rather scornful
> tone, "it means just what I choose it to mean—neither more nor
> less."
> "The question is," said Alice, "whether you *can* make words mean
> so many different things."
> "The question is," said Humpty Dumpty, "which is to be master—
> that's all."[1]

When they speak of stipulative definitions, the analytical philosophers have in mind chiefly those of logic or of mathematics,
where everybody seems to be free to start when and where he
wants provided that he defines precisely the terms he employs in
his reasoning. Without entering into the complicated questions
relating to the nature of mathematical or logical procedures, we
feel obliged nonetheless to sound a note of warning against confusing these procedures with those of people who speak of matters like "freedom." A triangle is certainly a concept, whether or
not this concept is also something else—for instance, an object
of experience, of intuition, or the like. "Freedom," while pre-

---

[1] Lewis Carroll (Charles Lutwidge Dodgson), "Through the Looking Glass," in *The Lewis
Carroll Book,* ed. Richard Herrick (New York: Tudor Publishing Co., 1944), p. 238.

senting itself as a concept, is also what many people believe in as a reason for living, something they say they are ready to fight for, something they say they cannot live without. I do not think that people would fight for triangles. Perhaps a few mathematicians would do so. But many people say that they are prepared to fight for freedom just as they are prepared to fight for a piece of land or to protect the lives of their loved ones.

This is not intended to be a panegyric on behalf of freedom. The facts referred to here can easily be verified in the historical records of many countries or observed in everyday life. The fact that people are prepared to fight for what they call their "freedom" is related to the fact that they also say they have "maintained" or "lost" or "restored" their "freedom," although they never say that they have "maintained" or "lost" or "restored" triangles or other similar geometrical concepts. On the other hand, "freedom" cannot be actually pointed to; it is not a material thing. Even if considered as a material thing, "freedom" could not be the same for everybody, since there are different meanings of "freedom." Nevertheless, we probably can say that "freedom" is, at least for each person who speaks of it, a reality, a definite thing. "Freedom" may be a situation deemed suitable to those who praise it; it may be an object of nonsensorial experience inducing an awareness of nonmaterial things like values, beliefs, and so on. "Freedom" seems to be an object of psychological experience. This means that it is not conceived of by ordinary people simply as a word, as a nominal entity the meaning of which it is only necessary to agree on by means of a stipulation similar to those of mathematics or logic.

Under these circumstances, I wonder whether or not we can define "freedom" stipulatively. Of course, every definition is to some extent stipulative, since it implies a certain agreement about how a word is to be used. Even lexicographic definitions do not exclude stipulations concerning the way of describing, say, what people mean by a certain word of ordinary usage in France or in England or in both countries or all over the world. For instance, we can make stipulations about the languages to be taken into consideration in elaborating a lexicographic definition or about the choice to be made among the meanings of the same word when dictionaries give several. But in all such cases we never forget that there are some uses which are revealed by common dictionaries and which cannot be changed by stipulation without disregarding the meanings of the words as other people actually use them.

Stipulations are simply instrumental devices to convey to others something we want them to know. In other words, they are a means of communicating or transmitting information, but the information itself cannot be stipulated. We can stipulate that black shall be called "white," and white, "black," but we cannot make stipulations about the actual sensorial experiences which we communicate and to which we arbitrarily give the name "black" or "white." A stipulation is possible and also useful in so far as there is a *common factor* that makes its commun ition successful. This common factor may be an intuition in mathematics or a sensorial experience in physics, but it is never itself a subject of stipulation in its turn. Whenever a stipulation seems to be based on another stipulation, the problem of finding a common factor that permits the stipulation to function is simply postponed; it cannot be eliminated. This would be the limit of Humpty Dumpty's power if Humpty Dumpty were not a fictitious character in a children's tale, but a real person making stipulations with other persons about the use of a word.

It would be of little use, therefore, to make a stipulative definition of "freedom" that would not convey to other people some kind of information included in the very meaning of that word as already understood, and it may be questioned if the theorists, in speaking of stipulative definitions, had such a thing as "freedom" actually in mind.

Thus, if a stipulative definition of "freedom" is to have significance, it must transmit some information. It is doubtful whether information knowable only by the author of the definition would be of any interest whatever to other people who have no share in the content of that information. Being completely personal, it would be of little concern to others. Indeed, it would be impossible to reveal it to other people. An exclusively stipulative definition of "freedom" could not avoid this deficiency. Whenever political philosophers have proposed a stipulative definition of "freedom," they have not only wanted to transmit information about their personal feelings and beliefs, but also to remind others of feelings and beliefs that they considered as common to those whom they addressed. In this sense also the stipulative definitions of "freedom" proposed from time to time by political philosophers are more or less clearly concerned with some lexical use of the word "freedom" and therefore with some lexicographic research about it.

Thus, a really effective definition of "freedom" must be, in the last analysis, a lexicographic one, regardless of the fact that this will involve the difficulties of lexicographic research.

To sum up: "Freedom" is a word used by people in their ordinary language to mean special kinds of psychological experiences. These experiences are different at different times and in different places and are also connected with abstract concepts and technical words, but they cannot merely be identified with abstract concepts or reduced to a mere word. Finally, it is possible, and probably also useful or even necessary, to formulate a stipulative definition of "freedom," but stipulations cannot avoid lexicographic research because only the latter can reveal the meanings people actually attach to the word in ordinary usage.

"Freedom," by the way, is a word with favorable connotations. Perhaps it may be useful to add that the word "freedom" sounds good because people use it to point to their positive attitude toward what they call "being free." As Maurice Cranston has observed in his essay on *Freedom* (London, 1953) quoted above, people never use expressions such as "I am free" to mean that they are without something they consider to be good for them. No one says, at least in speaking of day-to-day affairs, "I am free from money" or "I am free from good health." Other words are used to express the attitude of people toward the absence of good things: they say that they lack something; and this applies, so far as I know, to all the European languages at present as well as in the past. In other words, to be "free" from something means "to be without something that is not good for us," while, on the other hand, to lack something means to be without something that is good.

Of course, freedom has little meaning when it is complemented only by the expression "from something," and we expect people to tell us also what it is that they are free to do. But the presence of a negative implication in the word "freedom" and in certain related words like "free" seems unquestionable. This negative implication is also present in derivative words connected with the term "liberty," which is simply the Latin counterpart of "freedom" and not a word with a different meaning.[2] For instance, "liberal" is a word that designates both in Europe and in America a negative attitude toward "constraint," regardless of the nature of the "constraint" itself, which in its turn is conceived of very differently by American and by European "liberals."

Thus, "freedom" and "constraint" in ordinary language are antithetical terms. Of course, one can like "constraint" or some kind of "constraint," like the Russian army officers of whom Tolstoy said that they liked military life because it turned out to be a sort of "commanded idleness." Many more people in the world like "constraint" than we probably imagine. Aristotle made a penetrating remark when he said at the beginning of his treatise on politics that people are divided into two broad categories, those who were born to rule and those who were born to obey rulers. But even if one likes "constraint," it would be an abuse of words to say that "constraint" *is* freedom. Nevertheless, the idea that "constraint" is something very closely connected with freedom is at least as old as the history of political theories in the Western world.

I think that the main reason for this is that no one can be said to be "free from" other people if the latter are "free" to constrain him in some way. In other words, everyone is "free" if he can constrain in some way other people to refrain from constraining him in some respect. In this sense, "freedom" and "constraint" are inevitably linked, and this is probably too often forgotten when people speak of "freedom." But "freedom" itself in ordinary language is never constraint, and the constraint that is linked inevitably with freedom is only a negative constraint; that is, a constraint imposed solely in order to make other people renounce constraining in their turn. All this is not merely a play on words. It is a very abridged description of the meaning of words in the ordinary language of political societies

---

[2] Notwithstanding the contrary opinion of Sir Herbert Read (quoted by Maurice Cranston, op. cit., p. 44).

whenever individuals have any power whatever to be respected or, as one might say, whenever they have any power of a negative kind entitling them to be called "free."

In this sense, we can say that the "free market" also inevitably implies the idea of a "constraint" in that all the members of a market society have the power to exercise restraint against people like robbers or thieves. There is no such thing as a "free market" with some constraining power superadded. A free market is rooted in a situation in which those engaged in market transactions have some power to constrain the enemies of a free market. This point probably is not emphasized sufficiently by those authors who, in focusing their attention on the "free market," end by treating it as the very antithesis of governmental constraint.

Thus, for instance, Professor Mises, an author whom I admire greatly for his adamant defense of the "free market" on the basis of lucid and compelling reasoning and a superb mastery of all the issues involved, says that "liberty and freedom are terms employed for the description of the social conditions of the individual members of a market society in which the power of the indispensable hegemonic bond, the state, is curbed lest the operation of the market be endangered."[3] We notice here that he has qualified as "indispensable" the hegemonic bond of the state, but he means by liberty, as he also says, "restraint imposed upon the exercise of the police power"[4] without adding exactly, as I would consider it reasonable to add from the point of view of a free-trader, that liberty means also restraint imposed on the exercise of the power of anyone else to interfere with the free market. As soon as we admit this meaning of liberty, the hegemonic bond of the state is not only something to be curbed, but also, and I would say first of all, something we make use of to curb other people's actions.

Economists do not deny, but also do not take into direct consideration, the fact that every economic act, as a rule, is also a legal act the consequences of which may be enforced by the au-

---

[3] Ludwig von Mises, *Human Action: A Treatise on Economics* (New Haven: Yale University Press, 1949), p. 281.

[4] Ibid.

thorities if, for instance, the parties to the transaction do not behave as they are expected to behave on the basis of their agreement. As Professor Lionel Robbins pointed out in his *The Nature and Significance of Economics,* studies of the connection between economics and the law are still rather unusual on the part of the economists, and the connection itself, although indisputable, is rather neglected. Many economists have debated about the distinction between productive and nonproductive work, but few have examined what Professor Lindley Frazer, in *Economic Thought and Language,* calls "misproductive" work— i.e., work that is useful for the worker, but not for those for whom, or *against* whom, he works. "Misproductive" work, such as that of beggars, blackmailers, robbers, and thieves, remains outside the scope of economics, probably because the economists take it for granted that "misproductive" work is usually against the law. In this way economists recognize that the utilities that they usually take into consideration are only those compatible with the existing law of most countries. Thus, the connection between economics and the law is implied, but it is rarely regarded by economists as a special object worthy of their research. They consider, for instance, the exchange of goods, but not the behavioral exchange that makes possible an exchange of goods, regulated and occasionally enforced for that purpose by the law of all countries. Hence, a free market seems something more "natural" than government or at least independent of government, if not, indeed, something that it is necessary to maintain "against" the government. In fact, a market is no more "natural" than government itself, and both are no more natural than, say, bridges. People who ignore this fact ought to take seriously a couplet once sung in a cabaret in Montmartre:

> *Voyez comme la nature a en un bon sens bien profond*
> *À faire passer les fleuves justement sous les ponts.*

(See how Nature had the extreme good sense
To make the rivers flow exactly under the bridges.)

To be sure, economic theory has not ignored the fact that it is the government that gives people the practical power to avoid constraint on the part of other people on the market. Robbins aptly emphasized this in his essay, *The Theory of Economic Policy in*

English Political Economy (London, 1952), noting that "we would get an entirely distorted view" of the significance of the doctrine of what Marshall called the system of economic freedom "unless we see it in combination with the theory of law and the functions of government which its authors (from Smith onwards) also propounded." As Robbins says, "the idea of freedom *in vacuo* was entirely alien to their conceptions." But Professor Robbins also pointed out, in *Economic Planning and International Order* (London, 1937), that the classical economists paid too little attention to the fact that international trade could not emerge as a simple consequence of the theorem of comparative costs, but required some kind of international legal organization to ward off the enemies of international free trade, who, to a certain extent, are comparable to such enemies of the free market within a nation as robbers or thieves.

On the other hand, the very fact that constraint is in some way inevitably linked with "freedom" in all political societies gave rise to or at least favored the idea that "increasing freedom" could be somehow compatible in those societies with "increasing constraint." This idea was, in its turn, connected with a confusion about the meaning of the terms "constraint" and "freedom" which is chiefly due, not to propaganda, but to the uncertainties that can arise about the meaning of these words in ordinary usage.

Professor Mises says that "freedom" is a human concept. We must add that it is human in so far as some preference on the part of men is always implied when we use that term in ordinary language. But this does not mean that a man can be said to be "free" only from the power of other men. A man also can be said to be "free" from a disease, from fear, from want, as these phrases are employed in ordinary language. This has encouraged some people to consider "freedom from other men's constraint" on a par with, say, "freedom from want," without observing that the latter kind of "freedom" may have nothing to do with the former. An explorer may be starving in the desert where he wanted to go alone without being constrained by anybody else. Now, he is not "free from hunger," but he is, as he was before, completely "free from coercion or constraint" on the part of other people.

Several thinkers, ancient as well as modern, have tried to connect the fact that some people are not free from hunger or from disease with the fact that other people in the same society are not free from the constraint of their fellow men. Of course, the connection is obvious when someone is in bondage to other people who treat him badly and let him die, for instance, through starvation. But the connection is not at all obvious when people are not in bondage to others. However, some thinkers have erroneously believed that whenever someone lacks something he needs or simply desires, he has been unjustly "deprived" of that very thing by the people who do have it.

History is so full of examples of violence, robbery, invasions of land, and so on, that many thinkers have felt justified in saying that the origin of private property is simply violence and that it is therefore to be regarded as irremediably illicit at present as well as in primitive times. The Stoics, for example, imagined that all the land on earth was originally common to all men. They called this legendary condition *communis possessio originaria*. Certain Fathers of the Christian Church, particularly in the Latin countries, echoed this assumption. Thus, Saint Ambrose, the famous archbishop of Milan, could write in the fifth century C.E. that while Nature had provided for things to be common to all, private property rights were due to usurpation. He quotes the Stoics, who maintained, as he says, that everything in the earth and in the seas was created for the common use of all human beings. A disciple of Saint Ambrose, called the Ambrosiaster, says that God gave everything to men in common and that this applies to the sun and to the rain as well as to the land. The same thing is said by Saint Zeno of Verona (for whom one of the most magnificent churches in the world is named) in reference to the men of very ancient times: "They had no private property, but they had everything in common, like sun, days, nights, rain, life, and death, as all those things had been given to them in equal degree, without any exception, by the divine providence." And the same saint adds, obviously accepting the idea that private property is the result of constraint and of tyranny: "The private owner is without doubt similar to a tyrant, having himself alone the total control of things that would be useful to several other people." Almost the same idea can be found some centuries later in the works of certain canonists. For instance, the author of the first systemization of the rules of the Church, the so-called *decretum Gratiani,* says: "Whoever is determined to keep more things than he needs is a robber."

Modern socialists, including Marx, have simply produced a revised version of this same idea. For instance, Marx distinguishes various stages in the history of mankind: a first stage, in which the production relations had been those of cooperation, and a second stage, in which some people acquired for the first time control of the factors of production, thereby placing a minority in the position of being fed by the majority. The old Archbishop of Milan would say in less complicated and more effective language: "Nature is responsible for a law of things in common; usurpation is responsible for private law."

Of course, we can ask how it is possible to speak of "things common to all." Who decreed that all things are "common" to all men, and why? The usual reply given by the Stoics and their disciples, the Christian Fathers in the first centuries after Christ, was that, just as the moon and the sun and the rain are common to all men, so there is no reason to maintain that other things, such as land, are not also common. These advocates of communism did not bother to make a semantic analysis of the word "common." Otherwise they would have discovered that land cannot be "common" to all men in the same sense in which the sun and the moon are and that it is therefore not altogether the same thing to let people cultivate land in common as it is to let them use moonlight or sunlight or fresh air when they go out for a walk. Modern economists explain the difference by pointing out that there is no scarcity of moonlight, while there is a scarcity of land. Notwithstanding the truistic nature of this statement, a purported analogy between scarce things like arable land and abundant things like moonlight has always been a good reason in the eyes of many people for maintaining that the "have-nots" have been "constrained" by the "haves," that the latter have illicitly deprived the former of certain things originally "common" to all men. The semantic confusion in the use of the word "common" introduced by the Stoics and the early Christian Fathers in this connection has been retained by modern socialists of all kinds and lies, I believe, at the origin of the tendency, manifested particularly in recent times, to use the word "freedom" in an equivocal sense that relates "freedom from want" with "freedom from other people's constraint."

This confusion is connected, in its turn, with another. When a grocer or a doctor or a lawyer waits for customers or clients, each of them may feel dependent on the latter for his living. This is quite true. But if no customer or client makes his appearance, it would be an abuse of language to assert that the customers or clients who do not appear constrain the grocer or the doctor or the lawyer to die by starvation. In fact, no one committed any constraint against him for the simple reason that no one put in an appearance. To put the matter in the simplest possible terms, the customers or clients did not exist at all. If we now suppose that a client puts in an appearance and offers a very small fee to the doctor or the lawyer, it is not possible to say that this particular client is "constraining" the doctor or the lawyer to accept his fee. We may despise a man who can swim and does not save a fellow man whom he sees drowning in a river, but it would be an abuse of language to assert that in failing to save the drowning man he was "constraining" the latter to drown. In this connection I must agree with a famous German jurist of the nineteenth century, Rudolph Jhering, who was indignant at the unfairness of the argument advanced by Portia against Shylock and on behalf of Antonio in Shakespeare's *Merchant of Venice*. We may despise Shylock, but we cannot say that he "constrained" Antonio or anybody else to make an agreement with him—an agreement that implied, under the circumstances, the death of the latter. What Shylock wanted was only to constrain Antonio to respect his agreement after he had signed it. Notwithstanding these obvious considerations, people are often inclined to judge Shylock in the same way as they would judge a murderer and to condemn usurers as if they were robbers or pirates, although neither Shylock nor any ordinary usurer can properly be accused of constraining anyone to go to him to ask for money at a usurious rate.

In spite of this difference between "constraint," in the sense of something actually done to cause harm to somebody against his will, and behavior like that of Shylock, many people, especially in the last hundred years in Europe, have tried to inject into ordinary language a semantic confusion the result of which is that a man who has never committed himself to perform a definite act in favor of other people and who therefore does nothing on their behalf is censured because of his purported "omission" and is blamed as if he had "constrained" others to do something against their will. This is not, in my opinion, in accordance with the proper usage of ordinary language in all the countries with which I am familiar. You do not "constrain" someone if you merely refrain from doing on his behalf something you have not agreed to do.

All socialist theories of the so-called exploitation of workers by employers—and, in general, of the "have-nots" by the "haves"—are, in the last analysis, based on this semantic confusion. Whenever self-styled historians of the Industrial Revolution in England in the nineteenth century talk about the "exploitation" of workers by employers, they imply precisely this idea that the employers were exercising "constraint" against workers to make them accept poor wages for hard jobs. When statutes such as the Trade Disputes Act of 1906 in England granted to the trade unions a privilege to constrain employers to accept their demands by unlawful acts, the idea was that the employees were the weaker party and that they could therefore be "constrained" by employers to accept poor wages instead of high wages. The privilege granted by the Trade Disputes Act was based on the principle familiar to the European liberals of that time, and corresponding also to the meaning of "freedom" as accepted in ordinary language, that you are "free" when you can constrain other people to refrain from constraining you. The trouble was that, while the constraint granted to the unions as a privilege by the Act had the usual meaning of this word in ordinary language, the "constraint" that the privilege was designed to prevent on the part of the employers was not understood in the sense that this word had and still has in ordinary language. If we consider things from this point of view, we must agree with Sir Frederick Pollock, who wrote in his *Law of Torts* that "legal science has evidently nothing to do with the violent empirical operation on the body politic" that the British legislature had thought fit to perform by the Trade Disputes Act of 1906. We have to say also that the ordinary use of language has nothing to do with the meaning of "constraint" that rendered it suitable, in the eyes of the British legislators, to inflict upon the body politic a violent operation of this kind.

Unprejudiced historians, such as Professor T. S. Ashton, have demonstrated that the general situation of the poor classes of the English population after the Napoleonic wars was due to causes that had nothing to do with the behavior of the entrepreneurs of the new industrial era in that country and that its origin is traceable far back into the ancient history of England. What is more, economists have often demonstrated, both by adducing cogent arguments of a theoretical nature and by examining statistical data, that good wages depend on the ratio between the amount of capital invested and the number of workers.

But this is not the main point of our argument. If one gives to "constraint" such different meanings as those we have just seen, one can easily conclude that the entrepreneurs at the time of the Industrial Revolution in England were "constraining" people to inhabit, for example, old and unhealthful houses only because they did not build for their workers a sufficient number of new and good houses. In the same way, one could say that the industrialists who do not make huge investments in machinery, regardless of the returns they can get, are "constraining" their workers to content themselves with low wages. In fact, this semantic confusion is fostered by several propaganda and pressure groups interested in making persuasive definitions both of "freedom" and of "constraint." As a result, people can be censured for the "constraint" they allegedly exercise over other people with whom they have never had anything to do. Thus, the propaganda of Mussolini and Hitler before and during the Second World War included the assertion that the people of other countries located as far from Italy or Germany as, say, Canada or the United States were "constraining" the Italians and the Germans to be content with their poor material resources and their comparatively narrow territories, although not even one single square mile of German or Italian territory had been taken by Canada or by the United States. In the same way, after the last World War we were told by many people—especially by those belonging to the Italian "intelligentsia"—that the rich landowners of Southern Italy were directly responsible for the misery of the poor workers there or that the inhabitants of Northern Italy were responsible for the depression of the deep South, although no demonstration could be seriously supplied to prove that the wealth of certain landowners in Southern Italy was the cause of the workers' poverty or that the reasonable standard of living enjoyed by the people of Northern Italy was the cause of the absence of such a standard in the South. The assumption underlying all these ideas was that the "haves" of Southern Italy were "constraining" the "have-nots" to make a poor living, in the same way as the inhabitants of Northern Italy were "constraining" those living in the South to be content with agricultural incomes instead of building industries. I must point out too that a similar semantic confusion underlies many of the demands made upon the peoples of the West (including the United States) and the attitudes adopted toward them by the ruling groups in certain former colonies like India or Egypt.

This results in occasional mutinies, riots, and all kinds of hostile actions on the part of the people who feel "constrained." Another no less important result is the series of acts, statutes, and provisions, at national as well as international levels, designed to help people allegedly "constrained" to counteract this "constraint" by legally enforced devices, privileges, grants, immunities, etc.

Thus, a confusion of words causes a confusion of feelings, and both react reciprocally on each other to confound matters even more.

I am not so naive as Leibniz, who supposed that many political or economic questions could be settled, not by disputes (*clamoribus*), but by a sort of reckoning (*calculemus*) through which it would be possible for all people concerned to agree at least in principle about the issues at stake. But I do maintain that semantic clarification is likely to be more useful than is commonly believed, if only people were put in a condition to benefit from it.

3

FREEDOM
AND THE RULE
OF LAW

It is not easy to state what English-speaking people mean by the expression "the rule of law." The meaning of these words has changed in the last seventy or even fifty years, and the phrase itself has acquired rather an obsolete sound in England as well as in America. Nevertheless, it once corresponded to an idea that (as Professor Hayek pointed out in his first lecture on freedom and the rule of law given at the National Bank of Egypt in 1955) "had fully conquered the minds if not the practice of all the Western nations," so that "few people doubted that it was destined soon to rule the world."[1]

The complete story of this change cannot be written yet, since the process is still going on. Moreover, it is a story to a certain extent complicated, fragmentary, tedious, and, above all, hidden from people who read only newspapers, magazines, or fiction and who have no special taste for legal matters or for such technicalities as, say, the delegation of judicative authority and legislative powers. But it is a story that concerns all the countries of the West that had and still have a share not only in the juridical ideal denoted by the expression "the rule of law," but also in the political ideal designated by the word "freedom."

---

[1] F. A. Hayek, *The Political Ideal of the Rule of Law* (Cairo: Fiftieth Anniversary Commemoration Lectures, National Bank of Egypt, 1955), p. 2. Virtually the entire substance of this book has been republished in *The Constitution of Liberty* by the same author.

58

I would not go so far as to say, as Professor Hayek does in the above-mentioned lecture, that "it is in the technical discussion concerning administrative law that the fate of our liberty is being decided." I would prefer to say that this fate is also being decided in many other places—in parliaments, on the streets, in the homes, and, in the last analysis, in the minds of menial workers and of well-educated men like scientists and university professors. I agree with Professor Hayek that we are confronted in this respect with a sort of silent revolution. But I would not say with him or with Professor Ripert of France that this is a revolution—nay, a *coup d'état*—promoted only, or even chiefly, by technicians like lawyers or the officials of ministries or of departments of state. In other words, the continuous and creeping change in the meaning of "the rule of law" is not the result of a "managerial" revolution, to use Burnham's apt expression. It is a much broader phenomenon connected with many events and situations the real features and significance of which are not easily ascertainable and to which historians refer by such phrases as "the general trend of our times." The process by which the word "freedom" began to assume several different and incompatible meanings in the last hundred years involved, as we have seen, a semantic confusion. Another semantic confusion, less obvious, but no less important, is revealing itself to those patient enough to study the silent revolution in the use of the expression "the rule of law."

Continental European scholars, notwithstanding their wisdom, their learning, and their admiration for the British political system, from the times of Montesquieu and Voltaire have not been able to understand the proper meaning of the British constitution. Montesquieu is probably the most famous of those who are open to this criticism, particularly as far as his celebrated interpretation of the division of powers in England is concerned, in spite of the fact that his interpretation (many people would say his misinterpretation) had, in its turn, an enormous influence in the English-speaking countries themselves. Eminent English scholars, in their turn, suffered a similar criticism because of their interpretations of European Continental constitutions. The most famous of these scholars is probably Dicey, whose misunderstandings of the French *droit administratif* have been considered by another well-known English scholar, Sir Carleton Kemp Allen, a "fundamental mistake" and one of the main reasons why the rule of law has evolved in the English-speaking countries of the present day in the way that it has. The fact is that the powers of government were never actually separated in England as Montesquieu believed in his day, nor was the *droit administratif* in France or, for that matter, the Italian *diritto amministrativo* or the German *Verwaltungsrecht* actually identifiable with the "administrative law" that Sir Carleton Kemp Allen and the generality of contemporary English scholars are thinking of when they speak of the recent changes in the respective functions of the judiciary and of the executive in the United Kingdom.

After long reflection on this subject, I am inclined to conclude that even more fundamental than the misinterpretations of Dicey, on the one hand, and of Montesquieu, on the other, have been those of the scholars and ordinary people who have tried to adopt, on the European Continent, the British "rule of law" and have imagined that the Continental imitation of the English or the American system (say, for instance, the German *Rechtsstaat* or the French *état de droit* or the Italian *stato di diritto*) is really something very similar to the English "rule of law." Dicey himself, who had a lucid view of some very important differences in this respect and who several thinkers believe was rather prejudiced against the French and generally against the constitutions of the European Continent, actually thought that at the beginning of the present century there was not a great deal of difference between the English or the American "rule of law" and the Continental constitutions:

> If we confine our observation to the Europe of the twentieth century, we might well say that in most European countries the rule of law is now nearly as well established as in England and that private individuals at any rate who do not meddle in politics have little to fear as long as they keep the law, either from the government or from anyone else.[2]

On the other hand, some Continental scholars—e.g., the great French *garantistes* like Guizot and Benjamin Constant and the

---

[2] Albert Venn Dicey, *Introduction to the Study of the Law of the Constitution* (8th ed.; London: Macmillan, 1915), p. 185.

German theorists of the *Rechtsstaat* like Karl von Rotteck, K. Welcker, Robert von Mohl, and Otto von Gierke—supposed (I would say, wrongly) that they were describing and recommending to their fellow citizens a type of state very similar to that of England. In our day Professor Hayek has tried to demonstrate that the German doctrine of the *Rechtsstaat,* before its corruption by the historicist and positivist *reactionnaires* at the end of the nineteenth century, contributed a great deal, in theory if not in practice, to the ideal of "the rule of law."

This ideal and that of the *Rechtsstaat* before its corruption did indeed have much in common. Almost all the features that Dicey described so brilliantly in the above-quoted book in order to explain what the English "rule of law" was, are traceable also in the Continental constitutions from the French constitution of 1789 to those of the present day.

The *supremacy of the law* was the chief characteristic cited in Dicey's analysis. He quoted the old law of the English courts: "La ley est la plus haute inheritance, que le roi had; car par la ley il même et toutes ses sujets sont rulés, et si la ley ne fuit, nul roi et nul inheritance sera" ("the law is the highest estate to which the king succeeds, for both he and all his subjects are ruled by it, and without it there would be neither king nor realm"). According to Dicey, the supremacy of the law was, in its turn, a principle that corresponded to three other concepts and therefore implied three different and concomitant meanings of the phrase "the rule of law": (1) the absence of arbitrary power on the part of the government to punish citizens or to commit acts against life or property; (2) the subjection of every man, whatever his rank or condition, to the ordinary law of the realm and to the jurisdiction of the ordinary tribunals; and (3) a predominance of the legal spirit in English institutions, because of which, as Dicey explains, "the general principles of the English constitution (as, for example, the right to personal liberty or the right to public assembly) are the result of judicial decisions. . . . ; whereas under many foreign constitutions the security given to the rights of individuals results or appears to result from the general (abstract) principles of the constitution."[3]

---

[3] Ibid., p. 191.

Americans may wonder whether or not Dicey considered the American system in the same class as the Continental systems of Europe. Americans derive or appear to derive their individual rights from the general principles laid down in their Constitution and in the first ten amendments. As a matter of fact, Dicey considered the United States a typical instance of a country living under "the rule of law" because she had inherited the English traditions. He was right, as one sees when one recalls, on the one hand, the fact that a written bill of rights was not considered necessary at first by the Founding Fathers—who did not even include it in the text of the Constitution itself—and, on the other hand, the importance that judicial decisions on the part of ordinary tribunals had and still have in the political system of the United States as far as the rights of individuals are concerned.

Professor Hayek, among more recent eminent theorists of "the rule of law," takes into consideration four features of it that correspond to a certain extent, although not entirely, to Dicey's description. According to Professor Hayek, the *generality,* the *equality,* and the *certainty* of the law, as well as the fact that administrative discretion in coercive action, i.e., in interfering with the person and the property of the private citizen, *must always be subject to review* by independent courts, are "really the crux of the matter, the decisive point on which it depends whether the Rule of Law prevails or not."[4]

Apparently, the theories of Professor Hayek and of Dicey coincide except for some minor details. Professor Hayek, it is true, emphasizes the difference between laws and orders in connection with the "generality" of the law and points out that the law must never concern particular individuals or be enacted when, at the moment of enactment, it can be predicted which particular individuals it will help or damage. But this may simply be considered as a special development of Dicey's idea that the "rule of law" means the absence of arbitrary power on the part of the government. *Equality,* in its turn, is an idea embodied in the Dicean description of the second characteristic of the rule of

[4] F. A. Hayek, op. cit., p. 45.

law, that is, that every man, whatever his rank or condition, is subject to the ordinary law of the realm.

In this connection we must notice a difference between Dicey's and Hayek's interpretations of equality or at least of its application in some respects. Professor Hayek agrees with Sir Carleton Kemp Allen in reproaching Dicey for a "fundamental mistake" relating to the interpretation of the French *droit administratif.* Dicey, according to Sir Carleton and Professor Hayek, was wrong in believing that the French and generally the Continental *droit administratif,* at least in its mature stage, was a sort of arbitrary law because it was not administered by ordinary tribunals. According to Dicey, only ordinary courts, in England as well as in France, could really protect citizens by applying the ordinary law of the land. The fact that special jurisdictions, like that of the *conseil d'état* in France, were given the power of judging in cases where private citizens litigated with officials employed in the service of the state, appeared in the eyes of Dicey as a proof that the equality of the law towards all citizens was not actually respected on the Continent. Officials, when litigating in their official capacity with ordinary citizens, were "to some extent exempted from the ordinary law of the land." Professor Hayek charges Dicey with having contributed a great deal to preventing or to delaying the growth of institutions capable of controlling, through independent courts, the new bureaucratic machinery in England because of a false idea that separate administrative tribunals would always constitute a denial of the ordinary law of the land and therefore a denial of "the rule of law." The fact is that the *conseil d'état* provides ordinary citizens in France as well as in most countries of Western Europe with a fairly unbiased and efficient protection against what Shakespeare would have called "the insolence of office."

Is it fair, however, to hold Dicey responsible for the fact that a process similar to that of the formation and functioning of the *conseil d'état* has not yet taken place in the United Kingdom? Perhaps what has hindered the development of an administrative court of appeals in England (which would correspond to the French *conseil d'état* or to the Italian *consiglio di stato*) is the fact, noticed by Allen, that in England "at the very mention of a 'new-found halliday' not a few hands are at once thrown up in horror at a 'foreign importation.' "[5] In fact, hostility toward un-British types of law and judicature is an old characteristic of the English people. The present inhabitants of the British Isles are, after all, the descendants of those who proudly proclaimed, many centuries ago, "nolumus leges Angliae mutari" ("we do not want any changes made in the laws of the Anglo-Saxons"). Dicey's role in the resistance to the importation of Continental forms of law into England was a comparatively small one. Allen himself, while cautiously suggesting how to adopt new means to protect citizens against British bureaucracy, hastily adds that "nobody in his right mind proposes to imitate in England the *conseil d'état*" and that people who still believe that " 'administrative law' (if they will even permit the term) is the same thing as *droit administratif* are living in an age long past."[6]

Incidentally, the amusing thing in this peroration by Sir Carleton is that he seems to imply here that "administrative law" is something much better than the foreign *droit administratif,* while at the beginning of his work he had reproached poor Dicey for his "complacent comparison with French administrative law," that is, with "that remarkable jurisprudence, at all events in its modern developments," and had charged Dicey with having "left the British public under the impression that the effect of administrative law in France was to place officials in a special privileged position rather than (as is the fact) to give the subject a large measure of protection against illegal state action."[7] One might add that this is a protection that the present English administrative law does not offer at all to the subjects of the British Crown because, as was pointed out recently by another English scholar, Ernest F. Row,

> whereas the French administrative courts are courts and administer a perfect code of law by a perfectly definite procedure akin to that of the other courts, the new English system [that is, that bestowal on the executive of judicial functions that the former Lord Chief Justice of England used to qualify as "administrative lawlessness" and as the

[5] Carleton Kemp Allen, *Law and Orders* (London: Stevens & Sons, 1956 ed.), p. 396.
[6] Ibid., p. 396.
[7] Ibid., p. 32.

"new despotism"] is nothing of the kind, for by it these disputes between individuals and the government are settled by the government, itself a party to the dispute, in a purely arbitrary manner, according to no regular and recognized principles and by no clearly defined legal procedure.[8]

Dicey and Hayek apparently differ only slightly in their respective interpretations of equality as a characteristic of the rule of law. Both maintain that independent courts are essential in order to grant to the citizens equality before the law. A minor difference between the two interpretations of the functions of the courts seems to be that while Dicey does not admit the existence of two different judiciary orders, one to settle disputes between ordinary citizens only and one to settle disputes between ordinary citizens, on the one hand, and state officials, on the other, Hayek thinks that the existence of two different judiciary orders is not objectionable in itself, provided that both orders are actually independent of the executive.

Things are probably not so simple as Professor Hayek's conclusion seems to imply. Of course, independent administrative tribunals are better than the simple bestowal of judiciary power on the executive in administrative matters, such as occurs in England today and, to a certain extent, in the United States as well. But the very presence of "administrative tribunals" gives added point to the fact (which Dicey disliked) that there is not one law for everybody in the country and therefore the equality of all citizens before the law is really not respected as it would be if there were only one law of the land and not also an administrative law side by side with the common law.

Dean Roscoe Pound pointed out in an essay cited by Professor Hayek[9] that contemporary tendencies in the exposition of public law subordinate the interests "of the individual to those of the public official" by allowing the latter "to identify one side of the controversy with the public interest and so give it a great value and ignore the others." This applies more or less to all kinds of

---

[8] Ernest F. Row, *How States Are Governed* (London: Pitman & Sons, 1950), p. 70. For the situation in the United States, *see* Walter Gellhorn, *Individual Freedom and Governmental Restraints* (Baton Rouge: Louisiana State University Press, 1956) and Leslie Grey, "The Administrative Agency Colossus," *The Freeman* (October, 1958), p. 31.

[9] F. A. Hayek, op. cit., p. 57.

administrative laws, whether they are administered by independent courts or not. A general principle that underlies all relations between private citizens and government officials acting in their official capacity is what the Continental theorists (like, for example, the German Jellinek or the French Hauriou or the Italian Romano) would call the *status subjectionis* of the individual in regard to the administration, and, correspondingly, the "supremacy" of the latter over the individual. State officials, as representatives of the public administration, are regarded as people having *eminentia jura* (pre-eminent rights) over other citizens. Thus, officials are entitled, for instance, to enforce their orders without any prior control whatever on the part of a judge over the legitimacy of these orders, whereas such a control would be prescribed if a private citizen demanded anything of another private citizen. It is true that Continental theorists admit as well that individuals have a right to personal liberty that limits the *eminentia jura* or, as they also say, the *supremacy* of the administration. But the principle of the supremacy of the administration is something that today qualifies the administrative law of all countries in Continental Europe and, to some extent, of all countries in the world.

It is exactly this principle that administrative tribunals take into account in judging controversies between private citizens and officials, whereas ordinary judges would consider all the private parties involved in a case as exactly on the same level. This fact, which has in itself nothing to do with the extent to which the administrative tribunals are independent of the executive or of state officials, is at the base of the existence of administrative tribunals as separate courts of judicature. Now, if we admit, with Dicey, that the only law to be taken into consideration in judging controversies between citizens (whether they are state officials or not) is one that is in accordance with the rule of law as Dicey conceives of it, his conclusion that a system of administrative courts (whether they are independent of the government or not) is to be avoided and that only ordinary courts are to be accepted is perfectly consistent.

Dicey's conclusion may or may not be applicable to present circumstances, but it is a consequence of the principle of equality before the law, that is, of one of the principles implied by both his and Professor Hayek's interpretation of the meaning of "the rule of law."

In England, Dicey wrote,

> the idea of legal equality, or of the universal subjection of all classes to one law administered by the ordinary courts, has been pushed to its utmost limit. With us every official, from the Prime Minister down to a constable or a collector of taxes, is under the same responsibility for every act done without legal justification as any other citizen. The reports abound with cases in which officials have been brought before the courts and made, in their personal capacity, liable to punishment or to the payment of damages for acts done in their official character but in excess of their lawful authority. A colonial governor, a secretary of state, a military officer, and all subordinates, though carrying out the commands of their official superiors, are as responsible for any act which the law does not authorize as is any private and unofficial person.[10]

The situation described by Dicey in 1885 is certainly not that which prevails at the present time, for a typical feature of the new "administrative law" in England is the removal from the jurisdiction of the ordinary courts of many cases in which the executive is or may be itself one of the parties to the dispute.

Dicey cannot be justly criticized for his condemnation of administrative tribunals on the basis of a principle he has so clearly enunciated, viz., the universal subjection of all classes to one law. Otherwise we ought to conclude that while all men are equal before the law, some men are "more equal than others."

In fact, we now know how far the interpretation of the principle of equality before the law can go in political systems in which the principle of the purely formal—nay, of the ceremonial— legality of any rule whatever, regardless of its content, has been substituted for the principle of the *Rechtsstaat* and, correspondingly, of "the rule of law" in its early meaning.

We can form as many categories of people as we want in order to apply the same laws to them. Within each category people will all be "equal" before the particular law that applies to them, regardless of the fact that other people, grouped in other categories, will be treated quite differently by other laws. Thus, we can

---

[10] Dicey, op. cit., p. 189.

create an "administrative law" before which all people grouped
in a certain category defined in the law will be treated in the
same way by administrative tribunals, and side by side with it we
can recognize a "common law" under which people, grouped in
other categories, will be no less equally treated by the ordinary
courts. Thus, by a slight change in the meaning of the principle
of "equality," we can pretend to have preserved it. Instead of
"equality before the law," all that we shall have will then be
*equality before each of the two systems of law enacted in the same coun-
try,* or, if we want to use the language of the Dicean formula, we
shall have *two laws of the land instead of one.* Of course, we can, in
the same way, have three or four or thousands of laws of the
land—one for landlords, one for tenants, one for employers, one
for employees, etc. This is exactly what is happening today in
many Western countries where lip service is still paid to the principle of "the rule of law" and hence of "equality before the law."

We can also imagine that the same courts are entitled to apply
all these laws of the land equally to all those included in the
categories concerned. This may still be called approximately
"equality before the law." But it is obvious that in such a case not
everybody will receive equal treatment under the law of the land
considered as a whole. For instance, in Italy, the third article of
the constitution states that "all citizens are equal before the
law." In fact, however, there are laws that constrain landlords to
keep tenants at a very low rent, notwithstanding previous agreements to the contrary, whereas other categories of people, who
entered into contracts in other capacities than those of landlords
or of tenants, are not interfered with by any special law and still
may—nay, must—keep the agreements that they have made. We
also have in my country other laws that constrain people to give
away a part of their land for a compensation fixed by the government itself and which the proprietors think in many cases to be
ridiculously low when compared with the market price of the
land. Other people—for instance, owners of buildings, of business firms, or of securities—are still left free to do what they
want with their property. The Italian Constitutional Court has
held valid in a recent decision a law that entitles the government
to pay a nominal price to proprietors expropriated by the land

reform laws, on the ground that this price was fixed with regard to the common interest of the country (and, of course, it is very difficult to ascertain what the "common interest" is). Theorists could probably elaborate a series of principles to explain all this and speak, for instance, of a *jus subjectionis* of the landlords or of *jura eminentia* or *supremacy* on the part of the tenants and the government officials who fix the amount to be paid to the expropriated landlords. But things remain as they are: people are not equally treated by the law of the land considered as a whole in the sense intended by Dicey in his famous book.

The possibility of several laws valid at the same time for different classes of citizens in the same country, but treating them differently (the most common example is that of progressive taxation according to the citizens' income, which has already become a general feature of the fiscal policy of all Western countries) is related in its turn to the principle of the *generality of the law*. Indeed, it is not easy to establish what renders one law *general* in comparison with another. There are many "genera" under which "general" laws may be contrived, and many "species" which it is possible to take into consideration within the same "genus."

Dicey considered "the legal spirit" a special attribute of English institutions. The whole British political system was based, according to him, on general principles resulting "from judicial decisions determining the rights of private persons in particular cases brought before the courts." He contrasted this with what happens on the Continent (and, he might have said, in the United States as well), where "the security given to the rights of individuals results or appears to result from the general principles of the constitution," emerging in its turn from a legislative act. Dicey explained with his usual lucidity what he meant by this:

> If it be allowable to apply the formulae of logic to questions of law, the difference in this matter between the constitution of Belgium and the English constitution may be described by the statement that in Belgium individual rights are deductions drawn from the principles of the constitution, whilst in England the so-called principles of the constitution are inductions or generalizations based upon partic-

ular decisions pronounced by the courts as to the rights of given individuals.[11]

Dicey also stated that, although "this was, of course, a formal difference" of no moment in itself, great practical differences had been revealed by historical evidence relating, for instance, to the French Constitution of 1791, which proclaimed a series of rights, while "there never was a period in the recorded annals of mankind when each and all of these rights were so insecure, one might almost say completely nonexistent, as at the height of the French Revolution." The reason for these differences between the English and the Continental systems was, according to Dicey, the lack of legal skill on the part of the legislators (and here Dicey seems to echo the well-known impatience of the English judges with the work of legislatures) required to contrive remedies to secure the exercise of rights on the part of the citizens. Dicey did not think that this skill was incompatible with written constitutions as such and declared with admiration that "the statesmen of America have shown unrivaled skill in providing means for giving legal security to the rights declared by the American constitutions," so that "the rule of law was as marked a feature of the United States as of England."[12] According to Dicey, the exercise of the rights of the individual under the English constitution was more *certain* than the exercise of similar rights under Continental constitutions; and this "certainty" was mainly due to greater legal skill on the part of the English-speaking people in contriving remedies connected with these rights.

Certainty is a feature that Professor Hayek also emphasizes in his recent analysis of the ideal of "the rule of law." He conceives it in a way that is only apparently different from that of Dicey, although this difference may be very important in some respects.

According to Professor Hayek,[13] the certainty of the law is probably the most important requirement for the economic activities of society and has contributed much to the greater prosperity of the Western world as compared with the Orient, where the certainty of the law was not so early achieved. But he does

[11] Loc. cit.
[12] Ibid., p. 195.
[13] F. A. Hayek, op. cit., p. 36.

not analyze what the term "certainty" properly means when referred to the law. This is a point that needs to be dealt with very accurately in a theory of "the rule of law," although neither Dicey nor Professor Hayek nor, for that matter, most other scholars enter very much into this matter. Different meanings of the expression "the certainty of the law" may be at the very foundation of most of the misunderstandings between Continental and English scholars relating to the rule of law and to apparently similar concepts like those of written constitutions, *Rechtsstaaten*, etc. Dicey did not have a completely clear conception of what the "certainty" of the law meant for him when he described the main features of the rule of law. Apparently, this fact is connected with the absence of written—and therefore, in a way, of *certain*—rules in the English traditional common law, including constitutional law. If certainty were connected only with written rules, neither the common law nor that part of it that can be called constitutional law would be certain at all. In fact, many of the recent attacks on the "uncertainty" of case law on the part of English-speaking and particularly of American lawyers and political scientists belonging to the so-called realistic school are based on a meaning of the term "certainty" that implies the existence of a definitely written formula the words of which ought not to be changed at will by the reader. This impatience with unwritten law is an outgrowth of the increasing number of statutes in contemporary legal and political systems and of the increasing weight that has been given to statutory law as compared with case law (that is, with the unwritten law) in England as well as in other countries of the British Commonwealth and in the United States of America.

The certainty of the law is connected with the idea of definitely written formulae, like those that the Germans would call *Rechtssaetze*, also in the meaning Professor Hayek gives to the word "certainty" in his lectures on the rule of law. He declares that even "the delegation of rule-making to some kind of nonelective authority need not be contrary to the rule of law so long as this authority is bound to state and publish the rules in advance of their application. . . . " He adds that "the trouble with the widespread modern use of delegation is not that the power of making general rules is delegated, but that authorities are in effect given power to wield coercion without rule, because no general rule can be formulated for the exercise of the powers in question."[14]

There is a sort of parallelism between what, according to Professor Hayek, is immaterial in relation to administrative law or administrative courts and what is really essential for him in the concept of "certainty." What matters for him is that administrative law be administered by *independent* courts, regardless of the fact that there is something peculiar called "administrative law" and no matter whether the courts administering it are special courts or not. In a similar way, Professor Hayek believes that no serious inconvenience can arise from the fact that rules are issued by parliaments or by some delegated authority, provided only that those rules be general, clearly stated, and published in advance.

General regulations laid down in due time and made known to all citizens make it possible for them to foresee what will happen on the legal stage as a consequence of their behavior, or, to use the words of Professor Hayek: "as a general rule, circumstances which are beyond his [the individual's] field of vision must not be made a ground for his coercion."

This is surely a classic interpretation of the certainty of the law. One can also add that it is probably the most famous one, for it has received many celebrated formulations since the days of ancient Greek civilization, as some quotations from the *Politics* and the *Rhetoric* of Aristotle could easily prove. When that philosopher praises the government of laws, he very probably has in mind those general rules, known in advance to all citizens, which were written in his day on the walls of public buildings or on special pieces of wood or stone, like the *kurbeis* that the Athenians used for that purpose. The ideal of a written law, generally conceived and knowable by every citizen of the small and glorious towns scattered all along the coasts of the Mediterranean Sea and inhabited by people of Greek descent, is one of the most precious gifts that the fathers of Western civilization have bequeathed to their posterity. Aristotle knew well the harm that an arbitrary, contingent, and unpredictable rule (whether a decree approved by the mob in the Athenian *agora* or the capricious

[14] Ibid., p. 38.

order of a tyrant in Sicily) could cause to ordinary people in his day. Thus, he considered laws, that is, general rules laid down in terms that were precise and knowable to everybody, as an indispensable institution for citizens who were to be called "free," and Cicero echoed this Aristotelian conception in his famous dictum in the *oratio pro Cluentio:* "omnes legum servi sumus ut liberi esse possimus" ("we must all obey the law if we are to remain free").

This ideal of certainty has been implanted and reinforced in the European Continent through a long series of events. Justinian's *Corpus Juris Civilis* was for several centuries the very book in which the ideal of the certainty of the law, understood as the certainty of a *written law,* appeared to be embodied, in the Latin as well as in the German countries. This ideal was not repudiated, but was even emphasized, in the seventeenth and eighteenth centuries in Continental Europe, when the absolutistic governments, as the late Professor Ehrlich has pointed out in his brilliant essay on legal reasoning (*Juristische Logik*), wanted to make sure that their judges did not alter the meaning of their rules. Everybody knows what happened in the nineteenth century in Continental Europe. All the European countries adopted written codes and written constitutions, accepting the idea that precisely worded formulae could protect people from the encroachments of all possible kinds of tyrants. Governments as well as courts accepted this interpretation of the idea of the certainty of the law as the precision of a written formula laid down by legislatures. This was not the only reason why Continental Europe adopted codes and constitutions, but it was at least one of the main reasons. In brief, the Continental idea of the certainty of the law was equivalent to the idea of a precisely worded, written formula. This idea of certainty was to a great extent conceived as *precision.*

Whether this is actually the notion that the English people had of the certainty of the law and whether this idea was actually implied in their ideal of "the rule of law" is not clear at first sight. We shall return to this question a little later.

The Greek or Continental notion of the certainty of the law actually corresponds to the ideal of individual liberty formulated by the Greek authors who speak of government by the laws.

There is no doubt that government by the laws is preferable to government by decrees of tyrants or of the mob. General laws are always more predictable than particular and sudden orders, and if the predictability of the consequences is one of the unavoidable premises of human decisions, it is necessary to conclude that the more that general rules render predictable, at least on the legal plane, the consequences of individual actions, the more these actions can be called "free" from interference on the part of other people, including the authorities.

From this point of view, we cannot help admitting that general rules, precisely worded (as they can be when written laws are adopted), are an improvement over the sudden orders and unpredictable decrees of tyrants. But unfortunately, all this is no assurance that we shall be actually "free" from interference by the authorities. We can set aside for the moment the questions arising from the fact that rules may be perfectly "certain" in the sense we have described, that is to say, precisely formulated, and be at the same time so tyrannical that nobody can be said to be "free" by behaving according to them. But there is another inconvenience that also results from adopting such general written laws, even when they do allow us considerable "freedom" in our individual behavior. The usual process of law-making in such cases is by way of legislation. But the legislative process is not something that happens once and for all. It takes place every day and is continually going on.

This is particularly true in our time. In my country the legislative process now means about two thousand statutes every year, and each of them may consist of several articles. Sometimes we find dozens or even hundreds of articles in the same statute. Quite frequently one statute conflicts with another. We have a general rule in my country that when two particular rules are mutually incompatible because of their contradictory content, the more recent rule abrogates the old one. But, according to our system, nobody can tell whether a rule may be only one year or one month or one day old when it will be abrogated by a new rule. All these rules are precisely worded in written formulae that readers or interpreters cannot change at their will. Nevertheless, all of them may go as soon and as abruptly as they came. The result is that, if we leave out of the picture the ambiguities of the text, we are always "certain" as far as the literal content of each rule is concerned at any given moment, but we are *never certain* that tomorrow we shall still have the rules we have today.

This is "the certainty of the law" in the Greek or Continental sense. Now I would not go so far as to say that this is "certainty" in the sense that one requires in order to foresee that the result of legal actions taken today will be free from legal interference tomorrow. This kind of "certainty," so much praised by Aristotle and by Cicero, has, in the last analysis, nothing to do with the certainty we should need to be actually "free" in the sense meant by these old and glorious representatives of our Western civilization.

However, this is not the only meaning of the expression "the certainty of the law" as used and understood in the West. There is another meaning that is much more in accord with the ideal of "the rule of law" as it was conceived by the English as well as the American people, at least in the times when "the rule of law" was an ideal undoubtedly connected with individual freedom understood as freedom from interference on the part of everybody, including the authorities.

FREEDOM AND THE CERTAINTY OF THE LAW

The Greek conception of the certainty of the law was that of a written law. Although we are not directly concerned here with problems of historical research, it may be interesting to recall that the Greeks, especially in earlier times, also had a conception of customary law and generally of unwritten laws. Aristotle himself speaks of the latter. These were not to be confused with the more recent concept of the law as a complex of written formulae in the technical sense that the word *nomos* assumed in the fifth and fourth centuries before Christ. But the ancient Greeks, in a more mature period of their history, also had an opportunity to become tired of their usual idea of the law as something written and enacted by such legislative bodies as the Athenian popular assembly.

The example of the ancient Greeks is particularly pertinent in this respect not only because they were the originators of the political systems later adopted by the countries of the West, but also because most of the Greek people, particularly the Athenians, were sincerely fond of political freedom in a sense perfectly understandable to us and comparable with our own. What, for instance, Thucydides has Pericles say in his famous Funeral Oration for the Athenian soldiers and sailors who were the first to fall in the Peloponnesian War could be repeated quite literally by such modern representatives of the political ideal of freedom as Jefferson, De Tocqueville, John Stuart Mill, Lord Acton, or

Spencer. The authenticity of the records that Thucydides made use of in order to reconstruct Pericles' speech is still an open question. But even if we imagine that Thucydides himself wrote this speech instead of Pericles, the authority of Thucydides, as far as the feeling of the Athenians and the conditions of his times are concerned, would not be inferior to that of Pericles in this respect. Thus, in the English translation of Crawley, Pericles, as quoted by Thucydides, uses these words to describe the Athenian political and civil system in the middle of the fifth century before Christ:

> Our constitution does not copy the laws of neighboring states. We are rather a pattern to others than imitators ourselves. Its administration favors the many instead of the few; this is why it is called a democracy. If we look to the laws, they afford equal justice to all in their private differences; if to social standing, advancement in public life falls to reputation for capacity, class considerations not being allowed to interfere with merit. Nor again does poverty bar the way. If a man is able to serve the state, he is not hindered by the obscurity of his condition. The freedom which we enjoy in our government extends also to our ordinary life. There, far from exercising a jealous surveillance over each other, we do not feel called upon to be angry with our neighbor for doing what he likes, or even to indulge in those injurious looks which cannot fail to be offensive, although they inflict no positive penalty. But all this ease in our private relations does not make us lawless as citizens. Against this, fear is our chief safeguard, teaching us to obey the magistrates and the laws, particularly such as regard the protection of the injured, whether they are actually on the statute books or belong to that code which, although unwritten, yet cannot be broken without acknowledged disgrace.[1]

This Greek idea of freedom, as reflected in Pericles' speech, is quite similar to our contemporary idea of freedom as maximum independence of constraint exercised by others, including the authorities, over our individual behavior. The old notion held by some scholars like Fustel de Coulanges that the ancient Greeks would not have given to the word "freedom" a sense similar to the one we now give to it in most instances has been successfully revised in recent times. There is, for example, a book entitled

---

[1] Thucydides, *The History of the Peloponnesian War*, II, 37–39, tr. by R. Crawley (London: J. M. Dent & Sons, 1957, p. 93).

The Liberal Temper in Greek Politics (1957), written by a Canadian scholar, Professor Eric A. Havelock, with the purpose of evidencing the splendid contribution that many Greek thinkers less famous than Plato and Aristotle gave to the ideal of political freedom as contrasted with bondage in all senses of the word. One of the conclusions emerging from this book is that Greek freedom was not "freedom from want," but *freedom from men.* As Democritus pointed out in a fragment that has been preserved to the present day, "poverty under a democracy is as much to be preferred above what an oligarchy calls prosperity as is liberty above bondage." Liberty and democracy come first in this scale of values; prosperity comes after. There is little doubt that this was also the scale of values of the Athenians. Certainly it was that of Pericles and of Thucydides. We also read in the Funeral Oration that those Athenians who had died in the war ought to be taken as a model by their fellow citizens, who, "judging happiness to be the fruit of freedom and freedom of valor, never would decline the dangers of war."[2]

Law-making was the business of popular legislative assemblies, and the general rules laid down in written form by those assemblies were contrasted with the arbitrary orders of tyrants. But the Greeks, and particularly the Athenians, were to realize fully in the second half of the fifth and in the fourth century before Christ the grave inconveniences of a law-making process by means of which all the laws were *certain* (that is, precisely worded in a written formula), but *nobody was certain that any law, valid today, could last until tomorrow* without being abrogated or modified by a subsequent law. Tysamenes' reformation of the Athenian constitution at the end of the fifth century offers us an example of a remedy against this inconvenience that could be usefully pondered by contemporary political scientists and politicians. A rigid and complex procedure was then introduced in Athens in order to discipline legislative innovations. Every bill proposed by a citizen (in the Athenian direct democracy every man belonging to the general legislative assembly was entitled to present a bill, whereas in Rome only the elected magistrates could do so) was thoroughly studied by a special committee of

[2] Loc. cit.

magistrates (*nomotetai*) whose task was precisely that of defending the previous legislation against the new proposal. Of course, proponents could freely argue before the general legislative assembly against the *nomotetai* in order to support their own bills, so that the whole discussion must have been based more on a comparison between the old and the new law than on a simple oration in favor of the latter.

But this was not the end of the story. Even when the bill had been passed at last by the assembly, the proponent was held responsible for his proposal if another citizen, acting as a plaintiff against the proponent himself, could prove, after the law had been approved by the assembly, that the new legislation had some grave defects or that it was in irremediable contradiction with older laws still valid in Athens. In that case, the proponent of the law could be legitimately tried, and the penalties could be very serious, including the death sentence, although, as a rule, unfortunate proponents suffered only fines. This is not a legend. We know all this from Demosthenes' accusation against one of these unfortunate proponents named Tymocrates. This system of fining proponents of unsuitable legislation was not in opposition to democracy, if we mean by that word a regime in which the people are sovereign and if we admit that sovereignty means also irresponsibility, as it does in many historical interpretations of it.

We must infer that the Athenian democracy at the end of the fifth century and during the fourth century before Christ was obviously not satisfied with the notion that the certainty of the law could be equated simply with that of a precisely worded formula in a written text.

Through Tysamenes' reform, the Athenians discovered at last that they could not be free from the interference of the political power only by obeying the laws of today; they also needed to be able to foresee the consequences of their actions according to the laws of tomorrow.

This is, in fact, the chief limitation of the idea that the certainty of the law can be simply identified with the precise wording of a written rule, whether general or not.

But the idea of the certainty of the law has not only the above-mentioned sense in the history of the political and legal systems of the West. It has also been understood in a completely different sense.

The certainty of the law, in the sense of a written formula, refers to a state of affairs inevitably conditioned by the possibility that the present law may be replaced at any moment by a subsequent law. The more intense and accelerated is the process of law-making, the more uncertain will it be that present legislation will last for any length of time. Moreover, there is nothing to prevent a law, certain in the above-mentioned sense, from being unpredictably changed by another law no less "certain" than the previous one.

Thus, the certainty of the law, in this sense, could be called the *short-run* certainty of the law. Indeed, there seems to be a striking parallel in our day between short-run types of provisions in matters of economic policy and the short-run certainty of the laws that are enacted to secure these provisions. In a more general way, the legal and political systems of almost all countries today could be defined in this respect as short-run systems, in contrast to some of the classic long-run systems of the past. The famous dictum of the late Lord Keynes that "in the long run we shall all be dead" could be adopted as the motto of the present age by future historians. Perhaps we have become increasingly accustomed to expect immediate results from the enormous and unprecedented progress in the technical means and scientific devices developed to perform many kinds of tasks and to achieve many kinds of results in material ways. Undoubtedly, this fact has created for many people who ignore or try to ignore the differences the expectation of immediate results also in other fields and in regard to other matters not dependent at all on technological and scientific progress.

I am reminded of a conversation I had with an old man who grew plants in my country. I asked him to sell me a big tree for my private garden. He replied, "Everybody now wants big trees. People want them immediately; they do not bother about the fact that trees grow slowly and that it takes a great deal of time and trouble to grow them. Everybody today is always in a hurry," he sadly concluded, "and I do not know why."

Lord Keynes could have told him the reason: people think that in the long run they will all be dead. This same attitude is also noticeable in connection with the general decline in religious belief that so many priests and pastors lament today. Christian religious beliefs used to emphasize, not the present life of man, but a future one. The less men believe now in that future world, the more they cling to their present life, and, believing that individual life is short, they are in a hurry. This has caused a great secularization of religious beliefs at the present time in the countries of both the Occident and the Orient, so that even a religion as indifferent to the present world as Buddhism is being given by some of its supporters a mundane "social," if not, in fact a "socialist," meaning. A contemporary American writer, Dagobert Runes, says in his book on contemplation, "Churches have lost the touch of the Divine and turned to book reviews and politics."[3]

This may help to explain why there is now so little attention given to a long-run conception of the certainty of the law or indeed to any other long-run conception that relates to human behavior. Of course, this does not mean that short-run systems are, in fact, more efficient than long-run ones in achieving the very ends that people endeavor to attain by devising, say, a new miraculous full-employment policy or some unprecedented legal provision or simply by asking from growers big trees for their gardens.

The short-run concept is not the only notion of the certainty of the law that the history of political and legal systems in the countries of the West presents to a student patient enough to recognize the principles that underlie institutions.

This was not so in ancient times. Although Greece could be described to a certain extent by historians as a country with a written law, it is doubtful that this was true of ancient Rome. We probably are so used to thinking of the Roman legal system in terms of Justinian's *Corpus Juris*, that is, in terms of a written law book, that we fail to realize how Roman law actually worked. A large part of the Roman rules of law was not due to any legislative process whatever. Private Roman law, which the Romans called *jus civile*, was kept practically beyond the reach of legisla-

---

[3] Dagobert D. Runes, *A Book of Contemplation* (New York: Philosophical Library, 1957), p. 20.

tors during most of the long history of the Roman Republic and
the Empire. Eminent scholars, such as the late Italian Professors
Rotondi and Vincenzo Arangio Ruiz and the late English jurist,
W. W. Buckland, repeatedly point out that "the fundamental notions, the general scheme of the Roman law, must be looked for
in the civil law, a set of principles gradually evolved and refined
by a jurisprudence extending over many centuries, with little
interference by a legislative body."[4] Buckland also remarks,
probably on the basis of Rotondi's studies, that "of the many
hundreds of *leges* [statutes] that are on record, no more than
about forty were of importance in the private law," so that at
least in the classical age of Roman law "statute, as far as private
law is concerned, occupies only a very subordinate position."[5]

It is obvious that this was not the result of any lack of skill on
the part of the Romans in devising statutes. They had many available types of statutes: the *leges*, the *plebiscita*, and the *Senatus
Consulta*, approved respectively by the people or by the Senate,
and they also had at their disposal several kinds of *leges*, such
as the *leges imperfectae*, the *minusquamperfectae*, and the *plus-
quamperfectae*. But, as a rule, they reserved statutory law to a field
in which legislative bodies were directly qualified to intervene,
namely, public law, *quod ad rem Romanam spectat*, relating to the
functioning of political assemblies, of the Senate, of the magistrates, that is to say, of their government officials. Statutory law
for the Romans was mainly constitutional law or administrative
law (and also criminal law), only indirectly relating to the private
life and private business of the citizens.

This meant that whenever a difference arose between Roman
citizens about their rights or their duties according to a contract,
for example, they could rarely base their claims on a statute, on a
written rule precisely worded, and therefore *certain* in the Greek
or short-run sense of the word. Thus, one of the most eminent
among contemporary historians of Roman legal science and law,
Professor Fritz Schulz, has pointed out that *certainty* (in the

---

[4] W. W. Buckland, *Roman Law and Common Law* (2nd ed. revised by F. H. Lawson; Cambridge University Press, 1952), p. 4. This book is a fascinating comparison of the two
systems.
[5] Ibid., p. 18.

short-run sense) was unknown to the Roman civil law. This does not mean at all that the Romans were not in a position to make plans about the future legal consequences of their actions. Everybody knows the enormous development of the Roman economy, and it is hardly necessary to refer here to the imposing work of Rostovtzeff on this subject.

On the other hand, it is well known to all students of Roman private law that, as Professor Schulz says, "the individualism of Hellenistic liberalism caused the private law to be developed on a basis of freedom and individualism."[6] As a matter of fact, most of our contemporary Continental codes, such as the French, the German, and the Italian, were written according to the rules of the Roman law recorded in Justinian's *Corpus Juris*. They have been labeled as "bourgeois" by some socialist reformers. So-called social "reforms" in European countries today can be brought about, if at all, only by modifying or canceling rules that very often go back to those of ancient Roman private law.

Thus, the Romans had a law sufficiently certain to enable citizens freely and confidently to make plans for the future, and this without being a written law at all, that is, without being a series of precisely worded rules comparable to those of a written statute. The Roman jurist was a sort of scientist: the objects of his research were the solutions to cases that citizens submitted to him for study, just as industrialists might today submit to a physicist or to an engineer a technical problem concerning their plants or their production. Hence, private Roman law was something to be described or to be discovered, not something to be enacted—a world of things that were there, forming part of the common heritage of all Roman citizens. Nobody enacted that law; nobody could change it by any exercise of his personal will. This did not mean absence of change, but it certainly meant that nobody went to bed at night making his plans on the basis of a present rule only to get up the next morning and find that the rule had been overturned by a legislative innovation.

The Romans accepted and applied a concept of the certainty of the law that could be described as meaning that the law was never to be subjected to sudden and unpredictable changes.

[6] Fritz Schulz, *History of Roman Legal Science* (Oxford: Clarendon Press, 1946), p. 84.

Moreover, the law was never to be submitted, as a rule, to the arbitrary will or to the arbitrary power of any legislative assembly or of any one person, including senators or other prominent magistrates of the state. This is the long-run concept, or, if you prefer, the Roman concept, of the certainty of the law.

This concept was certainly essential to the freedom that Roman citizens usually enjoyed in business and in all private life. To a certain extent, it put juridical relations among citizens on a plane very similar to that on which the free market put their economic relations. Law, as a whole, was no less free from constraint than the market itself. I cannot, in fact, conceive of a market actually free if it is not rooted in its turn in a legal system that is free from the arbitrary (that is, abrupt and unpredictable) interference of the authorities or of any other person in the world.

Some might object that the Roman legal system had to be based on the Roman constitutional system and that, therefore, indirectly if not directly, Roman freedom in business and in private life was in fact based on a statutory law. This, it might be argued, was submitted, in the last analysis, to the arbitrary will of the senators or of such legislative assemblies as the *comitia* or the *concilia plebis*, not to mention prominent citizens, who, like Sulla or Marius or Caesar, from time to time took control of all things and therefore had the actual power to overturn the constitution.

Roman statesmen and politicians, however, were always very cautious in using their legislative power to interfere with the private life of the citizens. Even dictators like Sulla behaved rather carefully in this respect, and probably they would have considered the idea of overturning the *jus civile* almost as strange as modern dictators would consider the idea of subverting physical laws.

True, men like Sulla made a great effort to change the Roman constitution in many respects. Sulla himself tried to wreak vengeance upon Italian peoples and on cities like Arretium or Volaterrae previously helpful to his chief enemy, Marius, by making the Roman legislative assemblies enact laws that suddenly deprived the inhabitants of these towns of the Roman *jus civitatis*, that is, of Roman citizenship, and of all the privileges it involved. We know all this from one of Cicero's orations in behalf of

Cecina, delivered by Cicero himself before a Roman court. But we also know that Cicero won his case by arguing that the law enacted by Sulla was not legitimate, since no legislative assembly could by a statute deprive a Roman citizen of his citizenship, any more than it could by a statute deprive a Roman citizen of his freedom. The law enacted by Sulla was a statute formally approved by the people, of the type the Romans used to call a *lex rogata*, that is, a statute whose approval had been requested and obtained from a popular assembly by an elected magistrate by due process of law. We are told by Cicero, in this connection, that all bills to be made into statute law used to contain, from very ancient times, a clause the meaning of which, although not completely understandable in a later age, obviously related to the possibility that the content of the bill, if it became a statute, might not be legal: "Si quid jus non esset rogarier, eius ea lege nihilum rogatum" ("if there is in this bill whose approval I am requesting of you," said the magistrate to the legislative assembly of the Roman people, "anything that is not legal, your approval of it is to be considered as not requested").

This seems to prove that there were statutes that could be contrary to law and that statutes like those depriving citizens of their freedom or of their citizenship were not considered as legal by Roman courts.

If Cicero is correct, we may conclude that Roman law was limited by a concept of legitimacy strikingly similar to that set forth by Dicey in regard to the English "rule of law."[7]

According to the English principle of the rule of law, which is closely connected with the whole history of the common law, rules were not properly the result of the exercise of the arbitrary will of particular men. They are the object of a dispassionate investigation on the part of courts of judicature, just as the Roman rules were the object of a dispassionate investigation on the part of the Roman jurists to whom litigants submitted their cases. It is now considered old-fashioned to maintain that courts

---

[7] I am indebted for this and other interesting remarks on the Roman legal system to Professor V. Arangio Ruiz, whose essay "La règle de droit dans l'antiquité classique," republished by the author in *Rariora* (Rome: Ed. di storia e letteratura, 1946, p. 233), is very informative and stimulating.

of justice *describe* or *discover* the correct solution of a case in the way that Sir Carleton Kemp Allen has pointed out in his rightly famous and stimulating book, *Law in the Making*. The contemporary so-called realistic school, while presuming to reveal all kinds of deficiencies in this process of discovery, is only too pleased to conclude that the work of the common-law judges was and is no more objective, and only less overt, than that of legislators. As a matter of fact, much more needs to be said on this topic than it is possible to say here. But one cannot deny that the attitude of common-law judges towards the *rationes decidendi* of their cases (i.e., the grounds of their decisions) has always been much less that of a legislator than that of a scholar trying to ascertain things rather than to change them. I do not deny that common-law judges may have sometimes deliberately concealed their desire to have something ruled in a certain way under cover of a pretended statement about an already existing rule of the law of the land. The most famous of these judges in England, Sir Edward Coke, is not exempt from this suspicion, and I dare say the most famous of American judges, Chief Justice Marshall, may be also compared in this respect with his celebrated predecessor in seventeenth-century England.

My point is merely that courts of judicature could not easily enact arbitrary rules of their own in England, as they were never in a position to do so directly, that is to say, in the usual, sudden, widely ranging and imperious manner of legislators. Moreover, there were so many courts of justice in England and they were so jealous of one another that even the famous principle of the binding precedent was not openly recognized as valid by them until comparatively recent times. Besides, they could never decide anything that had not been previously brought before them by private persons. Finally, comparatively few people used to go before the courts to ask from them the rules deciding their cases. As a result, judges were more in the position of spectators than of actors in the law-making process, and, moreover, of spectators not allowed to see all the things that happen on the stage. Private citizens were on the stage; common law was chiefly just what they commonly thought of as being law. Common citizens were the real actors in this respect, just as they still are the real actors in the formation of the language and, at least partially, in economic transactions in the countries of the West. The grammarians who epitomize the rules of a language or the statisticians who make records of prices or of quantities of goods exchanged in the market of a country could better be described as simple spectators of what is happening around them than as rulers of their fellow citizens as far as the language or the economy is concerned.

The increasing importance of the legislative process in the present age has inevitably obscured, both on the European Continent and in the English-speaking countries, the fact that law is simply a complex of rules relating to the behavior of the common people. There is no reason to consider these rules of behavior much different from other rules of behavior in which interference on the part of political power has been only exceptionally, if ever, exercised. True, in the present age language seems to be the only thing that the common people have been able to keep for themselves and to protect from political interference, at least in the Western world. In Red China today, for instance, the government is making a violent effort to change the traditional writing, and similar interference has already been successfully practiced in certain other countries of the East, such as Turkey. Thus, in many lands people have almost completely forgotten the days when bank notes, for example, were issued not only by a governmental bank, but also by private banks. Moreover, very few people know now that in other times the making of coins was a private business and that governments limited themselves to protecting citizens against bad practices on the part of counterfeiters simply by certifying the authenticity and the weight of the metals employed. A similar trend in public opinion is noticeable in regard to government-operated enterprises. In Continental Europe, where railroads and telegraphs have been monopolized by the governments for a long time, very few, even among well educated people, now imagine that in this country railroads and telegraphic communications are private businesses in the same way as movies or hotels or restaurants. We have become increasingly accustomed to considering law-making as a matter that concerns the legislative assemblies rather than ordinary men in the street and, besides, as something that can be done according to the personal ideas of certain individuals pro-

vided that they are in an official position to do so. The fact that
the process of lawmaking is, or was, essentially a private affair
concerning millions of people throughout dozens of generations
and stretching across several centuries goes almost unnoticed
today even among the educated elite.

It is said that the Romans had little taste for historical and
sociological considerations. But they did have a perfectly clear
view of the fact I have just mentioned. For instance, according to
Cicero, Cato the Censor, the champion of the traditional Roman
way of life against the foreign (that is, Greek) importation, used
to say that

> the reason why our political system was superior to those of all other
> countries was this: the political systems of other countries had been
> created by introducing laws and institutions according to the per-
> sonal advice of particular individuals like Minos in Crete and Lycur-
> gus in Sparta, while at Athens, where the political system had been
> changed several times, there were many such persons, like Theseus,
> Draco, Solon, Cleisthenes, and several others. . . . Our state, on the
> contrary, is not due to the personal creation of one man, but of very
> many; it has not been founded during the lifetime of any particular
> individual, but through a series of centuries and generations. For he
> said that there never was in the world a man so clever as to foresee
> everything and that even if we could concentrate all brains into the
> head of one man, it would be impossible for him to provide for
> everything at one time without having the experience that comes
> from practice through a long period of history.[8]

Incidentally, these words remind us of the much more famous,
but no more impressive, terms employed by Burke to justify his
conservative view of the state. But Burke's words had a slightly
mystical tone that we do not find in the dispassionate considerations of the old Roman statesman. Cato is merely pointing to
facts, not persuading people, and the facts he points out must
undoubtedly carry great weight with all who know something of
history.

The law-making process, so Cato says, is not actually that of
any particular individual, brain trust, time, or generation. If you
think that it is, you have worse results than you would have by

[8] Cicero *De republica* ii. 1, 2.

bearing in mind what I have said. Look at the fate of the Greek cities and compare it with ours. You will be convinced. This is the lesson—nay, I would say, the message—of a statesman about whom we commonly know only what we learned when we went to school, that he was a crusty bore, always insisting that the Carthaginians had to be killed and their city razed.

It is interesting to point out that when contemporary economists like Ludwig von Mises criticize central economic planning because it is impossible for the authorities to make any calculation regarding the real needs and the real potentialities of the citizens, they take a position that reminds us of that of the ancient Roman statesman. The fact that the central authorities in a totalitarian economy lack any knowledge of market prices in making their economic plans is only a corollary of the fact that central authorities always lack a sufficient knowledge of the infinite number of elements and factors that contribute to the social intercourse of individuals at any time and at any level. The authorities can never be certain that what they do is actually what people would like them to do, just as people can never be certain that what they want to do will not be interfered with by the authorities if the latter are to direct the whole law-making process of the country.

Even those economists who have most brilliantly defended the free market against the interference of the authorities have usually neglected the parallel consideration that no free market is really compatible with a law-making process centralized by the authorities. This leads some of these economists to accept an idea of the certainty of the law, that is, of precisely worded rules such as those of written law, which is compatible neither with that of a free market nor, in the last analysis, with that of freedom understood as the absence of constraint exercised by other people, including the authorities, over the private life and business of each individual.

It may seem immaterial to some supporters of the free market whether rules are laid down by legislative assemblies or by judges, and one may even support the free market and feel inclined to think that rules laid down by legislative bodies are preferable to the *rationes decidendi* rather unprecisely elaborated by a long series of judges. But if one seeks historical confirmation of the strict connection between the free market and the free law-making process, it is sufficient to consider that the free market was at its height in the English-speaking countries when the common law was practically the only law of the land relating to private life and business. On the other hand, such phenomena as the present acts of governmental interference with the market are always connected with an increase in statutory law and with what has been called in England the "officialization" of judiciary powers, as contemporary history proves beyond doubt.

If we admit that individual freedom in business, that is, the free market, is one of the essential features of political freedom conceived of as the absence of constraint exercised by other people, including the authorities, we must also conclude that legislation in matters of private law is fundamentally incompatible with individual freedom in the above-mentioned sense.

The idea of the certainty of the law cannot depend on the idea of legislation if "the certainty of the law" is understood as one of the essential characteristics of the rule of law in the classical sense of the expression. Thus, I think that Dicey was perfectly consistent in assuming that the rule of law implies the fact that judicial decisions are at the very foundation of the English constitution and in contrasting this fact with the opposite process on the Continent, where legal and judiciary activities appear to be based on the abstract principles of a legislated constitution.

Certainty, in the sense of the long-run certainty of the law, was just what Dicey bore more or less clearly in mind when he said, for instance, that whereas each and all of the guarantees that Continental constitutions afforded to citizens relating to their rights could be suspended or taken away by some power that was above the ordinary law of the land, in England "the constitution being based on the rule of law, the suspension of the constitution, as far as such a thing can be conceived, would mean . . . nothing less than a revolution."[9]

The fact that this very revolution is now taking place does not disprove, but rather confirms, the Dicean theory. A revolution is occurring in England by virtue of the gradual overturning of the

---

[9] Dicey, loc. cit.

law of the land by way of statutory law and through the conversion of the rule of law into something that is now increasingly coming to resemble the Continental *état de droit*, that is, a series of rules that are *certain* only because they are written, and *general,* not because of a common belief on the part of the citizens about them, but because they have been decreed by a handful of legislators.

In other words, the impersonal law of the land is coming more and more under the command of the sovereign in England, just as Hobbes and later Bentham and Austin had advocated, against the opinion of the English jurists of their day.

Sir Matthew Hale, a brilliant disciple of Sir Edward Coke and himself a Chief Justice after Coke, wrote towards the end of the seventeenth century in defense of his master against the criticism that Hobbes had elaborated in his little-known *Dialogue on the Common Law.* Hobbes had maintained, in his typical scientistic manner, that law is no product, as Coke had said in his curious way, of "artificial reason," and that everybody could establish general rules of law simply by using the ordinary reason common to all men. "Though it be true that no man is born with the use of reason, yet all men," said Hobbes, "may grow up to it as well as lawyers; and when they have applied their reason to the laws . . . may be as fit for and capable of judicature as Sir Edward Coke himself."[10] Surprisingly enough, Hobbes considered this argument consistent with his assertion that "none can make a law but he that has the legislative power." The dispute between Hobbes, on the one hand, and Coke and Hale, on the other, is highly interesting in connection with very important methodological questions arising from the comparison of the work of jurists with that of other people like physicists or mathematicians. Taking issue with Hobbes, Sir Matthew Hale pointed out that it is of no use to compare the science of the law with other sciences such as the "mathematical sciences" because for the "ordering of civil societies and for the measuring of right and

---

[10] Thomas Hobbes, *Dialogue between a Philosopher and a Student of the Common Laws of England* (1681) in Sir William Molesworth, ed., *The English Works of Thomas Hobbes of Malmesbury* (London: John Bohn, 1829–1845), VI, 3–161.

wrong" it is not only necessary to have correct general notions, but it is also necessary to apply them correctly to particular cases (which is, incidentally, just what judges try to do). Hale argued that

> they that please themselves with a persuasion that they can with as much evidence and congruitie make out an unerring system of laws and politiques [that is, we would say, written constitutions and legislation] equally applicable to all states [i.e., conditions] as Euclide demonstrates his conclusions, deceive themselves with notions which prove ineffectual when they come to particular application.[11]

One of the most striking remarks made by Hale reveals the consciousness that he as well as Coke had of the requirement of certainty as the long-run certainty of the law:

> 'Tis a foolish and unreasonable thing for any to find fault with an institution because he thinks he could have made a better, or expect a mathematical demonstration to evince the reasonableness of an institution or the selfe evidence thereof. . . . It is one of the thinges of the greatest moment in the profession of the common law to keepe as neare as may be to the *certainty* of the law, and the consonance of it to itselfe, that one age and one tribunal may speake the same thinges and carry on the same thred of the law in one uniforme rule as neare as possible; for otherwise that which all places and ages have contended for in laws, namely *certainty* [italics added] and to avoid arbitrariness and that extravagance that would fall out if the reasons of judges and advocates were not kept in their traces, would in half an age be lost. And this conservation of laws within their boundes and limitts could never be, unless men be well informed by studies and reading what were the judgements and resolutions and decisions and interpretations of former ages.[12]

It would be difficult to connect more clearly and more decidedly the concept of certainty to that of the uniformity of rules through the ages, and of continuity to the modest and limited work of courts of judicature instead of that of legislative bodies.

This is exactly what is meant by *the long-run certainty of the law,*

---

[11] Matthew Hale, "Reflections by the Lord Chief Justice Hale on Mister Hobbes, His *Dialogue of the Law,*" published for the first time by Holdsworth, *History of English Law* (London: Methuen & Co., 1924), Vol. V, Appendix, p. 500.

[12] Ibid., p. 505.

and it is incompatible, in the last analysis, with the short-run certainty implied by identifying law with legislation.

The former was also the Roman conception of the certainty of the law. Famous scholars have noted the lack of individuality of the Roman jurists. Savigny called them "fungible personalities." This lack of individuality was a natural counterpart of their individualistic view of the private laws they were studying. Private law was conceived of by them as a common inheritance of each and all of the Roman citizens. Therefore, nobody felt entitled to change it at his own will. When changes occurred, they were recognized by the jurists as having already happened in their environment rather than being introduced by the jurists themselves. For the same reason, like their modern successors, the English judges, Roman jurists never bothered about abstract principles, but were always concerned with "particular cases," to use the above-mentioned expression of Sir Matthew Hale. What is more, the lack of individuality on the part of the Roman jurists was of the same nature as that accepted by Sir Matthew Hale when he stated:

> It is a reason for me to preferre a law by which a kingdome hath been happily governed four or five hundred years than to adventure the happiness and peace of a kingdome upon some new theory of my own.[13]

In the same spirit, Roman jurists hated abstract theories and all the paraphernalia of the philosophy of law cultivated by Greek thinkers. As one Roman jurist (who was also a statesman), Neratius, wrote once in the second century after Christ: "Rationes eorum quae constituntur inquiri non oportet, alioquin multa quae certa sunt subvertuntur" ("we must avoid making inquiry about the rationale of our institutions, lest their certainty be lost and they be overthrown").[14]

To sum up very briefly: Many Western countries, in ancient as well as in modern times, have considered the ideal of individual freedom (the absence of constraint exercised by other people, including the authorities) essential to their political and legal sys-

---

[13] Ibid., p. 504.
[14] *Dig.* I, 3, 21.

tems. A conspicuous characteristic of this ideal has always been the certainty of the law. But the certainty of the law has been conceived in two different and, in the last analysis, even incompatible ways: first, as the precision of a written text emanating from legislators, and second, as the possibility open to individuals of making long-run plans on the basis of a series of rules spontaneously adopted by people in common and eventually ascertained by judges through centuries and generations. These two conceptions of "certainty" have rarely, if ever, been distinguished by scholars, and many ambiguities have been maintained in the meaning of the term by the common people in Continental Europe as well as in English-speaking countries. This is probably the chief reason why a comparison between European constitutions and the English constitution could be deemed easier than it was and why European political scientists could imagine that they were contriving good imitations of the English constitution without taking into consideration the significance that the peculiar kind of law-making process called the common law has always had for the English constitution.

Without this law-making process it is probably impossible to conceive of a rule of law in the classical English sense of the expression expounded by Dicey. On the other hand, without the legislative law-making process no Continental system would be what it is today.

In the present age the confusion of the meanings of "certainty" and "the rule of law" has particularly increased because of the emerging tendency in the English-speaking countries to emphasize law-making by way of legislation instead of by courts of judicature.

The obvious effects of this confusion have already begun to reveal themselves with respect to the idea of political freedom and freedom of enterprise. Once again semantic confusion seems to be at the very root of many troubles. I do not maintain that all our difficulties are due to semantic confusion. But it is a very important task of political scientists as well as of economists to analyze the different and contradictory meanings we imply in the English-speaking and in the European Continental countries respectively when we talk of "freedom" in connection with "the certainty of the law" and "the rule of law."

5

FREEDOM AND
LEGISLATION

A very important conclusion to be drawn from the preceding chapters is that the rule of law, in the classical sense of the expression, cannot be maintained without actually securing the certainty of the law, conceived as the possibility of long-run planning on the part of individuals in regard to their behavior in private life and business. Moreover, we cannot base the rule of law on legislation unless we have recourse to such drastic and almost absurd provisions as those contrived by the Athenians at the time of the *nomotetai*.

Typical of our times is the tendency to increase the powers that officials in the countries of the West have acquired and are still acquiring every day over their fellow citizens, notwithstanding the fact that these powers are usually supposed to be limited by legislation.[1] A contemporary author, E. N. Gladden, summarizes this situation as a dilemma which he formulates in the title of his book, *Bureaucracy or Civil Service.* Bureaucrats enter the scene as soon as civil servants seem to be above the law of the land regardless of the nature of that law. There are cases in which officials deliberately substitute their own will for the provisions of the law in the belief that they are improving on the law and achieving, in some way not stated in the law, the very ends they

---

[1] As far as Great Britain is concerned, cf. the very accurate analysis of Professor G. W. Keeton, *The Passing of Parliament* (London: E. Benn, 1952). In regard to the United States, *see* Burnham, *Congress and the American Tradition* (Chicago: Regnery, 1959), especially "The Rise of the Fourth Branch," p. 157, and Lowell B. Mason, *The Language of Dissent* (Cleveland, Ohio: World Publishing Co., 1959).

think the law was intended to achieve. There is often no doubt about the good will and the sincerity of the officials in these cases.

Permit me to cite an example taken from certain bureaucratic practices in my own country at the present time. We have legal regulations concerning vehicular traffic. These provide for a number of penalties for offenses committed by drivers of vehicles. The penalties are usually fines, although in exceptional cases those contravening the rules may be tried and put into prison. Moreover, in certain cases especially provided for by other legal regulations, offenders may be deprived of their driving licenses—if, for instance, their offenses against the traffic regulations cause personal injuries or grave damages to others or if they drive while drunk. As motor vehicle traffic of all kinds is constantly increasing in my country, accidents are becoming more and more frequent. The authorities are convinced that stricter discipline imposed on the drivers by the enforcement officers themselves is the best means, even though not a panacea, to reduce the number of traffic casualties all over the territory they control. Members of the executive, such as the minister of the interior and other state officials depending on his direction, the "prefects," the agents of the national police all over the country, the officers of the local police in the towns, and so on all down the line, try to apply this theory in dealing with offenses against traffic regulations. But some of them often do even more. They appear to be convinced that the law of the land in this connection (namely, the legal regulations concerning the penalties to be imposed by the judges on the offenders and the procedure to be followed for that purpose) is too mild and too slow to meet successfully the new exigencies of modern traffic conditions. Some officials in my country try to "improve" on the existing procedure to be followed in accordance with the law of the land in these respects.

One of the officials explained all this to me when I tried to intervene on behalf of some clients of mine against what I considered an illegal practice on the part of the authorities. A man was reported by the police as having passed a vehicle in violation of the traffic regulations. Immediately and unexpectedly he was deprived of his driving license by the "prefect." As a result, he could no longer drive his truck, which meant that he was practically without a job until the authorities consented to return his license. According to our written regulations, the "prefect" may deprive an offender of his driving license in a number of cases, but passing another vehicle against the traffic regulations and without causing any casualties is not one of them. When I brought this fact to the attention of the official concerned, he agreed with me that perhaps, according to a correct interpretation of the present rules, my client had not actually committed an offense punishable by depriving him of his license. The official also politely explained to me that, in several other cases, maybe in 70 percent of the cases, offenders were now being deprived of their driving licenses by the authorities without having actually committed an offense that deserved such a punishment according to the law. "But you see," he said, "if we do not do this, people in this country [sometimes officials seem to consider themselves natives of other countries] will not be sufficiently cautious, for they do not give a damn about penalties of a few thousand lire such as are imposed by our law. On the other hand, if you deprive them of their license for a while, offenders feel the loss more keenly and will be much more cautious in the future." He also said, rather in a philosophical vein, that he thought the injustice done to a comparatively small number of citizens could be justified by the general result obtainable, according to the opinion of the authorities, in improving the movement of vehicular traffic in the public interest.

An even more striking example in this connection was related to me by a colleague. He had gone to protest against the issuance by a district attorney on an order of imprisonment against a driver who had run over and killed somebody in the street. According to our law, casual homicides may be punished with prison sentences. On the other hand, district attorneys are entitled to issue orders of imprisonment before the trial only in special cases prescribed by the rules of our criminal procedure whenever they consider that imprisonment may be advisable under the circumstances. It should be obvious that imprisonment before trial is not a punishment, but a security measure designed to prevent, for instance, the possibility that a man who has been accused of committing a crime may escape before being tried or even that he may commit other crimes in the meantime. As this was obviously not true in the case of the above-mentioned man, my colleague asked the district attorney why he had issued an order of imprisonment under the circumstances. The reply of the district attorney was that in view of the increasing number of motor vehicle casualties it was legitimate and proper on his part to try to prevent offenders from causing further inconveniences by putting them into prison. Besides, ordinary judges are usually not very severe against people indicted for casual homicides; hence a little taste of prison before trial would be a salutary experience for offenders anyway. The official concerned candidly admitted that he was behaving this way in order to "improve" on the law, and he felt perfectly justified in employing means like imprisonment even though it was not properly prescribed by the law for that purpose, in order to achieve the desired end of reducing traffic casualties.

This is a typical case of the attitude of officials who substitute themselves for the law by so stretching the letter of the statute as to apply rules of their own under the pretext that the law would be insufficient if more scrupulously interpreted and applied to achieve its ends in a given circumstance. Incidentally, this is also a case of *illegal* behavior, that is, of behavior on the part of public officials in contravention of the law, and is not to be confused with *arbitrary* behavior, such as that eventually allowed to British officials at the present time in view of the lack of a definite set of administrative rules. As a good example of arbitrary behavior on the part of the British administration, one could probably cite the famous and rather complicated case of Crichel Down, which aroused so many strong protests in England some years ago. State officials who had legally requisitioned private property during the war in order to use it as a bombing range tried to dispose of the same property after the war for completely different purposes, such as conducting agricultural experiments and the like.

In cases of this kind, the existence of certain regulations, in the sense of precisely worded, written statutes, can be very useful, if not always in preventing officials from violating the law, at least in holding them legally responsible for their behavior before ordinary courts or before administrative tribunals such as the French *conseil d'état.*

But to move on to the important point of my argument: Individual freedom in all countries of the West has been gradually reduced in the last hundred years not only, or not chiefly, because of encroachments and usurpations on the part of officials acting against the law, but also because of the fact that the law, namely, the statutory law, entitled officials to behave in ways that, according to the previous law, would have been judged as usurpations of power and encroachments upon the individual freedom of the citizens.[2]

This is patently demonstrated, for example, by the history of the so-called English "administrative law," which may be summed up as a succession of statutory delegations of legislative and judiciary powers to executive officials. The fate of individual freedom in the West chiefly depends on this "administrative" process. But we must not forget that the process itself, without considering cases of sheer usurpation (which are probably not so important or so numerous as we may imagine), has been rendered possible by legislation.

I quite agree with some contemporary scholars, such as Professor Hayek, who are suspicious of executive officials, but I think that people who praise individual freedom ought to be even more suspicious of the legislators, as it is precisely through legislation that the increase in the powers (including the "sweeping powers") of officials has been and still is being achieved. Judges too may have contributed, at least in a negative way, to this result in recent times. We are told by so eminent a scholar as the above-quoted Sir Carleton Kemp Allen that the courts of judicature in England might have entered into a contest with the executive, as they were disposed to do in former ages, in order to assert and even to extend their authority in connection with an altered conception of the relationship between the individual and the state. In recent years, however, according to Sir Carleton, they have

---

[2] Cf., for instance, the new (1959) Italian traffic laws, which increase considerably the scope of the discretionary measures enforceable against drivers on the part of such executive officials as the "prefects."

done "precisely the opposite," as they have increasingly "tended
to keep their hands off the 'purely administrative' and to refrain
from any interference with executive policy."

On the other hand, so distinguished a magistrate as Sir Alfred
Denning, one of the present Lords of Her Majesty's Court of
Appeal in England, in his book, *The Changing Law*, first published in 1953, gives us a convincing account of several actions
on the part of British courts in recent years designed to maintain
the rule of law by keeping under ordinary judiciary control the
government departments (particularly after the Crown Proceedings Act of 1947) or such odd entities as nationalized industries,
departmental tribunals (against one of which the Court of the
King's Bench issued a writ of *certiorari* in the famous Northum-
berland case in 1951), private tribunals (like those set up by the
rules of such organizations as trade unions), and so on. It is
difficult to decide whether Sir Carleton is right in charging the
ordinary courts with indifference toward the new powers of the
executive or whether Sir Alfred Denning is right in pointing out
their activity in the same respect.

A great many powers have been conferred on state officials in
England as well as in other countries through the enactment of
statutes on the part of the legislature. It would be sufficient simply to scan, for instance, the history of the delegation of powers
in England in recent years to be quite convinced of this.

It is still one of the deeply rooted political beliefs of our age
that because legislation is passed by parliaments and because
parliaments are elected by the people, the people are the source
of the legislative process and that the will of the people, or at
least that part of the people identifiable with the electorate, will
ultimately prevail on all subjects to be determined by the government, as Dicey might have put it.

I do not know to what extent this doctrine has any validity if
we submit it to such criticisms as those suggested by my fellow
citizens, Mosca and Pareto, at the beginning of this century in
their famous theories of the significance of leading minorities,
or, as Pareto would say, of the elites, and still frequently quoted
by sociologists and political scientists in the United States. Regardless of any conclusion we may reach about these theories,
the "people" or the "electorate" is a concept not easily reducible

to or even compatible with that of the individual person as a particular citizen acting according to his own will and therefore "free" from constraint in the sense we have accepted here. Liberty and democracy have been concomitant ideals for the countries of the West since the times of the ancient Athenians. But it has been pointed out by several thinkers in the past, such as De Tocqueville and Lord Acton, that individual freedom and democracy may become incompatible whenever majorities are intolerant or minorities rebellious, and in general, whenever there are within a political society what Lawrence Lowell would have called "irreconcilables." Rousseau was aware of this when he pointed out that all majority systems must be based on unanimity, at least in regard to the acceptance of majority rule, if they are to be said to reflect the "common will."

If this unanimity is not merely a fiction of political philosophers, but also has to have actual meaning in political life, we must admit that whenever a decision taken by a majority is not freely accepted, but only suffered by a minority, in the same way as individuals may suffer coercive acts to avoid worse on the part of other people like robbers or blackmailers, individual freedom, in the sense of absence of constraint exercised by other people, is not compatible with democracy, conceived as the hegemonic power of numbers.

If we consider that no legislative process takes place in a democratic society without depending on the power of numbers, we must conclude that this process is likely to be incompatible with individual freedom in many cases.

Recent studies in the so-called science of policy and the nature of group decisions have tended to confirm this point in a rather convincing way.[3]

The attempts made by some scholars in recent times to compare such different forms of behavior as that of a buyer or a seller in the market and that, say, of a voter in a political election, with the object of discovering some common factor between them, seem to me rather stimulating, not only because of the

---

[3] I myself dealt with this subject on two other occasions, namely, in some lectures at Nuffield College, Oxford, and at the Department of Economics, University of Manchester, in 1957.

methodological questions involved, relating to economic and to political science respectively, but also because of the fact that the question whether there is a difference between the economic and the political (or the legal) position, respectively, of the individuals within the same society has been one of the main issues in dispute between liberals and socialists during the last hundred or hundred and twenty years.

This dispute may interest us in more than one respect, as we are trying to evidence a concept of freedom as absence of constraint exercised by other people, including the authorities, which implies freedom in business as well as in any other sphere of private life. Socialist doctrines have maintained that under a legal and political system which grants equal rights to everybody, no advantage in equal rights would accrue to those people who lack sufficient means to benefit from many of these rights. Liberal doctrines, on the contrary, have maintained that all the attempts at "integrating" political "freedom" with "freedom from want" on the part of the "have-nots," as suggested or imposed by the socialists, lead to such contradictions within the system that one cannot grant everybody "freedom," conceived as the absence of want, without bringing about the suppression of political and legal freedom, conceived as the absence of constraint exercised by other people. But liberal doctrines add something more. They maintain also that no "freedom from want" can be really achieved by decree or by the direction of the economic process on the part of the authorities, such as would be achieved on the basis of a free market.

Now what may be considered as a common assumption of both socialists and liberals is that a difference exists between the legal and political freedom of the individual, conceived as absence of constraint, on the one hand, and the "economic" or "natural" freedom of the individual, on the other, if we have to accept the word "freedom" also in the sense of "absence of want." This difference is appreciated from opposite points of view by liberals and by socialists, but in the last analysis both recognize that "freedom" may have different, if not also incompatible, meanings for individuals belonging to the same society.

There is no doubt that introducing "freedom from want" into a political or legal system implies a necessary alteration of the concept of "freedom," understood as freedom from constraint guaranteed by that system. This happens, as liberals point out, because of certain special provisions of the statutes and decrees of socialist inspiration that are incompatible with freedom in business. But it happens also, and above all, because the very attempt to introduce "freedom from want" has to be made—as all socialists admit, at least in so far as they want to deal with preexisting historical societies and do not limit their efforts to promoting societies of volunteers in some remote part of the world—first through legislation and therefore through decisions on the basis of majority rule, regardless of whether the legislatures are elected, as they are in almost all present-day political systems, or are the direct expression of the people, as they were in ancient Rome or in the old Greek cities and as they are in the present-day Swiss *Landsgemeinde*. No free-trade system can actually work if it is not rooted in a legal and political system that helps citizens to counteract interference with their business on the part of other people, including the authorities. But a characteristic feature of free-trade systems seems also to be that they are compatible, and probably compatible only, with such legal and political systems as have little or no recourse to legislation, at least as far as private life and business are concerned. On the other hand, socialist systems cannot continue to exist without the help of legislation. No historical evidence, as far as I know, supports the assumption that socialist "freedom from want" for all individuals is compatible with such institutions as the common-law system or the Roman system, where the law-making process is directly performed by each and all of the citizens, with only occasional help from judges and such experts as the Roman jurists, and without having recourse, as a rule, to legislation.

Only the so-called "utopians" who tried to promote special colonies of volunteers in order to realize socialistic societies imagined that they could do so without legislation. But they too actually managed to do without it only for short periods of time, until their voluntary associations turned into chaotic amalgams of old volunteers, ex-volunteers, and newcomers without special beliefs in any form of socialism.

Socialism and legislation seem to be inevitably connected if socialist societies are to keep alive. This is probably the main

reason for the increasing weight that is being given in common-
law systems like the English and the American not only to statutes and decrees, but also to the very idea that a legal system is,
after all, a legislative system and that "certainty" is the short-run
certainty of written law.

The reason why socialism and legislation are inevitably connected is that while a free market implies a spontaneous adjustment of demand and supply on the basis of the preference scales
of individuals, this adjustment cannot take place if the demand is
not such as to be met by supply on the same basis, that is, if the
preference scales of those who enter the market are not actually
complementary. This can happen, for instance, in all cases in
which the buyers think that the prices asked by the sellers are too
high, or where the sellers think that the prices offered by the
buyers are too low. Sellers who are not in a position to satisfy
buyers, or buyers who are not in a position to satisfy sellers
cannot make a market, unless sellers or buyers respectively have
some means at their disposal of coercing their counterparts in
the market into meeting their demands.

According to socialists, poor people are "deprived" by rich
people of what they need. This way of speaking is simply an
abuse of language, as it is not proved that the "haves" and the
"have-nots" were or are all entitled to the common possession of
all things. True, historical evidence supports the socialist point of
view in some cases like invasions and conquests, and generally in
cases of robbery, piracy, blackmail, and so on. But these never
occur in a free market, that is, in a system that enables individual
buyers and sellers to counteract constraint exercised by other
people. We have also seen, in this connection, that very few economists take into consideration such "misproductive" activities,
since they are generally regarded as completely outside the market and therefore not worthy of economic inquiry. If nobody
may be constrained, without the possibility of defending himself,
to pay for goods and services more than he would pay for them
without constraint, misproductive activities cannot take place,
since in such cases no corresponding supply of goods and services will be met by demand and no adjustment between buyers
and sellers will be obtained.

Legislation may achieve what a spontaneous adjustment could

never do. Demand may be obliged to meet supply, or supply may be obliged to meet demand, according to certain regulations enacted by legislative bodies, possibly deciding, as happens at present, on the basis of such procedural devices as the majority rule.

The fact about legislation that is immediately perceived by theorists no less than by the common people is that regulations are enforced upon everybody, including those who never participated in the process of making the regulations and who may never have had notice of it. This fact distinguishes a statute from a decision handed down by a judge in a case brought before him by the parties. The decision may be enforced, but it is not enforced automatically, that is, without the collaboration of the parties concerned or at least of one of them. At any rate, it is not directly enforceable on other people who were not parties to the dispute or who were not represented by the parties in the case.

Thus, theorists usually connect legislation with enforcement, while this connection is not directly emphasized, and in any case is ascertainable to a lesser extent, in decisions of courts of judicature. Very few people, on the contrary, have pointed out the fact that enforcement is connected with legislation not only as the result of the legislative process but also within the very process itself. Those who have a share in that process are themselves subject, in their turn, to the enforcement of procedural rules, and this very fact gives a coercive character to the whole activity of legislation as performed by a group of people according to a previously settled procedure. The same holds true of the activities of electorates, whose task may be defined as that of reaching a group decision about the people to be elected according to procedural rules that have been previously settled for all those participating in the formation of the decision itself.

The existence of a coercive procedure in the decision-making process whenever people are to decide, not as single individuals, but as members of groups, is precisely what renders it possible to distinguish between the process of making decisions on the part of individuals and the same process on the part of groups.

This difference has been ignored by those theorists who, like the English economist Duncan Black, have tried to elaborate a theory of group decisions that would include both the economic decisions of individuals in the market and group decisions on the

political stage. According to Professor Black, who has just published a new book about this subject, there is no substantial difference between these two kinds of decisions. Buyers and sellers
in the market may be compared, if taken as a whole, to the members of a committee whose decisions are the result of the interre-
lations of their preference scales according to the law of supply
and demand. On the other hand, individuals on the political
scene, at least in all those countries where political decisions are
taken by groups, may be considered as members of committees,
regardless of the special functions of each committee. The electorate could be considered one of these "committees" no less
than a legislative assembly or a council of ministers. In all these
cases, according to Professor Black, the preference scales of every member of the committee are confronted with the preference scales of every other member of the same committee. The
only difference—but a minor one, according to Professor
Black—is that whereas in the market preferences confront each
other according to the law of supply and demand, in political
preferences the selection of some of them rather than others
takes place according to a definite procedure. If we know this
procedure, Professor Black maintains, and moreover if we know
what political preferences are to confront each other, we are in
a position to calculate in advance which preferences will emerge
in the group decision, just as we are in a position to calculate
in advance, provided that we know the preferences at stake on
the market, which ones among them will emerge according to the
law of supply and demand.

As Professor Black assumes, one could speak of a tendency
toward an equilibrium of preference scales on the political stage
in the same way as one speaks of an equilibrium to which preference scales tend in the market.

In brief, we ought to consider, according to Black, both economics and political science as two different branches of the
same science, since they have the common task of calculating
which preferences will emerge in a market or on the political
scene, given a set of known preference scales and a definite law
governing their confrontation.

I do not want to deny that there is something correct in this conclusion. But what I do want to point out is that by putting political and economic decisions on the same level and considering them comparable, we deliberately ignore the differences that exist between the law of supply and demand in the market and any procedural law whatever governing the process of confrontation among political preferences (and the subsequent emergence of the preferences to be accepted by the group in its decision), like, for example, the majority rule.

The law of supply and demand is only a description of the way in which a spontaneous adjustment takes place, given certain circumstances, between several preference scales. A procedural law is completely different, notwithstanding the fact that it is also called a "law" in all European languages, just as the Greek language (at least since the fourth century before Christ) used the same word, *nomos*, to mean both a natural law and a man-made law, like a statute. Of course, we could say that the law of supply and demand is also a "procedural" law, but once again we would be confusing, under the same words, two very different meanings.

The main difference between individual decisions in the market and individual contributions to the decisions of groups on the political scene is that in the market, at least by virtue of the divisibility of the goods or services available in it, the individual not only can foresee exactly what the outcome of his decision is (for instance, what kind and quantity of chickens he will buy with a certain amount of money), but he can also put in a definite relation every dollar he spends with the corresponding things he can acquire. Group decisions, on the contrary, are of the all-or-none variety: if you are on the losing side, you lose your vote. There is no other alternative, just as there would be none if you went to the market and could find neither goods nor services nor even parts of them that could be bought with the money you have at your disposal.

As a distinguished American economist, Professor James Buchanan, acutely pointed out in this connection, "alternatives of market choice normally conflict only in the sense that the law of diminishing returns is operating. . . . If an individual desires more of a particular commodity or service, the market normally

requires only that he take less of another commodity or service."[4] By contrast, "alternatives of voting choice are more exclusive, that is, the selection of one precludes the selection of
another." Group choices, so far as the individuals belonging to
the group are concerned, tend to be "mutually exclusive by the
very nature of the alternative." This is the result not only of
the poverty of the schemes usually adopted and adoptable for
the distribution of the voting strength, but also of the fact (as
Buchanan points out) that many alternatives which we usually
call "political" do not allow those "combinations" or "composite
solutions" which render market choices so flexible in comparison with political choices. An important consequence, already
illustrated by Mises, is that in the market the dollar vote is never
overruled: "The individual is never placed in the position of being a member of a dissenting minority,"[5] at least so far as the
existing or potential alternatives of the market are concerned. To
put the point the other way round, there is a possible *coercion* in
voting which does not occur in the market. The voter chooses
only between potential alternatives; he may lose his vote and be
compelled to accept a result contrary to his expressed preference, whereas a similar sort of coercion is never present in market choice, at least on the assumption of production divisibility.
The political scene, which we have at least provisionally conceived as the *locus* of voting processes, is comparable to a market
in which the individual is required to spend the whole of his
income on one commodity or the whole of his work and resources in producing one commodity or service.

In other words, the voter is limited by some *coercive* procedures
in the utilization of his capacities for action. Of course, we can
approve or disapprove of this coercion, and we can occasionally
discriminate between different hypotheses in order to approve or
disapprove of it. But the point is that the voting process implies a
form of coercion and that political decisions are reached through
a procedure that implies coercion. The voter who loses makes
one choice initially, but eventually has to accept another that he

---

[4] James Buchanan, "Individual Choices in Voting and in the Market," *Journal of Political Economy*, 1954, p. 338.
[5] Loc. cit.

previously rejected; his decision-making process has been overthrown.

This is certainly the main, although it is not the only, difference between individual decisions in the market and group decisions taking place on the political scene.

The individual in the market can predict, with absolute certainty, the direct or immediate results of his choice. "The act of choosing," says Buchanan, "and the consequences of choosing stand in a one-to-one correspondence. On the other hand, the voter, even if he is fully omniscient in his foresight of the consequences of each possible collective decision, can never predict with certainty which of the alternatives presented will be chosen."[6] This uncertainty, of the Knightian type (that is, the impossibility of assigning any number to the probability of an event) must in some degree influence the voter's behavior, and there is no acceptable theory of the behavior of a decision-maker in uncertain conditions.

Moreover, the conditions under which group decisions occur seem to render it difficult to employ the notion of *equilibrium* in the same way in which it is employed in economics. In economics *equilibrium* is defined as equality of supply and demand, an equality understandable when the individual chooser can so articulate his choices as to let each single dollar vote successfully. But what kind of equality can exist between, for instance, supply and demand for laws and orders through group decisions when the individual can ask for bread and be given a stone? Of course, if the members of the groups are free to rank in changing majorities and can partake in revisions of earlier decisions, this possibility may be conceived of as a sort of remedy for the lack of equilibrium in group decisions, because it gives to each individual in the group, at least in principle, the possibility of having the group decision some time or other coincide with his personal choice. But this is not "equilibrium." Freedom to form part of changing majorities is a typical feature of democracy as traditionally understood in Western countries, and this is, incidentally, the reason why many authors feel that they may describe "political democracy" as similar to "economic democracy" (the market

[6] Loc. cit.

system). In fact, democracy appears to be, as we have seen, only a substitute for economic democracy, although it is probably its best substitute in many cases.

Thus, we reach the conclusion that legislation, being always—at least in contemporary systems—a product of group decisions, must inevitably imply not only a certain degree of coercion of those who have to obey the legislative rules, but also a corresponding degree of coercion of those who directly participate in the process of making the rules themselves. This inconvenience cannot be avoided by any political system where group decisions are to take place, including democracy, although democracy, at least as it is still conceived of in the West, gives to each member of the legislating body a chance to form a part sooner or later of winning majorities and so to avoid coercion by making the rules coincide with his personal choice.

Coercion is not, however, the only characteristic of legislation as compared with other law-making processes, such as that of the Roman law or of the common law. We have seen that uncertainty proves to be another characteristic of legislation, not only on the part of those who have to obey the legislated regulations, but also on the part of the members of the legislative body itself, since they vote without knowing the results of their vote until the group decision has been made.

Now the fact that coercion and uncertainty cannot be avoided by the members of the legislative bodies themselves in the process of legislation leads to the conclusion that not even political systems based on direct democracy allow individuals to escape coercion or uncertainty in the sense we have described.

No direct democracy could solve the problem of avoiding both coercion and uncertainty, since the problem is not itself related to direct or indirect participation in the law-making process through legislation resulting from group decisions.

This warns us also of the comparative futility of all attempts to secure more freedom or more certainty for the individuals in a country as far as the law of the land is concerned by letting them participate as frequently and as directly as possible in the law-making process through legislation by universal adult suffrage, proportional representation, referendum, initiative, recall of representatives, or even by other organizations or institutions revealing the so-called public opinion about as many subjects as possible and making the people more efficient in influencing the political behavior of the rulers.

On the other hand, representative democracies are much less efficient than direct democracies in obtaining the actual participation of individuals in the law-making process through legislation.

There are many senses in which representation may be thought of, and some of them certainly do give the people the impression that they are participating in a serious, although indirect, way in the process of law-making through the legislation of their country or even in the process of administering the affairs of the country through the executive apparatus.

Unfortunately, what is actually happening in all the countries of the West at present is something that does not afford us any real basis for gratification if we undertake a cold analysis of the facts.

6

FREEDOM AND
REPRESENTATION

It is frequently asserted that there is, or to put it more accurately, there once was, a classical concept of the democratic process that bears little resemblance to what is happening on the political scene at present either in Britain, where that process had its origin in the Middle Ages, or in other countries that have more or less imitated the "democratic" system of England. All economists, at least, will remember what Schumpeter clearly stated in this respect in *Capitalism, Socialism, and Democracy.* According to the classical concept of "democracy," as it was formulated towards the end of the eighteenth century in England, the democratic process was assumed to permit the people to decide issues for themselves through elected representatives in the parliament. This offered a supposedly efficient substitute for direct decision on general issues on the part of the people, such as the decisions that had taken place in the ancient Greek cities or in Rome or in the medieval Italian *comuni* or in the Swiss *Landsgemeinde.* Representatives had to decide for the people all the issues that the people could not decide themselves for certain technical reasons, as, for instance, the impossibility of meeting all together in a square to discuss policies and make decisions. Representatives were conceived of as mandataries of the people, whose task was to formulate and to carry out the people's will. In their turn, the people were not conceived of as a mythical entity, but rather as the ensemble of the individuals in their capacity as citizens, and the representatives of the people as persons were themselves citizens and therefore in a position to express what

112

all their fellow citizens felt about the general issues of the community.

According to Burke's interpretation,

> the House of Commons was supposed originally to be no part of the standing government of England. It was considered as a control issued *immediately* from the people, and speedily *to be resolved in the mass* from whence it arose. In this respect, it was in the higher part of government what juries are in the lower. The capacity of a magistrate being transitory and that of a citizen permanent, the latter capacity, it was hoped, would of course preponderate in all discussions, not only between the people and the standing authority of the Crown, but between the people and the fleeting authority of the House of Commons itself. . . . [1]

According to this interpretation, and aside from the so-called standing authority of the Crown, it is rather apparent that the deputies are to "discuss" and to decide more in their capacity as citizens than as magistrates, and moreover that the citizens as such are something permanent, from whom magistrates are to be chosen to effect their immediate and transitory expression.

Burke himself was not a man to be considered as a sort of gramophone record sent to the Parliament by his electors. He also took care to point out that

> to deliver an opinion is the right of all men; that of constituents is a weighty and respectable opinion, which a representative ought always to rejoice to hear and which he ought always most seriously to consider. But authoritative instructions, mandates issued, which the member is bound blindly and implicitly to obey, to vote and argue for, though contrary to the clearest conviction of his judgment and conscience, these are things utterly unknown to the laws of the land and which arise from a fundamental mistake of the whole order and tenor of our constitution.[2]

Generally speaking, it would be a mistake to think that towards the end of the eighteenth century the members of the Parliament heeded carefully the will of their fellow citizens. The second English revolution in the late seventeenth century was not a

---

[1] Edmund Burke, *Works* (1808 ed.), II, 287 ff.
[2] Edmund Burke, "Speech to the Electors of Bristol," December 3, 1774, in *Works* (Boston: Little, Brown & Co., 1894), II, 96.

democratic one. As a recent student of the development of the people's influence in the British government, Cecil S. Emden, has pointed out, "if a plebiscite had been taken in 1688 on the question of the substitution of William for James, the majority would have voted against the deposition of the latter."[3] The new regime of 1688 resembled an oligarchy of the Venetian type rather than a democracy. Notwithstanding the abolition of censorship of the press in 1695, the members of the House of Commons and the ministries proved many times indisposed to suffer free criticism by their fellow citizens. On some occasions—for instance, in 1712—they were so exasperated at the publication of certain pamphlets reflecting on the proceedings of the House that they decided to impose heavy duties on all newspapers and pamphlets in order to affect their sale adversely. Moreover, very little encouragement was given to the exercise of public opinion. The official publication of the determinations reached in proceedings in Parliament was not a regular procedure, and the objection to publishing information on the ground that it might imply an "appeal to the people" was frequent in the early eighteenth century in order to avoid the publication of the debates and the votes in Parliament. The same attitude influenced the House and the ministries in regard to matters of vital interest for the country in order to prevent opposition on the part of public opinion against the policy adopted by the government and by the House. In the eighteenth century, statesmen like Charles Fox, when a young man, could consider the House of Commons as the only revealer of the national mind, and Fox himself proclaimed once in the House:

> I pay no regard whatever to the voice of the people: it is our duty to do what is proper, without considering what may be agreeable; their business is to choose us; it is ours to act constitutionally and to maintain the independence of the Parliament.[4]

Nevertheless, it is generally admitted that, according to the classical theory of democracy, the Parliament was conceived of as

[3] Cecil S. Emden, *The People and the Constitution* (2nd ed.; Oxford: at the Clarendon Press, 1956), p. 34.
[4] Ibid., p. 53. The historians tell us that "as a result of this speech Fox himself was attacked by a mob as he drove down to the House and was rolled in the mud."

a committee whose functions "would be to voice, reflect, or represent the will of the electorate."[5] Incidentally, it was much easier to put this theory into effect at the end of the eighteenth century and before the Reform Act of 1832 than later on. Although representatives were as numerous as they are now, constituents were few. In 1830 the British Commons represented an electorate of about 220,000 out of a total population of approximately 14 million, or about 3 percent of the adult population. Members represented on the average 330 voters each. Now they represent in England an average of 56,000 electors each, on the basis of a universal adult suffrage of some 35,000,000 people. But at the beginning of this century, Dicey, while objecting to the alleged "legal" theory of Austin that the members of the House of Commons are merely "trustees for the body by which they were elected and appointed," and maintaining that no English judge could concede that Parliament is in any legal sense a "trustee" for the electors, had no difficulty in admitting that "in a political sense the electors are the more important part, or, we may even say, are actually the sovereign power, since their will is under the present constitution sure to obtain ultimate obedience." Dicey recognized that the language of Austin was therefore as correct in regard to "political" sovereignty as it was erroneous in regard to what he termed "legal" sovereignty and stated that "the electors are a part of and the predominant part of the politically sovereign power."[6]

> As things now stand, the will of the electorate, and certainly of the electorate in combination with the Lords and the Crown, is sure ultimately to prevail on all subjects to be determined by the British government. The matter indeed may be carried a little further, and we may assert that the arrangements of the constitution are now such as to ensure that the will of the electors shall by regular and constitutional means always in the end assert itself as the predominant influence in the country.[7]

All this was possible, according to Dicey, because of the *repre-*

---

[5] R. T. McKenzie, *British Political Parties* (London: Heineman, 1955), p. 588.

[6] Dicey, *Introduction to the Study of the Law of the Constitution* (9th ed.; London: Macmillan, 1939), p. 76.

[7] Ibid., p. 73.

sentative character of the English government, and he explained that "the aim and effect of such government is to produce a coincidence or at any rate diminish the divergence between the internal and the external limitations of the exercise of sovereign power,"[8] that is, between the wishes of the sovereign (and Parliament is in England legally a sovereign) and "the permanent wishes of the nation."[9] Dicey concluded on this subject that

> the difference between the will of the sovereign and the will of the nation was terminated by the foundation of a system of real representative government. Where a Parliament truly represents the people, the divergence between the external and the internal limit to the exercise of sovereign power can hardly arise, or if it arises, must soon disappear. Speaking roughly, the permanent wishes of the representative portion of Parliament can hardly in the long run differ from the wishes of the English people or at any rate of the electors: that which the majority of the House of Commons command, the majority of the English people usually desire.[10]

Of course, "representation" is rather a generic term. We could adopt only a "legal" concept of it, to conclude, as several lawyers do in regard to political representation in other countries, that this term means nothing more nor less than what it is supposed to mean in terms of constitutional law or, as in England, the constitutional conventions prevailing at a given time. But, as Dicey quite rightly pointed out, there is obviously also a "political" meaning of "representation," and it is this political meaning that political scientists emphasize in accordance with actual facts.

The verb "to represent,"[11] coming from the Latin *repraesentare,* that is, making present again, was given several meanings in early English, but its first political use in the sense of acting as an authorized agent or deputy of someone is traceable to a 1651 pamphlet of Isaac Pennington and later on, in 1655, to a speech by Oliver Cromwell on January 22 in Parliament, when he said: "I have been careful of your safety and the safety of those you

[8] Ibid., p. 82.
[9] Ibid., p. 83.
[10] Loc. cit.
[11] On this and other points mentioned in this chapter, cf. the clear and informative article on "Representation" by H. Chisholm in the *Encyclopaedia Britannica* (14th ed.).

represented." But as early as 1624, "representation" had come to mean "substitution of one thing or person for another," especially with a right or authority to act on the other's account. A few years later, in 1649, we find the word "representative" applied to the Parliamentary assembly in the act abolishing the office of king after the execution of Charles I. The act mentions the "representatives" of the "nation" as those by whom the people are governed and whom the people choose and entrust for that purpose according to their "just and ancient rights."

The thing itself was certainly older than the word. For instance, the famous principle, "no taxation without representation," the importance of which for the destiny of the United States it is unnecessary to underline, had been established in England as early as 1297 by the declaration *De tallagio non concedendo,* to be confirmed later by the Petition of Right in 1628. Even earlier, in 1295, Edward I's famous writ to the sheriff of Northamptonshire to summon to Parliament in Westminster elected representatives of the counties and boroughs applied for the first time to political practice (if we disregard a preceding similar writ of Henry III and a preceding Parliament of non-elected representatives in 1275) a device praised in more recent times as the most brilliant novelty in the field of politics since the days of the Greeks and the Romans.[12] Edward's writ to the sheriff read clearly that people had to be *elected (elegi facias)*—burgesses for boroughs, knights for counties, and citizens for cities —and pointed out that they must have "full and sufficient power for themselves and for the communities . . . for doing what shall then be ordained according to the Common Council in the premises, so that the aforesaid business [that is, doing what was necessary to avoid some grave dangers threatening the kingdom] shall not remain unfinished in any way for defect of this power."

---

[12] However, the political theory of representation in the Middle Ages seems to have been influenced by a similar theory of the Roman jurist Pomponius, contained in a fragment of the *Digest* ("deinde quia difficile plebs convenire coepit, populus certe multo difficilius in tanta turba hominum, necessitas ipsa curam reipublicae ad senatum deduxit," i.e., the senate was led to assume the responsibility of legislation because of the difficulties involved in assembling the plebeians and the even greater difficulty of holding an assembly of the vast multitude constituting the entire electorate). Cf. Otto Gierke, *Political Theories of the Middle Age,* tr. by Maitland (Cambridge University Press, 1922), pp. 168 ff.

Hence it is clear that people summoned by the king to Westminster were conceived of as proper attorneys and mandataries of their communities.

Very interesting from our point of view is the fact that "representation in Common Council" did not imply necessarily that decisions had to be taken according to the majority rule. As has been pointed out by some scholars (for instance, by McKechnie in his *Commentary in Magna Charta* [1914]), an early medieval version of the principle, "no taxation without representation," was intended as "no taxation without the consent of the individual taxed," and we are told that in 1221, the Bishop of Winchester, "summoned to consent to a scutage tax, refused to pay, after the council had made the grant, on the ground that he dissented, and the Exchequer upheld his plea."[13] We know also from the German scholar, Gierke, that in the more or less "representative" assemblies held among German tribes according to Germanic law, "unanimity was requisite" although a minority could be compelled to give way, and that the idea of a connection between representation and majority rule made its way into the political sphere through the church councils that adopted it from the law of corporations, although even in the Church the canonists held that minorities had certain irrefragable rights and that matters of faith could not be decided by mere majorities.[14]

Thus, it appears that the formation of decision groups and of group decisions according to a coercive procedure based on the idea of majority rule, whether the groups were only "presentative" or "representative" of other people, seemed at first to be unnatural, at least for a time, to our ancestors, both in religious and in political councils, and probably only expediency could have paved the way for its progress in more recent times. As a matter of fact, this procedure is somewhat unnatural, as it overrules some choices only because the people adopting them are less numerous than others, while this method of making decisions is never adopted in other circumstances, and, if adopted, would lead to patently unsuitable results. We shall go back to this point later on. Here it is sufficient to point out that political

[13] H. Chisholm, loc. cit.
[14] Gierke, op. cit., p. 64.

representation was closely connected in its origin with the idea that the representatives act as agents of other people and according to the latter's will.

When, in modern times, the principle of representation, in England as well as in other countries, was extended practically to all the individuals in a political community, at least to all the adults belonging to it, three great problems arose which needed to be solved if the representative principle was actually to work: (1) that of making the number of citizens entitled to choose representatives correspond to the real structure of the nation; (2) that of getting candidates to stand for the office of representatives who were adequate exponents of the will of the people represented; and (3) that of adopting a system of choosing representatives that would result in their adequately reflecting the opinions of the people represented.[15]

It can hardly be said that these problems have so far received a satisfactory solution. None has thus far been solved in any country; no nation has been able to preserve the spirit of representation as an activity performed according to the will of the people represented. Let us set aside such important questions as those raised in the famous essay of John Stuart Mill on *Representative Government* (1861) relating to what people are entitled to be represented and to the different weight to be possibly given to the people represented according to their abilities or to their contribution to the expenses of the community, and so on. Let us also for the moment set aside another question that is undoubtedly very important and difficult to solve, viz., whether or not a representation of the will of people could be consistent in regard to a great many issues, or, in other words, whether it is actually possible to speak of a "common will" on the part of the people in a number of instances where choices are of alternative nature and where there is no probability of discovering a way of allowing people to agree about any choice whatever. Schumpeter has pointed out this difficulty in his essay on *Capitalism, Socialism, and Democracy* and concluded that the "common will" is an ex-

---

[15] For a recent discussion of the problems of representation in connection with the majority rule, *see* Burnham, *The Congress and the American Tradition* (Chicago: Regnery, 1959), particularly the chapter entitled "What Is a Majority?" pp. 311 ff.

pression whose content must be inevitably contradictory when referred to individual members of a community that is said to have a "common will." If political matters are precisely those that do not allow of more than one choice, and if, moreover, there is no way of discovering by some objective method which is the most suitable choice for a political community, we ought to conclude that political decisions always imply an element that is not compatible with individual freedom, and therefore not compatible with a true representation of the will of those people whose choice has possibly been rejected in the decision adopted. Finally, let us set aside, as not important for our purposes, certain special questions relating to different systems of choosing. We must notice that voting is not the only system of choosing representatives. We have other historically important systems, such as the ballots cast in some cases by the ancient Greek cities or by the aristocratic republic of Venice in medieval and in modern times, and therefore relating to different systems of voting, if voting is the way adopted for making the choice.

These questions may be considered to some extent as technicalities that lie beyond the field of our inquiry. We have to deal now with other difficulties.

True, the extension of the principle of representation through the extension of the franchise to all citizens seems to correspond perfectly to an individualistic conception of representation, according to which every individual must be represented in some way in the decisions to be taken on the general issues of the nation. Every individual must exercise his right of choosing, entrusting, and instructing representatives in order to make political decisions through a free manifestation of his will. Of course, as Disraeli would say, the will of some people may be perfectly represented in some cases by other people who guess the wishes of the former without having been instructed by them, as, according to Schumpeter, Napoleon did when he terminated all religious struggles in his country at the time of his consulate. We can also imagine that the *real* interests of some people (that is, at least the interests some people later recognize as their own true interests, notwithstanding any contrary opinion they may have held before) may be better represented by some competent and incorruptible exponents of their will who never would have been entrusted or instructed by them. This is the case, for instance, with parents who act in the capacity of representatives of their children in private life and in business. But it seems to be obvious, from an individualistic point of view, that nobody is more competent to know what one's own will is than one is oneself. Therefore, the true representation of that will must be the result of a choice on the part of the individual who is to be represented. The extension of representation in modern times seems to correspond to this consideration. So far, so good.

But very serious difficulties arise when the principle of representation through individual choice of representatives is applied in political life. In private life, as a rule, these difficulties do not exist. Anybody may contact anybody else whom he trusts and engage him as an agent to negotiate a contract, for example, according to instructions that can be clearly stated, clearly understood, and clearly carried out.

In political life nothing of the kind takes place, and this seems to be also a consequence of the very extension of representation to as many individuals as possible in a political community. It seems to be a great misfortune of this principle that, the more one tries to extend it, the more one defeats its purpose. It must be observed that political life is not the only field in which these inconveniences have emerged in recent times. Economists and sociologists have already drawn our attention to the fact that representation in big private corporations works badly. Shareholders are said to have little influence on the policy of the managers, and the discretionary power of the latter, being a result as well as a cause of the "managerial revolution" in our times, is the greater, the more numerous are the shareholders that the managers "represent" in a business.[16] The story of representation in political as well as in economic life teaches us a lesson that people have not yet learned. There is in my country a saying, *chi vuole vada,* which means that if you really want something, you must go and see for yourself what is to be done instead of sending a

---

[16] This is true in spite of the fact, noted by Professor Milton Friedman, that shareholders may ultimately get rid of the stock of those firms whose policy they are not sufficiently allowed to control, whereas the citizenry cannot so easily do the same with their citizenship.

messenger. Of course, your action cannot have good results if you are not wise, skilled, or sufficiently well-informed to achieve the result you desire. And this is what managers and representatives in politics as well as in business would say if only they bothered to explain to the people they represent how things are actually being done.

John Stuart Mill pointed out the fact that representation cannot work unless the people represented participate in some way in the activity of their representatives.

> Representative institutions are of little value, and may be a mere instrument of tyranny or intrigue, when the generality of electors are not sufficiently interested in their own government to give their vote, or, if they vote at all, do not bestow their suffrages on public grounds, but sell them for money, or vote at the beck of someone who has control over them or whom for private reasons they desire to propitiate. Popular election, as thus practised, instead of a security against misgovernment, is but an additional wheel in its machinery.[17]

But in political representation many difficulties arise that are very probably not due to lack of wisdom or to the ill will or the apathy of the people represented. It is a truism that issues at stake in political life are too many and too complicated and that very many of them are actually unknown both to the representatives and to the people represented. Under these conditions, no instructions could be given in most cases. This happens at any moment in the political life of a community when the self-styled representatives are not in a position to represent the actual will of the alleged "people represented" or when there are reasons for thinking that the representatives and the people represented do not agree about the issues at stake.

In pointing out this fact, I am not referring only to the usual way of choosing representatives at the present time, that is, by voting. All the difficulties I have pointed out before remain whether or not voting is the method of choosing representatives.

But voting itself seems to increase the difficulties relating both to the meaning of "representation" and to the "freedom" of the individuals in making their choice. All the difficulties relating to decision groups and group decisions remain when we consider the

---

[17] John Stuart Mill, *Considerations on Representative Government* (New York: Henry Holt & Co., 1882).

process of voting in present-day political systems. Election is the result of a group decision where all the electors are to be considered as the members of a group, for instance, of their constituencies or of the electorate as a whole. We have seen that group decisions imply procedures like majority rule which are not compatible with individual freedom of choice of the type that any individual buyer or seller in the market enjoys as well as in any other choice he makes in his private life. The effects of coercion in the machinery of voting have been repeatedly pointed out by politicians, by sociologists, by political scientists, and especially by mathematicians. Certain paradoxical aspects of this coercion have been especially emphasized by the critics of such classical methods of representation as the so-called single-member system which still is in effect in the English-speaking countries. I wish to draw your attention to the fact that these criticisms are chiefly based on the alleged fact that the system is not in accordance with the principle of "representation," namely, when, as John Stuart Mill said, political issues are decided "by a majority of the majority who may be, and often are, but a minority of the whole." Let me quote the passage of Mill's essay on this subject:

> Suppose then that, in a country governed by equal and universal suffrage, there is a contested election in every constituency, and every election is carried by a small majority. The parliament thus brought together represents little more than a bare majority of the people. This parliament proceeds to legislate and adopts important measures by a bare majority of itself. What guarantee is there that these measures accord with the wishes of a majority of the people? Nearly half the electors, having been outvoted at the hustings, have had no influence at all in the decision, and the whole of these may be—a majority of them probably are—hostile to the measures; having voted against those by whom they have been carried. Of the remaining electors nearly half have chosen representatives who, by supposition, have voted against the measures. It is possible, therefore, and not at all improbable, that the opinion which has prevailed was agreeable only to a minority of the nation.[18]

This argument is not completely convincing, as the case cited by Mill is probably theoretical only, but there is some truth in the argument, and we all know the devices that have been in-

---

[18] Ibid., p. 147.

vented, such as proportional representation, of which there are no less than three hundred varieties, in order to render elections more "representative" of the supposed will of the electors. But it is also known that no other electoral system avoids these unsurmountable difficulties, as is proved by the very existence of such devices as referenda, initiatives, and so on, that have been introduced, not in order to improve on representation, but rather to replace representation by some other system, based on a different principle, namely, that of direct democracy.

In fact, no representative system based on elections can work properly while elections are held with the object of reaching group decisions by way of majority rule or any other rule of which the effect is to coerce the individual on the losing side of the electorate.

Thus, "representative" systems as usually conceived of, in which election and representation are connected, are incompatible with individual freedom, in the sense of freedom to choose, empower, and instruct a representative.

Nevertheless, "representation" has been retained to the present day as one of the alleged characteristic features of our political system by simply emptying the word of its historical meaning and using it as a catchword or, as the contemporary English analytic philosophers would say, a "persuasive" word. In fact, the word "representation" in politics still has a favorable connotation, as people inevitably understand it to mean a sort of relation between "cestui qui trust" and a trustee, just like that in private life and in business and like what Austin supposed it to be under the constitutional law of England. As one of the most recent students of present-day political parties, R. T. McKenzie, has pointed out,

> Lip service is still paid to the classical conception of democracy even by many who are aware of the extent to which it has proved unworkable. . . . It has also become increasingly evident that the classical theory attributed to the electorate an altogether unrealistic degree of initiative; it came near to ignoring completely the importance of leadership in the political process.[19]

[19] R. T. McKenzie, op. cit., p. 588.

Meanwhile a process of *monocratization* (to use Weber's word) is continually going on within groups like political parties, at least in Europe, in fulfillment of the prophecy made by my fellow citizen, Roberto Michels, who, in his famous essay published in 1927 in the *American Political Science Review* on the sociological character of political parties, formulated the so-called iron law of oligarchy as the chief rule of the internal evolution of all present-day parties.

All this affects the fate not only of democracy, but also of individual freedom in so far as the individual is involved in the so-called democratic process and in so far as the ideas of democracy are compatible with that of individual freedom.

The tendency is to accept things as they are, not only because people cannot see anything better, but also because they are frequently not aware of what is really going on. People justify present-day "democracy" because it seems to secure at least a loose participation of individuals in the process of legislation and in the administration of their country—a participation that, loose as it may be, is considered to be the best obtainable under the circumstances. In a similar vein, R. T. McKenzie writes: "It is . . . realistic to argue that the essence of the democratic process is that it should provide a free competition for political leadership." He adds that "the essential role of the electorate is not to reach decisions on specific issues of policy but to decide which of two or more competing teams of potential leaders shall make the decisions."[20] However, this is not very much for a political theory that still uses terms like "democracy" or "representation." It is not very much either if we consider that "representation" is something other than what these new theories imply, or at least it has been conceived of as something else until recent times in politics and it is still conceived of as something else in private life and business.

Valid objections can be raised against the arguments of those who accept this emasculated version of the individualistic point of view and think that the "representative system" as it works at present is better than any other system enabling people to participate in some way in the formation of policies and especially in

[20] Ibid., p. 589.

the formation of the law in accordance with the individual's freedom of choice.

People may be said to have a share in these processes only by
way of group decisions like, for instance, those of a constituency
or of a council of representatives such as Parliament. But to say
this is to take a strictly *legal* point of view, i.e., one based on the
present legal regulations, without taking into consideration all
that is or is not behind the official rules. This legal point of view
becomes untenable as soon as we discover that legislation and
constitutions, on the basis of which we ought to decide whether
something is "legal," are themselves frequently rooted in something that is not "legal" at all. The American Constitution, that
great achievement of so many first-rate statesmen in the late
eighteenth century, was the result of an *illegal* action taken at the
Philadelphia Convention in 1787 by the Founding Fathers, who
had not had conferred upon them any power of the kind by the
legal authority on which they were dependent, namely, the Continental Congress. The latter, in its turn, had an *illegal* origin,
since it had been set up as a result of a rebellion on the part of
the American colonies against the legal power of the British
Crown.

The origin of the recent constitution of my country can
scarcely be said to be any more legal than that of its American
counterpart, although many people in my country are not even
aware of this.

In fact, the present constitution of Italy was drawn up by a
constituent assembly whose creation was, in its turn, due to a
decree of June 25, 1944, issued by the hereditary prince of Italy,
Humbert, who had been appointed "lieutenant general" of the
Kingdom of Italy, without any limits of competence, by his father, King Victor Emmanuel III, in a royal decree of June 5,
1944. But neither the lieutenant general of the Kingdom of
Italy nor the king himself had any legal power to change the
constitution or to summon an assembly to do so. Moreover, the
promulgation of the above-mentioned decree stemmed from the
so-called Salerno Agreement, which took place, under the aus-
pices of the Allied powers, between King Victor Emmanuel III
and the "representatives" of Italian parties whom nobody had
chosen in our country through the usual way of election. The

constituent assembly was, therefore, to be considered *illegal* from the point of view of the existing law of the kingdom, for the act that had originated the assembly was itself illegal, since its author, the "lieutenant general," had promulgated it *ultra vires*. On the other hand, it would have been very difficult to avoid "illegal" acts in a situation like that. None of the institutions foreseen by the constitutional laws of the kingdom survived until June, 1944. The Crown had changed its character after the nomination of the lieutenant general; one of the branches of the parliament, the Chamber of Fasces and Corporations, had been suppressed without being replaced by any other, and the other branch, the Senate, was not in condition to function at that time. Such is the lesson for those who speak of what is *legal* and what is not on the basis of alleged "legal" constitutions and do not bother about what lies behind them.

Leslie Stephen pointed out rather well the limits of the legal point of view:

> Lawyers are apt to speak as though the legislature were omnipotent, as they do not require to go beyond its decisions. It is, of course, omnipotent in the sense that it can make whatever law it pleases, inasmuch as a law means any rule which has been made by the legislature. But from the scientific point of view, the power of legislation is, of course, strictly limited. It is limited, so to speak, both from within and from without: from within, because the legislature is the product of a certain social condition, and determined by whatever determines the society; and from without, because the power of imposing laws is dependent upon the instinct of subordination, which is itself limited. If a legislature decided that all blue-eyed babies should be murdered, the preservation of blue-eyed babies would be illegal; but legislators must go mad before they could pass such a law, and subjects be idiotic before they could submit to it.[21]

While agreeing with Leslie Stephen, I wonder, incidentally, whether idiocy begins only at this point on the part of the "subjects" and whether contemporary "subjects" are not likely to accept decisions like this in the future if the ideals of "representation" and "democracy" are still to be seriously identified for a long time with the power of simply deciding (as R. T. McKenzie

---

[21] Leslie Stephen, *The Science of Ethics,* quoted by Dicey, op. cit., p. 81.

would say) "which of two or more competing teams of potential leaders shall make the decisions" for every kind of action and behavior on the part of their fellow citizens.

Of course, choosing between potential competitors is the proper activity of a free individual in the market. But there is a great difference. Market competitors, if they are to keep their position, are necessarily working for their voters (that is, for their customers), even when both they and their voters are not completely aware of it. Political competitors, on the other hand, are not necessarily working for their voters, since the latter cannot actually choose in the same way the peculiar "products" of the politicians. Political producers (if I may use this word) are at the same time the sellers and the buyers of their products, both in the name of their fellow citizens. The latter are not expected to say, "I do not want that statute, I do not want that decree," since, according to the theory of representation, they have already delegated this power of choice to their representatives.

To be sure, this is a *legal* point of view, which does not coincide necessarily with the actual attitude of the people concerned. In my country citizens frequently distinguish between the *legal* point of view and other points of view. I have always admired countries in which the legal point of view coincides as much as possible with any other and I have become convinced that their great achievements in politics have been chiefly owing to this coincidence. I still remain convinced of this, but I wonder whether this virtue cannot become a vice whenever the legal point of view results in the blind acceptance of inadequate decisions. A saying in my country may explain why our political theorists, from Machiavelli to Pareto, Mosca, and Roberto Michels, were little concerned with the *legal* point of view, but always tried to go beyond it and see what was going on behind it. I do not think that the German- or English-speaking peoples have a similar saying: *Chi comanda fa la legge,* that is, "Whoever has the power makes the law." This sounds like a Hobbesian sentence, but it lacks the Hobbesian emphasis on the *necessity* of a supreme power. It is rather, unless I am wrong, a cynical sentence, or, if you prefer, a realistic one. The Greeks, of course, had a similar doctrine, although I do not know whether they had a similar saying.

Please do not think that I am recommending such political cynicism. I am merely pointing out the scientific implications of this cynicism, if we may indeed qualify the doctrines as cynical. He who has the power makes the law. True, but what about people who do not have the power? The saying is apparently silent about this, but I suppose that a rather critical view of the limits of the law as centered on political power is the natural conclusion to be drawn from the doctrine. This is probably the reason why my fellow countrymen do not know by heart their written constitution as many Americans do. My fellow country-men are convinced, I would say instinctively, that written laws and constitutions are not the end of the political story. Not only do they change and may change rather frequently, but also they do not always correspond to the *law written in living tables,* as Lord Bacon would have said. I dare say that there is a sort of cynical common-law system which underlies the written-law system of my country and which differs from the English common-law system in so far as the former is not only unwritten but also officially unrecognized.

Moreover, I am inclined to think that something similar is happening and will happen perhaps to an even greater extent in the future in other countries where the coincidence between the legal point of view and other views has been so perfect until recent times. Blind acceptance of the contemporary legal point of view will lead to the gradual destruction of individual freedom of choice in politics as well as in the market and in private life, for the contemporary legal point of view means the increasing substitution of group decisions for individual choices and the progressive elimination of spontaneous adjustments between not only individual demands for and supplies of goods and services, but all kinds of behavior, by such rigid and coercive procedures as that of the majority rule.

To sum up my views on this subject: There is far more legislation, there are far more group decisions, far more rigid choices, and far fewer "laws written in living tables," far fewer individual decisions, far fewer free choices in all contemporary political systems than would be necessary in order to preserve individual freedom of choice.

I do not say that we ought to do entirely without legislation and give up group decisions and majority rules altogether in order to recover individual freedom of choice in all the fields in which we have lost it. I quite agree that in some cases the issues involved concern everybody and cannot be dealt with by the spontaneous adjustments and mutually compatible choices of individuals. There is no historical evidence that there ever existed an anarchistic state of affairs of the kind that would result if legislation, group decisions, and the coercion of individual choices were to be altogether eliminated.

But I am convinced that the more we manage to reduce the large area occupied at present by group decisions in politics and in the law, with all their paraphernalia of elections, legislation, and so on, the more we shall succeed in establishing a state of affairs similar to that which prevails in the domain of language, of common law, of the free market, of fashion, of customs, etc., where all individual choices adjust themselves to one another and no individual choice is ever overruled. I would suggest that at the present time the extent of the area in which group decisions are deemed necessary or even suitable has been grossly overestimated and the area in which spontaneous individual adjustments have been deemed necessary or suitable has been far more severely circumscribed than it is advisable to do if we wish to preserve the traditional meanings of most of the great ideals of the West.

I suggest that the maps of the above-mentioned areas have to be redrawn, as many lands and seas appear now to be indicated on them in places where in the old classical maps nothing was marked. I also suspect, if I may continue to use this metaphor, that there are signs and marks on the present-day maps that actually correspond to no newly discovered land at all and that some lands are not to be located where they have been placed at present by inaccurate geographers of the political world. In fact, some of the marks appearing on the present-day political maps are only little spots with nothing real behind them, and our behavior toward them is like that of the skipper who mistook for an island on his map what a fly had left on it several days before and kept on searching for that presumed "island" in the ocean.

In redrawing these maps of the areas occupied respectively by group decisions and by individual decisions, we ought to take into account the fact that the former include decisions of the all-or-none variety, as Professor Buchanan would say, while the latter include articulate decisions which are compatible—nay, complementary—with other people's decisions.

A golden rule in this reform—unless I am wrong—ought to be that all individual decisions that have proved to be not incompatible with one another ought to be substituted for corresponding group decisions in regard to alternatives among which incompatibilities have been wrongly assumed to exist. It would be silly, for instance, to submit individuals to a group decision in regard to such questions as whether they should go to the movies or take a walk whenever there is no incompatibility between these two forms of individual behavior.

Supporters of group decisions (for instance, of legislation) are always inclined to think that in such or such a case individual choices are mutually incompatible, that the issues concerned are necessarily of the all-or-none variety, and that the only way to make a final choice is to adopt a coercive procedure like majority rule. These people pretend to champion democracy. But we ought always to remember that whenever majority rule is unnecessarily substituted for individual choice, democracy is in conflict with individual freedom. It is this particular kind of democracy that ought to be kept to a minimum in order to preserve a maximum of democracy compatible with individual freedom.

Of course, it would be necessary to avoid misunderstandings at the very outset of the reform I am proposing. Freedom could not be conceived of indifferently as "freedom from want" and "freedom from men," just as constraint ought not to be understood as "constraint" exercised by people who have done absolutely nothing to constrain anybody else.

The assessment of various forms of behavior and decisions in order to ascertain the area to which they properly belong and to locate them in that area, if consistently performed, would obviously involve a great revolution in the field of present-day constitutions and of legislative and administrative law. This revolution would for the most part consist in the displacement of rules from the area of the written to the area of the unwritten law. In this process of displacement great attention should be paid to the concept of *the certainty of the law,* understood as a long-run certainty, in order to render it possible for individuals to make free choices in view not only of the present, but also of the future. In the process judicature ought to be separated as much as possible from other powers, as it was in Roman times and in the Middle Ages, when *jurisdictio* was separated as much as possible from the *imperium.* Judicature should address itself much more to discovering what the law is than to imposing on the parties to the dispute what the judges want the law to be.

The law-making process ought to be reformed by making it mainly, if not only, a spontaneous process, like that of trading or of speaking or of keeping other compatible and complementary relations on the part of individuals with other individuals.

It may be objected that such a reform would be equivalent to the creation of a utopian world. But such a world was, taken all in all, certainly not utopian in several countries and at several historical times, some of which have not yet vanished altogether from the memory of living generations. On the other hand, it is probably much more utopian to continue addressing appeals to a world where old ideals are perishing and only old words remain, as empty shells, that everybody can fill up with his favorite meanings, regardless of the final results.

7

FREEDOM AND
THE COMMON
WILL

To a superficial observer my suggestion of a redrawing of the maps of the areas occupied respectively by individual choices and by group decisions may resemble more a daring attack on the present system, with its emphasis on decision groups and group decisions, than a convincing argument in favor of another system emphasizing individual decisions.

In politics there seem to be many issues on which, at least at first, agreement cannot be unanimous, and therefore group decisions, with their appendage of coercive procedures, majority rule, and so on, are unavoidable. This may be true of present systems, but it does not hold true of the same systems after a thorough assessment is made of the issues to be decided by groups in accordance with coercive procedures.

Decision groups often remind us of groups of robbers, about whom the eminent American scholar, Lawrence Lowell, once remarked that they do not constitute a "majority" when—after having waited for a traveler in a lonely place—they deprive him of his purse. According to Lowell, a handful of people are not to be called a "majority" in comparison with the man they rob. Nor can the latter be called a "minority." There are constitutional protections and, of course, criminal legislation in the United States as well as in other countries, tending to prevent the formation of such "majorities." Unfortunately, many majorities in our time often have much in common with the peculiar "majority"

described by Lawrence Lowell. They are *legal* majorities, constituted according to written law and to the constitutions, or at
least according to some rather elastic interpretations of the
constitutions, of many present-day countries. Whenever, for
instance, a majority of the purported "representatives of the
people" manage to obtain a group decision, for example, the
present Landlord and Tenant Acts in England or similar statutes
in Italy or elsewhere, designed to force landlords to keep in their
houses, against their will and against all previous agreements, at
a low rent, tenants who could easily pay, in most cases, a rent in
accordance with market prices, I cannot see any reason to distinguish this majority from that described by Lawrence Lowell.
There is only one difference: the latter is not permitted by
the written law of the country, while the former at present is
permitted.

In fact, the one characteristic that both "majorities" have in
common is the constraint exercised on the part of certain more
numerous people against other less numerous people to make
the latter suffer what they never would suffer if only they could
make free choices and free agreements with the former. There is
no reason to suppose that the individuals belonging to these majorities would have a different feeling from that of their present
victims if the former belonged to the minorities they have managed to constrain. Thus, the Gospel dictum, which goes back at
least as far as the Confucian philosophy, and which is probably
one of the most strikingly concise rules of the philosophy of
individual freedom—"Do not do unto others what you do not
wish others to do unto you"—is being modified by all majorities
of the Lowell kind as follows: "Do unto others what you do not
wish others to do unto you." In this respect, Schumpeter was
correct when he said that the "common will" is a sham in modern political communities. We must agree with him if we consider
all the cases of group decisions like those I have mentioned.
People who belong to the winning side of the group say that they
are deciding for the common interest and according to the
"common will."

But whenever decisions are at issue constraining minorities to
give up their money or to keep in their houses other people
whom they do not want to keep there, there will be no unanimity

on the part of all the members of the group. True, many people consider this very lack of unanimity as a good reason for invoking decision groups and coercive procedures. However, this is not a serious objection against the reform I am proposing. If we consider that one of the chief ends of such a reform would be to restore individual freedom as freedom from other people's constraint, we shall find no reason to grant a place in our system to those decisions which involve the exercise of constraint over less numerous people on behalf of other, more numerous people. There could be no "common will" in these kinds of decisions unless one simply identifies the "common will" with the will of the majorities regardless of the freedom of the people belonging to the minorities.

On the other hand, the "common will" has a meaning much more convincing than that adopted by supporters of group decisions. It is *the will that emerges from the collaboration of all the people concerned, without any recourse to group decisions and decision groups.* This common will creates and keeps alive words in the ordinary language as well as agreements and engagements among various parties without any need of coercion in relations among individuals; exalts popular artists, writers, actors, or wrestlers; and creates and keeps alive fashions, rules of courtesy, moral rules, and so on. This will is "common" in the sense that all those individuals who participate in manifesting and exercising it in a community are free to do so, while all those who eventually do not agree are equally free to do so in their turn without being forced by other people to accept their decision. Under such a system, all the members of the community appear to agree in principle that feelings, actions, forms of behavior, and so on, on the part of individuals belonging to the community are perfectly admissible and permissible without disturbing anybody, regardless of the number of individuals who feel like behaving or acting in these ways.

True, this is more a theoretical model of the "common will" than a situation historically ascertainable in all details. But history offers us a number of examples of societies in which a "common will" may be said to have existed in the sense I have described. Even at present and even in those countries where coercive methods are widely applied, there are still many situations in which a true common will emerges and nobody would seriously contest its existence or desire a different state of affairs.

Let us now see whether we can imagine a "common will" that reflects itself not only in a common language or in a common law, in common fashions, tastes, and so on, but also in group decisions, with all their paraphernalia of coercive procedures.

Strictly speaking, we ought to conclude that no group decision, if it is not unanimous, is the expression of a will common to all the people who participate in that decision at a given time. But decisions are taken in some cases against minorities, as, for instance, when a verdict is reached by a jury against a robber or a murderer, that would not hesitate in their turn to adopt or to favor the same decision if they had been the victims of other people in the same respect. It has been noticed repeatedly since the time of Plato that even pirates and robbers must actually admit a law *common* to all of them, lest their band be dissolved or destroyed from within. If we take these facts into consideration, we can say that there are decisions which, although not reflecting at every moment the will of all the members of the group, can be considered as "common" to the group, in so far as everybody admits them under similar circumstances. I think that this is the nucleus of truth in certain paradoxical considerations by Rousseau that appear rather silly to his adversaries or to his superficial readers. When saying that a criminal wants his own condemnation, since he has agreed previously with other people to punish all criminals and himself too if that were the case, the French philosopher makes a statement that, literally taken, is nonsense. But it is no nonsense to presume that every criminal would admit and even request condemnation for other criminals in the same circumstances. In this sense, there is a "common will" on the part of every member of a community to hinder and eventually to punish certain kinds of behavior that are defined as crimes in that society. The same applies more or less to all other kinds of behavior called torts in the English-speaking countries, that is, forms of behavior that, according to a commonly shared conviction, are not allowed in the community.

There is an obvious difference between the object of group decisions relating to the condemnation of such forms of behavior as crimes or torts and decisions relating to other forms of behavior such as those imposed upon landlords in the above-mentioned statutes. In the former case, sentences are pronounced by the group against an individual or a minority of individual members of the group who have committed robbery within the group itself. In the latter case, decisions are made that simply consist in committing some robbery against other people, namely, against people belonging to a minority of the group. In the former case, everybody, including each member of the minority being condemned for robbery, would approve condemnation in any other instance than his own; whereas in the latter case, just the contrary happens: the decision (for instance, to rob a minority within a group) would not be approved by the very members of the winning majority in any instance in which they themselves were the victims of it. But in both cases all the members of the groups concerned do feel, as we have seen, that some forms of behavior are condemnable. This is what allows us to say that actually there are group decisions which may correspond to a "common will" whenever we may presume that the object of those decisions would be approved under like circumstances by all the members of the group, including the minority members that are their present victims. On the other hand, we cannot consider as corresponding to the "common will" of a group such decisions as would not be approved under like circumstances by any member of the group, including the majority members who are now the beneficiaries.

Group decisions of the latter type would have to be removed altogether from the map describing the area of suitable or necessary group decisions in contemporary society. All the group decisions of the former type should be left on the map after a rigorous assessment of their objective. Of course, I do not imagine that eliminating such group decisions would be an easy task on the part of anybody at the present time. Eliminating all group decisions taken by majorities of the Lowell type would mean terminating once and for all the sort of legal warfare that sets group against group in contemporary society because of the perpetual attempt of their respective members to constrain, to their own benefit, other members of the community to accept misproductive actions and treatment. From this point of view, one could apply to a conspicuous part of contemporary legislation the definition that the German theorist Clausewitz applied to war, namely, that it is a means of attaining those ends that it is no longer possible to attain by way of customary bargaining. It is this prevailing concept of the law as an instrument for sectional purposes that suggested, a century ago, to Bastiat his famous definition of the state: "L'État, la grande fiction à travers laquelle tout le monde s'efforce de vivre au dépens de tout le monde" ("that great fictitious entity by which everyone seeks to live at the expense of everyone else"). We must admit that this definition holds good also in our own time.

An aggressive concept of legislation to serve sectional interest has subverted the ideal of political society as a homogeneous entity, nay, as a society at all. Minorities constrained to accept the results of legislation they would never agree to under other conditions feel unjustly treated and accept their situation only in order to avoid worse or consider it as an excuse for obtaining on their behalf other laws that in turn injure still other people. Perhaps this picture does not apply to the United States in such full measure as it does to several nations in Europe in which socialistic ideals have covered so many sectional interests of transitory as well as of lasting majorities within each country. But I need only refer to such laws as the Norris-La Guardia Act to convince my readers that what I am saying applies also to this country. Here, however, legal privileges in favor of particular groups are usually paid for, not by another particular group, as is the case in European countries, but by all the citizens in their capacity as taxpayers.

Fortunately for all the people who hope that the reform I have suggested will take place some time or other, group decisions in our society are not all of the vexatious kind I have just considered nor are all majorities of the Lowell variety.

Group decisions figuring in our present-day political maps concern also objects that would be more properly located on the map of individual decisions. Such objects, for instance, are covered by contemporary legislation whenever the latter limits itself to epitomizing what is commonly held as a right or a duty by the people of a country. I suspect that many of those who invoke written laws against the arbitrary powers of individual men, whether tyrants or state officials or even transitory majorities

such as those that prevailed in Athens in the second half of the
fifth century B.C., more or less consciously think of laws as simply
epitomizing unwritten rules already adopted by all the people in
a given society. In fact, many written regulations could and still
may be considered simply as epitomes of unwritten rules, at least
with reference to their content, if not to the intention of the
legislators concerned. A classical case is Justinian's *Corpus Juris*.
This is true notwithstanding the fact that, according to the explicit intention of that emperor, who (we must not forget) belonged to a country and to a people inclined to identify the law
of the land with its *written* law, the whole of the *Corpus Juris* had
to be adopted by his subjects as an enacted statute of the emperor himself.

But a strict connection between the ideal of the *Corpus Juris* as
a written law and the common or unwritten law actually embodied in it was strikingly evidenced by the content of the *Corpus*.
Indeed, the central and more lasting part of it, the so-called
Pandectae or *Digesta*, consisted entirely of statements of the old
Roman jurists relating to the unwritten law. Their works were
now collected and selected by Justinian (who may be considered,
incidentally, as the editor of the most famous *Reader's Digest* of
all times) in order to be presented to his subjects as a particular formulation of his own personal orders. True, according to
modern scholars, Justinian's compilation, selection, and diges-
tion must have been rather a tricky one, at least in several cases
when reasonable doubts may arise about the authenticity of the
texts included in the *Corpus* and allegedly belonging to the work
of old Roman jurists like Paulus or Ulpian. But there is no doubt
among scholars about the authenticity of the selection as a
whole. Even doubts about the authenticity of the selection in
particular cases have been abandoned to some extent in recent
times by most scholars.

In its turn, the Justinian selection was the object of a similar
process on the part of the Continental jurists in the Middle Ages
and in modern times, before our present age of codes and of
written constitutions. For the Continental jurists of those days, it
was not a question of "selecting" in the Justinian way, but of
"interpreting," that is, of stretching the meaning of the Justinian
texts whenever it was necessary to give expression to new exigen-

cies, while leaving the whole of it essentially valid, until recent times, as the law of the land in most of the Continental countries of Europe. Thus, while the old emperor had transformed the common law ascertained by the Roman jurists into a written law formally enacted by him, the medieval and the modern Continental jurists, before the enactment of present-day codes, transformed in their turn the formally enacted law of Justinian into a new law ascertained by the jurists, into a *Juristenrecht*, as the Germans used to call it, which was approximately a revised edition of the Justinian *Corpus* and therefore of old Roman law.

Much to his surprise, an Italian colleague of mine discovered some years ago that the Justinian *Corpus* was still literally valid in some countries of the world—for instance, in South Africa. A client of his, a lady resident in Italy who had some property in South Africa, had put him in charge of the transactions concerned, which he duly undertook to carry out. Later on he was requested by his correspondent from South Africa to send him a declaration signed by the lady stating that she renounced availing herself in the future of the privilege conferred upon women by the *Senatus Consultum Velleianum*, that is, a provision enacted by the Roman Senate nineteen centuries ago in order to authorize women to go back on their word and in general to refuse to keep certain engagements towards other people. Those wise Roman senators were aware of the fact that women were inclined to change their mind and that therefore it would have been unfair to seek from them the same consistency that was usually required of men by the law of the land. The result of the Senate's provision had been, I gather, slightly different from that expected by the senators. People had very little desire to enter into agreements with women after the enactment of the *Senatus Consultum*. A remedy for this inconvenience was finally found by admitting that women could renounce the privilege of the *Senatus Consultum* before engaging in some contracts, such as the sale of land. My colleague sent to South Africa the waiver of his client's right to invoke the *Senatus Consultum Velleianum*, signed by the lady, and the sale was performed in due course.

When I was told this story, I reflected with amusement that there are people who think that all we need to be happy are new laws. On the contrary, we have impressive historical evidence to support the conclusion that even legislation in many cases, after centuries and generations, has reflected much more a spontaneous process of law-making than the arbitrary will of a majority decision by a group of legislators.

The German word *Rechtsfindung,* i.e., the operation of *finding* the law, seems to render well the central idea of the *Juristenrecht* and of the Continental European jurist's activity as a whole. Law was conceived of, not as something *enacted,* but as something *existing,* which it was necessary to find, to *discover.* This operation was not to be performed directly by ascertaining the meaning of human engagements or of human feelings relating to rights and duties, but, first of all (at least apparently), by ascertaining the meaning of a written text two thousand years old, like the Justinian compilation.

This idea is interesting from our point of view as it offers us evidence of the fact that *written law is itself not always necessarily legislation,* that is, *enacted law.* The Justinian *Corpus Juris* in Continental Europe was not legislation any longer, at least in the technical meaning of the word, i.e., law enacted by the legislative authority of the European countries. (This, incidentally, could please those people who cling to the ideal of the certainty of the law in the sense of a precisely worded formula, without sacrificing the ideal of the certainty of the law understood as the possibility of making long-run plans.)

The codes of Continental Europe offer another example of a phenomenon very few people are aware of today, viz., the strict connection between the ideal of a formally enacted law and the ideal of a law the content of which is actually independent of legislation. These codes may be considered, in their turn, chiefly as epitomes of the Justinian *Corpus Juris* and of the interpretations that the Justinian compilation had undergone on the part of European jurists for several centuries during the Middle Ages and in modern times before the enactment of the codes.

We could compare the codes of Continental Europe to some extent with the official pronouncements that the authorities, for instance in the Italian *municipia* of Roman times, used to issue certifying to the purity and the weight of the metals employed by private people in making coins, while present-day legislation may be compared as a rule to the interference by all contemporary

governments in the determination of the value of their incon-
vertible legal tender notes. (Incidentally, legal tender money is
itself a striking example of legislation in the contemporary sense,
that is, of a group decision the result of which is that some members of the group are sacrificed for the benefit of others, while
this could not happen if the former could freely choose which
money to accept and which to refuse.)

The codes of Continental Europe, like the Code Napoléon or
the Austrian Code of 1811 or the German Code of 1900, were
the result of several criticisms to which the Justinian compilation,
already transformed into the *Juristenrecht*, had been subjected. A
desire for certainty of the law, in the sense of verbal precision,
was one of the chief reasons for the suggested codification. The
Pandectae appeared to be rather a loose system of rules, many of
which could be considered as particular instances of a more general rule that the Roman jurists had never bothered to formulate. Indeed, they had deliberately eschewed such formulations
in most instances in order to avoid becoming prisoners of their
own rules whenever they had to deal with unprecedented cases.
In fact, there was a contradiction in the Justinian compilation.
The emperor had attempted to transform into a *closed* and
planned system what the Roman lawyers had always considered
as an *open* and spontaneous system, but he tried to do so by
making use of the work of these very lawyers. Thus, the Justinian
system proved to be too open for a closed system, while the
Juristenrecht in its turn, working in its characteristic piecemeal
fashion, had increased, rather than reduced, the original contradiction in the Justinian system.

The codification represented a considerable step in the direction of Justinian's idea that law is a closed system, to be planned
by experts under the direction of the political authorities, but it
implied also that the planning ought to relate more to the form
of the law than to its content.

Thus, an eminent German scholar, Eugen Ehrlich, wrote that
"the reformation of the law in the German Code of 1900 and in
the preceding Continental codes was more apparent than real."[1]
The *Juristenrecht* passed almost untouched into the new codes,

---

[1] Eugen Ehrlich, *Juristische Logik* (Tübingen: Mohr, 1918), p. 166.

although in a rather abridged form, the interpretation of which still implied substantial knowledge of the preceding juridical literature of the Continent.

Unfortunately, after a certain time the newly adopted ideal of giving a legislative form to a nonlegislative content proved self-contradictory. Nonlegislative law is always changing, although slowly and in a rather clandestine way. It can no more be transformed into a closed system than can ordinary language, although the attempt has been made by scholars in several countries, such as the founders of Esperanto and of other artificial languages. But the remedy adopted for this inconvenience proved rather inefficient. New written laws had to be enacted to modify the codes, and, gradually, the original closed system of the codes became surrounded and overburdened with an enormous amount of other written rules, the accumulation of which is one of the most striking features of present-day European legal systems. Nevertheless, the codes are still considered in European countries as the nucleus of the law, and so far as their original content has still been preserved, we can recognize in them the connection between the ideal of a formally enacted law and a content tracing back to unwritten law that had first actuated Justinian's compilation.

If we consider, on the other hand, what has happened in comparatively recent times in the English-speaking countries, we can easily find examples of the same process. Several acts of Parliament are more or less epitomes of the *rationes decidendi* elaborated by courts of judicature during a long process stretching over the whole history of the common law.

Those familiar with the history of the English common law will agree on being reminded, for instance, that the Infant Relief Act of 1874 did nothing but reinforce the common-law rule that infants' contracts are voidable at the infant's option. To take another instance, the Sale of Goods Act of 1893 rendered statutory the common-law rule that when goods are sold by auction, in the absence of a contrary expressed intention the highest bid constitutes the offer, and the fall of the hammer constitutes the acceptance. In their turn, several other acts like the Statute of Frauds of 1677 or the Law of Property Act of 1925 rendered statutory other rules of common law (such as the rule that certain contracts were unenforceable unless evidenced in writing), and the Companies Act of 1948 binding promoters of companies to disclose certain specific matters in their prospectuses merely constituted an application to a particular case of some rules ascertained by the courts relating to the misinterpretation of contracts. It would be supererogatory to cite the other examples that could be mentioned.

Finally, as Dicey already pointed out, many modern constitutions and bills of rights may be considered, in their turn, not as creations *de nihilo* on the part of modern Solons, but as more or less diligent epitomes of a set of *rationes decidendi* that courts of judicature in England had discovered and applied step by step in decisions concerning the rights of given individuals.

The fact that both written codes and constitutions, although presenting themselves in the nineteenth century as enacted law, actually reflect in their content a law-making process based essentially on the spontaneous behavior of private individuals through centuries and generations could and still can induce liberal thinkers to consider written law (conceived of as a set of precisely worded general rules) as an indispensable means for the preservation of individual freedom in our time.

In fact, the rules embodied in written codes and in written constitutions could appear as the best expression of the liberal principles in so far as they reflected a long historical process the result of which was not, in its essence, a legislator-made law, but a judge-made or a jurist-made law. This is like describing it as an "everybody-made" law of the variety that old Cato the Censor had exalted as the main cause of the greatness of the Roman system.

The fact that enacted rules, although generally formulated, precisely worded, theoretically impartial, and also "certain" in some respects, could also have a content quite *incompatible* with individual freedom was disregarded by the Continental proponents of written codes and especially of written constitutions. They were convinced that the *Rechtsstaat* or the *état de droit* corresponded perfectly to the English *rule of law* and was also preferable to it because of clearer, more comprehensive, and more certain formulation. When the *Rechtsstaat* was corrupted, this conviction was soon revealed to be a delusion.

In our time subversive parties of all kinds have found it easy, while trying to change altogether the content of the codes and the constitutions, to pretend that they were still respecting the classical idea of the *Rechtsstaat*, with its concern for the "generality," "equality," and "certainty" of the written rules approved by the "representative" deputies of the "people" according to majority rule. The nineteenth-century idea that the *Juristenrecht* of the Continent had been reinstated successfully and even more clearly rewritten in the codes (and that, moreover, the principles underlying the judge-made constitution of the English people had been successfully transferred into written constitutions enacted by legislative bodies) now paved the way for a new, emasculated concept of the *Rechtsstaat*—a state of law in which all the rules had to be enacted by the legislature. The fact that in the original codes and constitutions of the nineteenth century the legislature confined itself chiefly to epitomizing a law that had not been enacted was gradually forgotten or considered as of little significance compared with the fact that both codes and constitutions had been enacted by legislatures, the members of which were the "representatives" of the people.

Concomitant with this fact was another, also pointed out by Professor Ehrlich. The *Juristenrecht* introduced into the codes had been abridged, but in a form that contemporary lawyers were able to understand easily by reference to a judicial background with which they had been perfectly familiar before the enactment of the codes.[2] However, the lawyers of the second generation no longer were able to do this. They became accustomed to refer much more to the code itself than to its historical background. Aridity and poverty were, according to Ehrlich, the characteristic features of the commentaries of the second and subsequent generations of Continental lawyers—evidence of the fact that the activity of lawyers cannot remain at a high level if based only on a written law without the background of a long tradition.

The most important consequence of the new trend was that people on the Continent and to a certain extent also in the English-speaking countries accustomed themselves more and more

[2] Ibid., p. 167.

to conceiving of the whole of the law as *written law*, that is, as a single series of enactments on the part of legislative bodies according to majority rule.

Thus, the law as a whole began to be thought of as the result of group decisions instead of individual choices, and some theorists—like Professor Hans Kelsen—went so far as to deny that it is even possible to speak of juridical or political behavior on the part of individuals without reference to a set of coercive rules by which all behavior is to be qualified as "legal" or not.

Another consequence of this revolutionary concept of the law in our times was that the law-making process was no longer regarded as chiefly connected with a theoretical activity on the part of the experts, like judges or lawyers, but rather with the mere will of winning majorities within the legislative bodies. The principle of "representation" appeared to secure in its turn a purported connection between those winning majorities and each individual conceived of as a member of the electorate. Thus, the participation of individuals in the law-making process has ceased to be effective and has become more and more a sort of empty ceremony taking place periodically in the general election of a country.

The spontaneous law-making process before the enactment of the codes and constitutions of the nineteenth century was by no means unique if considered in relation to other spontaneous processes like that of the ordinary language or of day-to-day economic transactions or of changing fashion. A characteristic feature of all these processes is that they are performed through the voluntary collaboration of an enormous number of individuals each of whom has a share in the process itself according to his willingness and his ability to maintain or even to modify the present condition of economic affairs, of language, of fashion, etc. There are no group decisions in this process that constrain anybody to adopt a new word instead of an old one or to wear a new type of suit instead of an old-fashioned one or to prefer a moving picture instead of a play. True, the present age does offer the spectacle of huge pressure groups whose propaganda is designed to make people engage in new economic transactions or adopt new fashions or even new words and languages such as Esperanto or Volapuk. We cannot deny that these groups may play a large part in modifying the choices of particular individuals, but this is never done through constraint. To confuse pressure or propaganda with constraint would be a mistake similar to that which we observed in analyzing certain other confusions relating to the meaning of "constraint." Some forms of pressure can be associated with and even identified with constraint. But these are always connected with constraint in the proper sense of the word, such as occurs, for instance, when the inhabitants of a country are forbidden to import foreign newspapers and magazines or to listen to foreign broadcasts or simply to go abroad at all. In such cases propaganda and pressure inside a country are very similar to forms of constraint properly so called. People cannot hear the propaganda they would like better, cannot make a selection of information, and sometimes cannot even avoid listening to the broadcasts or reading the newspapers edited under the direction of their rulers inside the country.

A similar situation arises in the economic field when monopolies are set up within a country with the help of legislation (that is, of group decisions and constraints) the purpose of which, for instance, is to hinder or to limit the importation of goods produced by potential competitors in foreign countries. Here too individuals are coerced in some way, but the cause of this coercion is not traceable to any action or behavior on the part of single individuals in the ordinary process of spontaneous collaboration I have already described.

Special cases, such as those of subliminal devices or invisible advertising through infra-red rays acting on our eyes and therefore on our brains or obsessive advertisement and propaganda that one could not avoid seeing or hearing, may be considered as contrary to the rules already commonly accepted in every civilized country in order to protect everyone against other people's constraint. Such cases may be rightly considered, therefore, as instances of constraint to be avoided by applying rules already existing on behalf of individual freedom.

Now, legislation proves to be in the end a much less obvious and a much less usual device than it would appear to be if we did not pay attention to what is happening in other important fields of human action and of human behavior. I would even go so far as to say that legislation, especially if applied to the innumerable

choices that individuals make in their daily life, appears to
be something absolutely exceptional and even contrary to the
rest of what takes place in human society. The most striking contrast between legislation and other processes of human activity
emerges whenever we compare the former with the proceedings
of science. I would even say that this is one of the greatest paradoxes of contemporary civilization: it has developed scientific
methods to such an astonishing degree while at the same time
extending, adding, and fostering such antithetic procedures as
those of decision groups and majority rule.

No truly scientific result has ever been reached through group
decisions and majority rule. The whole history of modern science
in the West evidences the fact that no majorities, no tyrants, no
constraint can prevail in the long run against individuals whenever the latter are able to prove in some definite way that their
own scientific theories work better than others and that their
own view of things solves problems and difficulties better than
others, regardless of the number, the authority, or the power of
the latter. Indeed, the history of modern science, if considered
from this point of view, constitutes the most convincing evidence
of the failure of decision groups and group decisions based on
some coercive procedure and more generally of the failure of
constraint exercised over individuals as a pretended means of
promoting scientific progress and of achieving scientific results.
The trial of Galileo, at the dawn of our scientific era, is in this
sense a symbol of its whole history, for many trials have since
actually taken place in various countries up to the present day in
which attempts have been made to constrain individual scientists
to abandon some thesis. But no scientific thesis has ever been
established or disproved in the end as a result of any contraint
whatever exercised upon individual scientists by bigoted tyrants
and ignorant majorities.

On the contrary, scientific research is the most obvious example of a spontaneous process involving the free collaboration of
innumerable individuals, each of whom has a share in it according to his willingness and abilities. The total result of this collaboration has never been anticipated or planned by particular
individuals or groups. Nobody could even make a statement
about what the outcome of such a collaboration would be with-

out ascertaining it carefully every year, nay, every month and every day throughout the whole history of science.

What would have happened in the countries of the West if scientific progress had been confined to group decisions and majority rule based on such principles as that of the "representation" of the scientists conceived of as members of an electorate, not to speak of a "representation" of the people at large? Plato outlined such a situation in his dialogue *Politikos* when he contrasted the so-called science of government and the sciences in general with the written rules enacted by the majority in the ancient Greek democracies. One of the characters in the dialogue proposes that the rules of medicine, of navigation, of mathematics, of agriculture, and of all the sciences and techniques known at his time be fixed by written rules (*syngrammata*) enacted by legislatures. It is clear, so the rest of the characters in the dialogue conclude, that in such a case all sciences and techniques will disappear without any hope of reviving again, being banished by a law that would hinder all research, and life, they add sadly, which is so hard already, would become impossible altogether.

Yet the final conclusion of this Platonic dialogue is rather different. Although we cannot accept a state of affairs like this in the scientific field, we must, said Plato, accept it in the field of our law and of our institutions. Nobody would be so clever and so honest as to rule over his fellow citizens in disregard of fixed laws without causing many more inconveniences than a system of rigid legislation.

This unexpected conclusion is rather similar to that of the authors of the written codes and written constitutions of the nineteenth century. Both Plato and these theorists contrasted written laws with the arbitrary actions of a ruler and maintained that the former were preferable to the latter, since no individual ruler could behave with sufficient wisdom to secure the common welfare of his country.

I do not object to this conclusion *provided we accept its premise*: namely, that the arbitrary orders of tyrants are the only alternative to written rules.

But history supplies us with abundant evidence to support the conclusion that this alternative is neither the only nor even the most significant one open to people who value individual freedom. It would be much more consistent with the historical evidence to point out another alternative—for instance, that between arbitrary rules laid down by particular individuals or groups, on the one hand, and spontaneous participation in the law-making process on the part of each and all of the inhabitants of a country, on the other.

If we view the alternative in this light, there is no doubt about the choice in favor of individual freedom, conceived of as the condition of each man making his own choices without being constrained by anybody else to do unwillingly what the latter imposes.

Nobody likes arbitrary orders on the part of kings, state officials, dictators, and so on. But legislation is not the appropriate alternative to arbitrariness, for arbitrariness may be and actually is exercised in many cases with the help of written rules that people must endure, since nobody participates in the process of making them except a handful of legislators.

Professor Hayek, who is one of the most eminent supporters of written, general, and certain rules at the present time as a means of counteracting arbitrariness, is himself perfectly aware of the fact that the rule of law "is not sufficient to achieve the purpose" of safeguarding individual freedom, and admits that it is "not a sufficient condition of individual freedom, as it still leaves open an enormous field for possible action of the State."[3]

This is also the reason why free markets and free trade, as a system as much as possible independent of legislation, must be considered not only as the most efficient means of obtaining free choices of goods and services on the part of the individuals concerned, *but also as a model for any other system of which the purpose is to allow free individual choices, including those relating to the law and legal institutions.*

Of course, systems based on the spontaneous participation of each and all of the individuals concerned are not a panacea. Minorities exist in the market as well as in any other field, and their participation in the process is not always satisfactory, at least until their members are sufficiently numerous to induce

---

[3] F. A. Hayek, op. cit., p. 46.

producers to meet their demands. If I want to buy a rare book or a rare phonograph record in a small town, I may have to give up after some attempts, as no local seller of books or of records may be able to satisfy my request. But this is not at all a defect that coercive systems could avoid, unless we think of those supposedly utopian systems contrived by socialist reformers and dreamers and corresponding to the motto: Everything to everybody according to his needs.

The land of Utopia has not yet been discovered. Thus, it would be of little use to criticize a system by contrasting it with nonexisting systems that, perhaps, would avoid the defects of the former.

To sum up what I have said in this lecture: Individual freedom cannot be consistent with the "common will" whenever the latter is only a sham to conceal the exercise of constraint by majorities of the Lawrence Lowell variety over minorities that, in turn, would never accept the resulting situation if they were free to reject it.

But individual freedom is consistent with the common will whenever the object of it is compatible with the principle formulated by the rule: "Do not do unto others what you do not wish others to do unto you." In this case, group decisions are compatible with individual freedom in so far as they punish and offer redress for kinds of behavior that all members of the group would disapprove of, including the persons evincing such behavior if they were themselves the victims of it.

Moreover, individual freedom may be consistent with decision groups and group decisions in so far as the latter reflect the results of a spontaneous participation of all the members of the group in the formation of a common will, for instance, in a lawmaking process independent of legislation. But the compatibility between individual freedom and legislation is a precarious one because of the potential contradiction between the ideal of the spontaneous formation of a common will and that of a statement about the latter arrived at by way of a coercive procedure, such as usually happens in legislation.

Finally, individual freedom is perfectly compatible with all those processes the result of which is the formation of a common will without recourse to decision groups and group decisions. Ordinary language, day-to-day economic transactions, customs, fashions, spontaneous law-making processes, and, above all, scientific research are the most common and most convincing examples of this compatibility—indeed, of this intimate connection—between individual freedom and the spontaneous formation of a common will.

In contrast to this spontaneous mode of determining the common will, legislation appears as a less efficient device for arriving at such a determination, as becomes evident when we pay attention to the imposing area within which the common will has been spontaneously determined in the countries of the West in the past as well as at present.

History evidences the fact that legislation does not constitute an appropriate alternative to arbitrariness, but that it often ranks alongside the vexatious orders of tyrants or of arrogant majorities against all kinds of spontaneous processes of forming a common will in the sense I have described.

From the point of view of the supporters of individual freedom it is not only a question of being suspicious of officials and rulers, but also of legislators. In this sense, we cannot accept the famous definition that Montesquieu gave of freedom as "the right to do all that the laws allow us to do." As Benjamin Constant remarked in this connection: "No doubt there is no liberty when people cannot do all that the laws allow them to do; but laws could forbid so many things as to abolish liberty altogether."[4]

<hr/>

[4] B. Constant, *Cours de politique constitutionnelle* (Brussells, 1851), I, 178.

8

SOME
DIFFICULTIES
ANALYZED

Let us consider some of the objections that might be raised against a system in which group decisions and decision groups would play a much less important role than is now commonly deemed necessary in political life.

No doubt present-day governments and legislatures and a large percentage of the well-educated and of the people in general have gradually grown accustomed, during the last hundred years, to considering interference by the authorities with private activities as much more useful than they would have deemed it in the first half of the nineteenth century.

If anyone at present dares to suggest that big governments and paternal legislatures ought to give up in favor of private initiative, the usual criticisms heard are that "we cannot put the clock back," that the times of *laissez faire* have gone forever, and so on.

We ought to distinguish carefully between what people believe can be done and what it would be possible to do towards restoring the maximum area of free individual choice. Of course, in politics as well as in many other areas, if we try to achieve our ends in accordance with liberal principles, nothing can be done without the consent of our fellow citizens, and this consent depends, in its turn, on what people believe. But it is obviously important to ascertain, if possible, whether people are right or wrong in maintaining any opinion whatever. Public opinion is not everything, not even in a liberal society, although opinion is certainly a very important thing, especially in a liberal society. I am reminded of what one of my fellow citizens wrote several years ago: "A fool is a fool, two fools are two fools, five hundred fools are five hundred fools, but five thousand, not to say five million, fools are a great historical force." I do not deny the truth of this cynical statement, but a historical force may be contained or modified, and this is the more likely to be so the more the facts turn out to disprove what people believe. What Hippolyte Taine once said, that ten million instances of ignorance do not make knowledge, is true of every kind of ignorance, including that of people belonging to contemporary political societies, with all their appendages of democratic procedures, majority rules, and omnipotent legislatures and governments.

The fact that people in general still believe that governmental intervention is suitable or actually necessary even in cases where many economists would deem it useless or dangerous is not an insurmountable obstacle for supporters of a new society. Nor is there anything wrong if that new society in the end resembles many older, successful societies.

True, socialistic doctrines, with the more or less overt condemnation, on the part of governments and legislators, of individual freedom from constraint, are still proving to be more palatable to the masses of the present day than the cool reasoning of the economists. The case for freedom under these conditions seems to be hopeless in most countries of the world.

Nevertheless, it is doubtful whether or not the masses are actually the protagonists in the contemporary drama of public opinion relating to individual freedom. If I must choose sides among the supporters of the liberal ideal in our time, I should prefer to join Professor Mises rather than the pessimists:

> The main error of widespread pessimism is the belief that the destructionist ideas and policies of our age sprang from the proletarians and are a "revolt of the masses." In fact, the masses, precisely because they are not creative and do not develop philosophies of their own, follow leaders. The ideologies which produced all the mischiefs and catastrophes of our century are not an achievement of the mob. They are the feats of pseudo scholars and pseudo intellectuals. They were propagated from the chairs of universities and from the pulpits; they were disseminated by the press, by novels, by plays, by

the movies, and the radio. The intellectuals are responsible for converting the masses to socialism and interventionism. What is needed to turn the flood is to change the mentality of the intellectuals. Then the masses will follow suit.[1]

I would not go so far as to think, as Professor Mises seems to do, that to change the mentality of the so-called intellectuals would be an easy task. Professor Mises has pointed out in his recent book, *The Anti-Capitalistic Mentality*, that what causes many so-called intellectuals to range themselves among the enemies of individual freedom and free enterprise are not only or mainly wrong arguments or insufficient information about the whole subject, but rather emotional attitudes, for instance, envy of successful businessmen or feelings of inferiority to them. If this is so, cool reasoning and better information will prove as useless in converting the intellectuals as they would be in converting directly the "dull and mentally inert people" belonging to the masses that crowd the political scene.

Fortunately, not all uneducated men are so "dull" as to be unable to understand or to reason correctly for themselves, particularly when this relates to ordinary experience in daily life. In many obvious cases their experience does not confirm the theories advanced by the enemies of individual freedom. In many other cases the socialistic interpretation has as little cogency as other sophistical arguments that have proved more convincing to the so-called intellectuals than to uneducated people judging solely by common sense. The trend of socialistic propaganda in the present day seems to confirm this fact. The strange and complicated theory of so-called "surplus value" is no longer expounded to the public by contemporary agents of Marxian socialism, notwithstanding the fact that Marx had assigned to this very theory the task of supporting theoretically all his attacks against the alleged exploitation of the workers on the part of capitalistic employers.

Meanwhile, Marxian philosophy is still recommended to the intellectuals of today as an up-to-date interpretation of the world. Much more emphasis now seems to be placed on the pur-

---

[1] Ludwig von Mises, *Planning for Freedom* (South Holland, Ill.: Libertarian Press, 1952), last chapter.

portedly philosophical than on the political content of the works of such representatives of communism as V. I. Lenin.

On the other hand, many economic teachings relating to the suitability of individual freedom for all kinds of people, including socialists, are such simple developments of common-sense assumptions in special fields that their correctness cannot escape, in the end, the common sense of common people, regardless of the teachings of demagogues and of socialistic propaganda of all kinds.

All these facts encourage the hope that people in general may become persuaded, at some time or other, to adopt liberal principles (in the European sense of the word) in many more matters and in a more consistent way than they do today.

A different question is to ascertain whether liberal principles are always based on cogent reasoning on the part of the representatives of the peculiar science called economics, on the one hand, and of representatives of that older discipline called political science, on the other.

This is a significant and important question on the solution of which may well depend the possibility of speaking of a system of individual freedom in politics as well as in economics.

Let us set aside the problem of the relations between science, on the one hand, and political or economic ideals, on the other. Science is not to be confused with ideology, although the latter may consist of a set of choices relating to possible political or economic systems inevitably connected in many ways with the results of economic and political science conceived of as "neutral" or "value-free" activities, according to Weber's theory of the social sciences. I think that Weber's distinction between "value-free" activities and ideologies as sets of value judgments is still valid, but we need not discuss this particular topic at length.

Much more difficult, it seems to me, is the methodological question of the cogency of economic and of political reasoning if compared with other kinds of reasoning—for example, that in mathematics or in the natural sciences.

I am convinced personally that the chief reason why political and economic issues are so frequently a cause of disagreements and disputes is precisely the lack of the same cogency on the part of the corresponding theories that reasoning and demonstration have in other scientific fields. I do not agree with Hobbes that arithmetic would be completely different from what it is if only it were important for some motivating power that two plus two be equal to five and not four. I doubt that any power whatever could transform arithmetic according to its interests or desires. On the contrary: I am convinced that it is important for any power whatever to make no attempt to transform arithmetic into the curious kind of science it would become on Hobbes' supposition. On the other hand, some power may indeed find some profit in supporting this or that purportedly scientific thesis whenever, but only whenever, there is no certainty about the final result of the scientific process itself.

In this connection, a restatement of what we call a scientific demonstration in our time would be worthwhile. Perhaps the situation of the social sciences as a whole would be improved a great deal by a dispassionate and extensive analysis in this field. But in the meantime things are what they are. Several limitations attach to economic as well as political theories, even if we consider them empirical or aprioristic inferences.

Methodological problems are important because of the connection they have with the possibility of economists' reaching unequivocal conclusions and therefore inducing other people to accept these conclusions as premises for their choices, not only in regard to their daily action in private life and business, but also in regard to the political and economic systems to be adopted by the community.

Economics as an empirical science has not yet, unfortunately, attained the ability to offer indubitable conclusions, and the attempts so frequently made in our time by economists to play the role of physicists are probably much more damaging than useful in inducing people to make their choices according to the results of that science.[2]

Of particular interest is some recent methodological research concerning economics, as presented by Professor Milton Friedman in his brilliant *Essays in Positive Economics*.

I quite agree with Professor Friedman when he says that

---

[2] Perhaps one should also take account of the damage resulting from physicists' playing the role of economists!

"the denial to economics of the dramatic and direct evidence of the *crucial* experiment does hinder the adequate testing of hypotheses," and that this places a considerable "difficulty . . . in the way of achieving a reasonably prompt and wide *consensus* on the conclusions justified by the available evidence."

Professor Friedman points out in this connection that this "renders the weeding-out of unsuccessful hypotheses slow and difficult" so that "they are seldom downed for good and are always cropping up again." He quotes, as a very convincing example, "the evidence from inflations on the hypothesis that a substantial increase in the quantity of money within a relatively short period is accompanied by a substantial increase in prices." Here, as Professor Friedman points out,

> the evidence is dramatic, and the chain of reasoning required to interpret it is relatively short. Yet, despite numerous instances of substantial rises in prices, their essentially one-to-one correspondence with substantial rises in the stock of money, and the wide variation of other circumstances that might appear to be relevant, each new experience of inflation brings forth vigorous contentions, and not only by the lay public, that the rise in the stock of money is either an incidental effect of a rise in prices produced by other factors or a purely fortuitous and unnecessary concomitant of the price rise.[3]

In principle, too, I agree with what Professor Friedman maintains in this analysis of the role of empirical evidence in the theoretical work of economics and of the social sciences as well as of other sciences in general, namely, that empirical assumptions are not to be tested on the basis of their presumed description of reality, but on the basis of their success in rendering possible sufficiently accurate predictions.

But I do object to the assimilation, which Professor Friedman proposes, of hypotheses in physical theory with hypotheses in economics, in disregard of certain relevant and important differences between them.

Friedman takes as an example of the first type the hypothesis that the acceleration of a body falling in a vacuum is a constant and is independent of the shape of the body, the manner of

---

[3] M. Friedman, *Essays in Positive Economics* (University of Chicago Press, 1953), p. 11.

dropping it, and so on. All this is expressed by the well-known formula:

$S = \dfrac{gt^2}{2}$, where S is the distance traveled by a falling body in any

specified time, g is the constant indicating the acceleration, and t is the time in seconds. This hypothesis works well in predicting the motion of a falling body in the air, regardless of the fact that other relevant factors, such as the density of the air itself, the shape of the body, and so on, are neglected. In this sense, the hypothesis is useful, not because it describes accurately what actually happens when a body is falling in the air, but because it renders it possible to make successful predictions about its movements.[4]

On the other hand, Professor Friedman (with Professor Savage) takes as a parallel example involving human behavior that of shots made by an expert billiard player—shots to be predicted in some way by the spectators through some kind of hypotheses.

According to Friedman and Savage,

> it seems not at all unreasonable that *excellent predictions* [italics added] would be yielded by the hypothesis that the billiard player made his shots *as if* he knew the complicated mathematical formulae that would give the optimum directions of travel, could estimate accurately by eye the angles, etc. . . . , describing the location of the balls, could make lightning calculations from the formulae, and could then make the balls travel in the direction indicated by the formulae.[5]

Professor Friedman states quite rightly in this respect that

> our confidence in this hypothesis is not based on the belief that billiard players, even expert ones, can or do go through the process described; it derives rather from the belief that, unless in some way or other they were capable of reaching essentially the same result, they would not in fact be expert billiard players.[6]

The only trouble with this comparison, in my opinion, is that

[4] Ibid., pp. 16–18.
[5] Ibid., p. 21.
[6] Loc. cit.

in the former case our hypothesis could allow us to predict, say, the speed of a falling body at any instant whatever with a reasonable approximation, while in the latter case we are not able to predict anything, much less make "excellent predictions" about the shots of a billiard player other than that they will probably be "good shots." In fact, the mere hypothesis that the billiard player will behave as if he knew all the physical laws connected with a billiard game tells us very little about those laws and even less about the position of the balls after any future shot by our brilliant player. In other words, we are not permitted a prevision of the kind allowed by the application of the hypothesis relating to a body falling in air.

The way in which the comparison is made seems to me to imply or to suggest that we could make any calculation whatever in order to predict, for instance, the future position of the balls on the billiard table after any shot by our player. But this is not the case. A friend of mine, Eugenio Frola, professor of mathematics at the University of Turin, and I, after considering the problem, came to some rather amusing conclusions.

To begin with, any billiard player may locate the ball—or find it located—in an infinite number of initial positions defined by a system of Cartesian co-ordinates corresponding to two edges of the billiard plane. Each of these positions is a combination of the infinite numbers that may be assumed by these two co-ordinates, and the total may therefore be mathematically symbolized as ∞^2. Moreover, we ought to take into account the inclination and the direction of the stick at the moment when the player hits the ball. Here we are again confronted with an infinite number of combinations of these factors that may be symbolized, in their turn, as ∞^2. Besides, the ball may be hit on an infinite number of points, each of them being defined by a latitude and by a longitude on the surface of the ball. Again we have another infinite number of combinations that may be symbolized as before by ∞^2. Another factor to be taken into consideration in order to make predictions about the final position of the ball is the force of the impact when the ball is hit by our player. We are here once more in the presence of an infinite number of possibilities, corresponding to the impulse applied and designated by the symbol ∞.

If we bring together all the factors we ought to take into consideration to predict what will happen to the ball at the moment of impact, we obtain a result that may be symbolized as ∞^7, which means that the possible factors to be taken into consideration are as numerous as the *points of a seven-dimensional space.*

Nor is this the end of the story. For each shot we ought also to determine the motion, that is, the way the ball will rotate on the billiard table's plane, and so on, which would require a system of differential nonlinear equations that is not easy to solve. Moreover, we ought to take into consideration the way the ball will hit the edges of the table, how much speed it will lose because of it, what will be the new rotation of the ball as a consequence of the hit, and so on. Finally, we ought to express the general solution, in order to calculate how many successful cases an expert player ought to consider each time before hitting the ball, in terms of the rules of the game, the physical nature of the table, and the probable ability of the player's adversaries to exploit the resulting situation on their own behalf.

All this indicates how different are such examples of working hypotheses as those formulated in some parts of physics (like that relating to falling bodies) from hypotheses relating to apparently not very complicated problems like those of a billiard game, the difficulties of which escape the attention of most people.

It is safe to say that our hypothesis that a good billiard player will behave as if he knew how to solve the scientific problems involved in his game, far from allowing any real prediction of the future shots of our player, is but a metaphor to express confidence that he will make "good shots" in the future as he did in the past. We are like a physicist who, instead of applying his hypotheses relating to the bodies falling in air in order to predict, for instance, their speed at any moment, would simply say that the body will fall as if it knew the laws relating to its motions and obeyed them, while the physicist himself would be unable to formulate these laws in order to make any calculation whatever.

Professor Friedman states that

> it is only a short step from these examples to the economic hypothesis that under a wide range of circumstances individual firms behave as if they were seeking rationally to maximize their expected returns, and had full knowledge of the data needed to succeed in this attempt; as if, that is, they knew the relevant cost and demand func-

tions, calculated marginal cost and marginal revenue from all actions open to them, and pushed each line of action to the point at which the relevant marginal cost and marginal revenue were equal.[7]

I agree that there is only a short step from the preceding example to the new one, provided that we consider both as merely *metaphors* expressing our generic confidence in the ability of good business men to remain in the market, in the same way as we could express our confidence that a good billiard player will win as many games in the future as he did in the past.

But there would be more than a short step from the example of the billiard player to the example of a firm in the market if it is implied that we could calculate in some scientific way the results of the activity of that firm at any given time in the future.

The difficulties of such a calculation are much more formidable than the problems relating to successful solutions of a billiard game. Human activity in business is not only related to the maximization of returns in monetary terms. Many other factors relating to human behavior must be taken into consideration and cannot be ignored in favor of a numerical interpretation of maximization. This renders the problem of calculating such maxima in economics much more complicated than the numerical problems relating to the successful cases in a billiard game. In other words, while the maximization of success in a billiard game may be a numerical problem, the maximization of success in the economy is not identifiable with the maximization of monetary returns; i.e., it is not a numerical problem. Maximization problems in the economy are not mathematical problems at all, and the concept of a maximum in economic behavior is not identical with the concept of a maximum as this is employed in mathematics. We are here confronted with a semantic confusion comparable to that of a man who, having heard about the existence of the most beautiful girl in the city, would undertake a mathematical calculation of the maximum beauty possible to all girls in order to discover her.

If we continue our comparison of the problems of a billiard player with economic problems, we ought to take into consideration a situation (comparable to that prevailing in the economic

---

[7] Loc. cit.

domain) in which the billiard table itself would move, the edges would expand and contract without any regularity, the balls would go and come in their turn without waiting for the hits of the players, and, above all, somebody sooner or later would change the laws governing all these processes, as happens so frequently when legislatures and governments intervene to change the rules of the economic "game" in a given country.

Economics as an aprioristic science would be no less doomed to failure, even if we could expect, from its tautologies alone, to find all the conclusions needed to settle questions vital to the lives of particular individuals as well as members of a political and economic community. In this respect I agree completely with Professor Friedman when he says that while "the canons of formal logic alone can show whether a particular language is complete and consistent . . . factual evidence alone can show whether the categories of the analytical filing system have an empirical counterpart, that is, whether they are useful in analyzing a particular class of concrete problems." And I agree, too, when he cites, as an example, the use of the categories of demand and supply, the usefulness of which "depends on the empirical generalizations that an enumeration of the forces affecting demand in any problem and of the forces affecting supply will yield two lists that contain few items in common." But as soon as we enter the field of empirical assumptions, all the limitations we have seen relating to the empirical approach in economics will emerge, the result being that so far neither the empirical nor the aprioristic approach in economics is fully satisfactory.

This implies, of course, that the choice of a system of individual freedom on the part of educated people as well as of people in general certainly cannot be brought about by economic arguments of which the cogency would be comparable to that of corresponding arguments in mathematics or in several parts of physics.

The same considerations apply to political science, whether or not we consider it a science on the same level as economics.

There is still a wide fringe of questionable points, a sort of no-man's land, that superficial thinkers and demagogues of all countries are carefully cultivating in their way, to grow in it every kind of mushrooms, including many poisonous ones, served up to their fellow citizens as if they were the products of scientific work.

We must admit frankly that it is difficult not only to teach people scientific conclusions, but also to find appropriate arguments to convince people that our teachings are correct. There is some consolation in the fact that, according to liberal ideals, only a few general assumptions need to be accepted in order to found and to carry out a liberal system, for it belongs to the very nature of such a system to let people work as they think best, provided that they do not interfere with the similar work of other people.

On the other hand, free collaboration on the part of the individuals concerned does not necessarily imply that the choices of each individual are worse than they would be under the direction of economists or political scientists. I was once told that a famous economist of our time had almost ruined his aunt by giving her, at her insistent request, confidential advice about the stock market. Everyone knows his personal situation and is probably in a better position than anybody else to make decisions about many questions relating to it. Everyone probably has more to gain from a system in which his decisions would not be interfered with by the decisions of other people than he has to lose by the fact that he could not interfere in turn with other people's decisions.

Moreover, a system of free choice in the economic as well as in the political domain gives to each individual the precious possibility, on the one hand, of abstaining from all concern with questions he finds too complicated and too difficult and, besides, rather unimportant, and, on the other hand, of asking for the collaboration of other people in order to solve problems that it would be both difficult and important for him to solve. There is no reason to think that people would not behave in this respect as they do in any other similar circumstance, when they go, for instance, to their lawyer or their doctor or their psychiatrist. This does not mean, of course, that there are experts who can solve every kind of problem. It is hardly necessary to remind ourselves in this connection of what we have said about economic reasoning. But whenever there is no possibility of any objective solution of a problem, the conclusion to be drawn is not that individuals ought to act under the direction of the authorities, but, on the contrary, that the authorities should refrain from giving instructions that cannot be based on objective solutions of the problems concerned.

Few advocates of contemporary socialistic solutions would admit that their theories are not based on objective reasoning. But it is quite sufficient, in most cases, to conclude that their objections to a maximum area of individual choice are based on philosophical, or rather, on ethical, postulates of dubious validity and also on economic arguments that are even more dubious.

The often-heard slogan that "we cannot put the clock back" in economics or in politics, besides being a proud boast that socialistic ideas are widespread, seems also to imply that the particular socialistic clock indicates not only the right time, but also a time that is conceived of as right without need of any demonstration. We cannot be very happy with this implication.

The adversaries of a free economic system in our day have not added a single new, solid item to the agenda on the part of governments and legislatures that had been already compiled by those classical economists who recommended a liberal system.

As far as the economy is concerned, and the economy is actually a favorite field for all the advocates of coercive procedures at the present time, the nationalization of several kinds of industries is often deemed a necessary or, at least, a suitable substitute for private enterprises regulated according to laws and orders issued by the authorities.

Many reasons are alleged in support of such nationalization. Some of them are perhaps acceptable, although they are not new, while others that are new are not acceptable at all on the basis of the arguments that their advocates present.

From a statement of the policy and principles of the so-called British democratic socialism, published by the British Labour Party in 1950, we learn that there are three main principles supporting the idea of nationalization or public ownership of industries:

(1) To ensure that monopolies—whenever they are "unavoidable"—do not "exploit" the public, which would necessarily happen, according to these socialists, if monopolies were private.

(2) To "control" basic industries and services on which the economic life and welfare of the community depend, because control cannot be "safely" left in the hands of private owners "not answerable" to the community.

(3) To deal with industries in which "inefficiency" persists and where the private owners lack either the will or the capacity to make improvements.

None of these principles is really convincing, if submitted to careful analysis. Monopolies, whenever necessary, may be easily controlled by the authorities without any necessity for the latter to substitute their initiative for that of the monopoly controlled by them. On the other hand, there is no valid demonstration that public monopolies, that is, monopolies exercised by public authorities or by other people delegated by them, would not exploit the public or would exploit the public less than private monopolies. Indeed, historical evidence in many countries proves that monopolies exercised by public authorities may exploit the public much more consistently and much less precariously than private ones. Controlling the authorities through other authorities or through private persons proves to be much more difficult than controlling private monopolists through the authorities or even through other private individuals or groups.

The second principle, that so-called control of basic industries cannot be left in the hands of private owners, implies both the idea that private owners cannot be made answerable in some way to the community for their control of the basic industries and that public owners are answerable to the community in any respect. Unfortunately for the advocates of nationalization, on the basis of this principle neither the former nor the latter implication can be demonstrated by any valid argument. Private owners are answerable to the community for the simple reason that they must depend on it both to sell their products and to buy raw materials, plants, services, capital, equipment, and so on, in order to produce what they intend to sell. If they refuse to meet the exigencies of the community, they lose their customers and cannot remain in the market. They must then give way to other, more "answerable" controllers of basic industries. On the other hand, the public authorities do not depend at all on the community in the same way, since they can impose, in principle, through laws and orders, in a coercive way, prices of goods and services so as to take advantage, if necessary, both of other sellers and of other buyers. Moreover, they are not doomed to failure, as they can always compensate, at least in principle, for the losses they happen to cause to their industries by imposing further taxation on the citizens, that is, on the community they are purportedly "answerable" to. Of course, the advocates of public ownership of basic industries will maintain that the authorities must be elected, that they therefore "represent" the community, and so on. But we know this story already and have seen what it means: a rather empty ceremony and a mostly symbolic control of a handful of rulers on the part of the electorate.

The third principle is no less dubious than the preceding ones. There is no valid argument to demonstrate either that industries owe their possible inefficiency to their private ownership or that efficiency will be recovered through the initiative of public authorities when private ownership gives way to public ownership.

The underlying assumption of all these principles is that public authorities are not only more honest, but also wiser, more skilled, and more efficient than private persons in conducting economic activities. This assumption is obviously not proved, and there is much historical evidence against it.

Other distinctions, for example, like that between "wants," for which the individual consumer could pay, and "needs," for which the individual could not or even would not pay, made by several people in order to justify the nationalization of industries for the purpose of satisfying these "needs" instead of the "wants" that private industries supposedly would satisfy, are based on a similar undemonstrated idea, namely, that the authorities are better qualified to discover and even to satisfy individual "needs" that private citizens would not be able or even might not want to satisfy if they were free to choose.

Of course, some old arguments in favor of nationalization still hold good. This is the case with industries or services of which the whole cost cannot be paid by charging the consumers because of the difficulties involved in assessing them individually (as, for instance, in the case of lighthouses) or because of complications arising from the collection of the charges (as in the case of busy roads, bridges, and so on). In these cases, perhaps, private industry would not find it profitable to supply goods or services, and some other system must step in. But it is interesting to notice that in these cases the principle of free choice in economic activities is not abandoned or even put in doubt. It is admitted that people who freely chose these services would be willing to pay for them if it were possible and that therefore they can be taxed with reference to their presumed benefit and to the cost of it. Taxation can never be completely identifiable with the payment of a price under the market system, but it may be considered in this case as a good approximation to the payment of a price under that system. The same cannot be said of other impositions brought about on the socialist assumption that the authorities know better than individuals what those individuals ought to do.

It may be that modern technology and modern ways of life have rendered more frequent cases of services that cannot easily or cannot at all be paid for by the public through the usual system of prices. But it is also true that in several instances this system is still workable and that private enterprise may be kept efficient anyway under new circumstances. The enormous increase in the traffic on the usual roads and bridges in industrialized countries has rendered it difficult or even impossible to keep privately operated turnpikes, but present-day motor roads are bringing back again similar conditions for collecting charges. Another example to be cited in this connection is television and broadcasting. The advocates of public ownership of these enterprises often contend, for instance, that private ownership would be unsuitable because of the impossibility of charging prices, while private enterprise in this sector in the United States has already solved the problem by selling its services to the firms that want to advertise their products to the general public and are prepared to pay for this purpose an amount of money sufficient to defray all the expenses of the broadcast. Even here, some enterprisers might find a way to charge for television if the authorities permitted them to try!

On the other hand, new technological conditions may limit individual freedom—for instance, with reference to the right of property in land—but the general principle that choices are to be left to the individual and not to the authorities may be retained rather satisfactorily under modern conditions in this respect as well. This is demonstrated, for example, by the efficiency of the American system of exploiting oil and mineral resources in accordance with the principle that private property in land must be respected—a principle that has been decidedly disregarded in other countries of the world because of the alleged incompatibility of private ownership with such activities as mining.

Other difficulties may arise from a different kind of consideration. We have tried to define coercion as direct action on the part of some people with the object of hindering others from reaching certain ends and, generally, of inducing them to make choices they would not otherwise have made.

Direct action may be conceived of as physical action, and in all the cases in which coercion is identifiable with physical action we have a simple method of defining what coercion is. But in most cases coercion is exercised through the threat of some kind of physical action that actually does not take place. Coercion is more a feeling of intimidation than a physical event, and the identification of coercion is more difficult than we would imagine at first sight. Threats and the feelings relating to threats constitute a chain of which the links are not easily traceable under all circumstances nor easily definable by other people than the individual concerned. In all such cases the assumption that some action or form of behavior is coercive of the action or the behavior of others is not clear or objective enough to form the basis of an empirically ascertainable statement about it. This is an embarrassment for all supporters of a system of individual freedom, in so far as freedom has a negative character that cannot help being accurately stated without reference to coercion. If we have to state what behavior or action would be "free" in a given case, we must also state what corresponding behavior or action would be coercive, that is, what action would deprive people of their freedom in that case. Whenever there is no certainty about the nature of the corresponding coercion to be avoided, the ascertainment of the circumstances under which we can secure "freedom" for an action and the definition of the content of the latter are very difficult indeed.

To the extent that freedom is not something ascertainable either by empirical or by aprioristic methods, a political and economic system based on "freedom" understood as absence of "constraint" will be subject to a criticism similar to that which we have made in connection with the empirical approach in economics.

This is the reason why a political system based on freedom

includes always at least a minimum amount of coercion, not only in the sense of hindering constraint, but also in the sense of determining—for instance, by a majority rule—through a group decision what the group will admit as free and what it will forbid as coercive in all the cases that are not susceptible of an objective determination.

In other words, a system of political or economic freedom is based, above all, on the empirical approach in economics and politics, but it cannot be based completely on it. Thus, there is always some victim of coercion in this "free" system. You may try to convince people to behave in the way you deem "free" and to restrain them from behaving in the way you deem "coercive." But you cannot always demonstrate that what you deem to be free is actually free or that what you deem to be coercive is actually coercive in an objective sense of the word.

Religious intolerance may be cited as an example of what I mean. There are some people who become indignant if you behave in a way that they deem incompatible with their religious feelings, even if you behave in a way that you yourself would never deem coercive of them. Nevertheless, the latter feel offended by your behavior because, in their eyes, you do something against their God or you fail to do something which you ought to do on behalf of their God and which could possibly bring down the wrath of God upon all concerned. In fact, their God, according to their religion, is also yours, and they are likely to think that your behavior is offensive to them in the same way as it is offensive to the God you have in common with them.

I do not say, of course, that all religions are intolerant. Hinduism, Buddhism, the old Greek and Roman religions were not intolerant, as far as I know, since their supporters would be inclined to admit that you might have your gods just as they had theirs. This is not always the case with other religions. There was a law in England, enacted at the time of Queen Elizabeth I, that forbade people to enjoy entertainment on Sundays. Offenders could be punished, and the victims of the "scandal" could request an indemnification. This law is no longer observed, but several years ago I read in the newspapers that an English girl had filed a suit for damages on this basis against an English movie firm that showed motion pictures, as was customary, on

Sundays. According to the newspaper, the girl was rather poor, but she had taken care to select, as the perpetrator of the scandal, a very big movie firm in the center of London. The request for damages—a rather large one—was perfectly adequate to the importance of the firm, although probably not so if compared with the "damages" suffered by the "victim." I do not remember how the English court concerned decided this case, but I think the Elizabethan law on which it was based may be cited as a good example of what I mean by religious intolerance and by the corresponding "constraint" that some religious people may feel they are suffering because of behavior that nobody else would consider coercive of anybody.

I was reminded of this Elizabethan law some weeks ago as I was sitting outside a coffee house on the main street of a little Italian village. A procession was just passing along the road, and I did not pay any attention to the fact that everybody stood up while the procession went by. A nun in the procession looked at me and, seeing that I was still sitting down without bothering about the action of the other people, reproached me by pointing out that one *must* stand up when the procession is passing. I do not think that this poor nun was usually an arrogant person. Probably she was a very mild and charitable creature. But she could not admit that anybody should remain seated outside a coffee house while the procession, her procession, the procession of her God, was passing. My being seated in that case was to her an offensive form of behavior, and I am sure that she felt constrained somehow in her feelings, nay, almost insulted, just as I might feel unjustly constrained if somebody were to speak to me with insolence.

Fortunately, the law of my country thus far does not forbid people to sit by the side of the road while a procession is passing by, but I am sure that the nun would immediately approve of a law forbidding such behavior and would, moreover, approve of it in the same way as I would approve of a law that would forbid insults or similar things.

I think there is a lesson in this. But I have finished mine.

CONCLUSION

Perhaps the best procedure to follow in writing this conclusion is to try to reply to some of the questions that my readers would probably ask me if they could. In fact, I was asked such questions when the contents of this book were delivered as lectures.

1. *What do I mean when I say (in chapter 8) that public opinion "is not everything"?*
2. *Is there any possibility of applying the "Leoni model" to present-day society?*
3. *Supposing that the above-mentioned possibility exists, how can the "golden rule" referred to here enable us to distinguish the area of legislation from the common-law area? What are the general boundaries of the domains to be respectively allotted to legislation and to the common law according to the model?*
4. *Who will appoint the judges or lawyers or other* honoratiores *of that kind?*
5. *If we admit that the general trend of present-day society has been more against individual freedom than in favor of it, how could the said* honoratiores *escape the trend?*

Of course, we could take into consideration many other questions, but those mentioned above seem to be the salient points arising from a possible discussion of the whole matter.

   1. *What do I mean when I say (in chapter 8) that public opinion "is not everything"?* As far as the first question is concerned, I maintain that not only may public opinion be wrong, but it may also be corrected by resorting to reasonable argument. True enough, this may be a long-drawn-out process. It took more

172

than a century for people to become acquainted with socialist ideas; it will certainly take a considerable time for them to reject these ideas, but this is no reason to give up the attempt.

While the trend against individual freedom is still the prevailing one in countries comparatively undeveloped according to Western standards, it is already possible to realize from several symptoms that people have learned some lessons in those countries of the West in which the limitation of individual freedom through a corresponding expansion of enacted law, preached more or less openly by socialist leaders as a necessary condition for the advent of a "better world," has proved to be very little counter-balanced by the alleged advantages of such legislation. Today we can already observe, for instance, a recession of socialism in England, Germany, and possibly France, as far as the so-called nationalization of industry is concerned. It is obvious that as a result of this recession individual initiative in the economic field is being gradually liberated from the threat of further interference on the part of the government. Recent books, like that of an ex-Labourite in England, Mr. R. Kelf-Cohen, are rather illuminating in this regard.

What is characteristic of the socialistic solution of the so-called social problem is not the end of promoting public welfare and eliminating, as far as possible, poverty, ignorance, and squalor, for this end is not only perfectly compatible with individual freedom, but may also be considered as complementary to it. The very core of the socialist solution is the peculiar way its supporters propose to reach that end, namely, by resorting to a host of officials acting in the name of the state and limiting accordingly, if not suppressing altogether, private initiative in economics as well as in several other fields that are inextricably connected with the economic domain.

If socialism consisted chiefly, as many persons still believe, in its declared aims, it would probably be difficult to convince people to give it up in the near future. It is quite possible, on the other hand, to convince people that what is wrong with socialism is not its professed aims, but the means purportedly necessary for their achievement. The naïveté of the socialist view as far as the means are concerned is really surprising. As the above-mentioned author points out,

There was magic in the words "public board" or "public corporation." They were to be staffed by selfless men of outstanding ability,
devoted to the national interest. We assumed that such men were to
be found in large numbers; naturally they had no chance to come
forward in the degenerate capitalistic era in which we were living.

We also assumed that the workers in the industries would be transformed by the Act of Nationalization and devote themselves to the
national interest.

Thus, the combination of selfless management and selfless workers would bring about the brave new world of socialism—so utterly
different from capitalism.[1]

A similarly incredible naïveté has been typical of such famous
leaders of the Labour movement in Great Britain as Sidney and
Beatrice Webb, who placed, as Kelf-Cohen says, great reliance on
"independent and disinterested experts" in the new socialist
state. They had, as the same author says,

> great faith in the reasonableness of the human being who could al-
> ways be swayed by facts duly collected and published. . . . They, of
> course, believed that once the personal element represented by the
> capitalists had disappeared, the character of all persons connected
> with these industries would be so profoundly changed that the indus-
> tries would in fact represent a new way of life. . . . As the Webbs had
> little understanding of the function of management and the respon-
> sibility for making decisions, which is a vital part of that function,
> they failed to realise that a conglomeration of committees and
> disinterested experts would still leave it necessary for responsible
> management to do the work. They tended to identify at the back of
> their minds the responsibility of management with the greed of
> capitalism.[2]

Finally, Kelf-Cohen proves quite conclusively that the same
naïveté was shown by the members of the Labour Government in
the period from 1945–1950. In fact, the British Labourites are
not alone in this attitude, which is common to all advocates of
publicly owned enterprises that are to be operated on a commercial basis. In the long run this attitude cannot last. The innumerable failures of publicly owned enterprises are being slowly but

---

[1] R. Kelf-Cohen, *Nationalization in Britain: The End of a Dogma* (London: Macmillan,
1958), Preface, p. v.
[2] Ibid., p. 12.

surely realized by people at large. Public opinion will be forced to change accordingly.

2. *Is there any possibility of applying the "Leoni model" to present-day society?* What I said above gives me the opportunity to answer the second question relating to the possibility of applying in present-day society what some of my dear friends and auditors at Claremont humorously called the "Leoni model." The displacement of the center of gravity of legal systems from legislation to other kinds of law-making processes cannot be attained in a short time. It can, however, be the result of a change in public opinion concerning the scope and significance of legislation with reference to individual freedom. History shows us other examples of a similar process. Classical Greek law, based on legislation, gave way to Roman law, based mainly on the authority of the jurisconsults, customs, and judiciary law. When a Roman emperor of Greek descent, Justinian, tried later to revive the Greek idea of legislative law by putting in force, as if it were a statute, a huge collection of opinions of classical Roman jurisconsults, his attempt eventually underwent a similar fate by becoming the basis of a lawyers' law that lasted for centuries until modern times.

True, history never repeats itself in the same way, but I would not go so far as to say that it does not repeat itself in other ways. There are countries at present in which the judiciary function performed by judges officially appointed by the government and based on the enacted law is so slow and cumbrous, not to say expensive, that people prefer to resort to private arbiters for the settlement of their disputes. Further, whenever the enacted law appears to be too complicated, arbitration is often likely to abandon the basis of enacted law for other standards of judgment. On the other hand, businessmen like to resort, whenever possible, to bargaining rather than to official judgments based on the enacted law. Although we lack statistical figures relating to most countries, it seems reasonable to think that this trend is increasing and could be deemed as a symptom of a new development.

Another indication of a trend in the same direction may be seen in the behavior of people who willingly renounce in some countries, at least to a certain extent, their right to take advantage of discriminatory statutes like the Landlord and Tenant

Acts, which enable one of the parties to violate previous agreements, for example, by the renewal or nonrenewal of leases, the ability of the landlord to increase the rent, etc. In these cases, the deliberate attempt made by the legislators to disrupt, through an enacted law, previous engagements freely entered into and kept, proves a failure, notwithstanding the obvious interest that one of the parties could have in invoking the law.

A characteristic feature of some legislative measures in this respect, at least in certain countries, is the fact that the discriminatory practices introduced by the enacted law were and/or are obligatory, i.e., have or had to take place even in the face of previous agreements between the parties concerned, while in other cases agreements reached later in spite of the enacted law could be violated according to that law by one of the parties, the other party being left defenseless. In such cases the legislators were obviously concerned about the—for them—unwelcome possibility that the privileged party might renounce his privileges by making and keeping other agreements, not only because of his ideas of honesty in entering into or keeping agreements, but also because his valuation of his own interests might differ from that of the legislators. In such cases we see apparently paradoxical instances of nonlegislated law prevailing over legislated law, as a sort of unrecognized, but still effective, "common law."

A more general phenomenon that must be taken into consideration in this respect is the evasion of the enacted law in all cases in which the evaders feel that they have been unjustly treated by contingent majorities within legislative assemblies. This happens notably in connection with heavy progressive taxation. True, one must distinguish between one country and another in this respect, but there are many reasons to think that the phenomenon of evasion of heavy progressive taxation is much more general and widespread in the countries of the West than is officially admitted or possibly recognized. One could also refer, in this respect, to the increasing practice in the United States of creating foundations and other tax-exempt organizations, the purpose of which, among others, is the transference of both "capital and annual income away from a corporation."[3]

[3] Cf., in this connection, M. Friedman, op. cit., pp. 290 ff. and quotations therein.

No less interesting in this connection is the real attitude of people as compared with the legislative law prohibiting habits and forms of behavior that are commonly considered, on the other hand, as falling within the field of morality and left to private judgment.

As signs of a possible recession of legislation in these fields one could cite, for instance, the strictures of some contemporary American sociologists against the attempts to enforce morals by way of the law (as still happens in some states where, for instance, people "vote dry and drink wet") or the recommendations of a very recent British report, in which it is stated:

> It is not in our view the function of the law to intervene in the private lives of citizens or to seek to enforce any particular pattern of behavior further than is necessary to carry out the purposes we have outlined. . . . to preserve public order and discipline, to protect the citizen from what is offensive or injurious, and to provide sufficient safeguards against exploitation and corruption of others. . . . [4]

Finally, ignorance of what very many statutes entail or even of their very existence and a corresponding negligence in abiding by the enacted law on the part of the man in the street (notwithstanding the classic rule that ignorance of the law is no defense) must also be brought into the picture to give an adequate idea of the limits of the legislation which is officially "in force," but not effective in many cases.

The more that people become aware of these limits of legislation, the more they will accustom themselves to the idea that present-day legislation, with its pretense of covering all patterns of human behavior, is actually much less capable of organizing social life than its supporters seem to believe.

3. *Supposing that the above-mentioned possibility exists, how can the "golden rule" referred to here enable us to distinguish the area of legislation from common-law area? What are the general boundaries of*

---

[4] Wolfenden Report, the Committee on Homosexual Offences and Prostitution (1959). However, as an example of a contrary, "reactionary" view, we may cite the Maccabean lecture in jurisprudence delivered at the British Academy by the Hon. Sir Patrick Devlin, March, 1959, and published by the Oxford University Press under the title, *The Enforcement of Morals.*

the domains to be respectively allotted to legislation and to the common law according to the model? To the third question I wish to reply that the "golden rule" mentioned in the preceding pages could not be changed into a rule of thumb sufficient in itself to enable us to say when legislation is to be resorted to instead of common law. Other requirements are obviously needed to decide whether legislation is necessary or not in any particular situation. The "golden rule" has only a negative meaning, since its function is not that of organizing society, but that of avoiding as far as possible the suppression of individual freedom in organized societies. It enables us, however, to sketch some boundaries in this respect, to which I referred in the introductory chapter in summarizing in advance some of the points to be made in these lectures when I said that we should reject legislation whenever (a) it is used merely as a means of subjecting minorities in order to treat them as losers in the field, and (b) it is possible for individuals to attain their own objectives without depending upon the decision of a group and without actually constraining any other people to do what they would never do without constraint.

Another criterion already anticipated in the introductory chapter and resulting from the "golden rule" is that the presumed profitability of the legislative process as compared with other law-making processes should be assessed very carefully in all cases where the legislative process is not to be rejected for the above-mentioned reasons. Whatever is not positively proved as worthy of legislation should be left to the common-law area.[5]

I would agree that the attempt to define on these bases the boundaries between the areas to be allotted respectively to legislation and to common law is likely to be very difficult in many

---

[5] A practical way of reducing the scope of legislation could be that of resorting to legislation itself—for instance, by introducing a clause in the written constitutions of the countries concerned, with the object of preventing legislatures from enacting statutes about certain kinds of matters and/or prescribing unanimity or qualified majorities before certain statutes could be put into effect. The requirement of qualified majorities in particular could prevent groups within a legislature from bribing other groups in order to sacrifice dissenting minorities, by rendering the consent of these minorities indispensable for the approval of the law. This procedure was suggested by Professor James Buchanan at the meeting of the Mont Pèlerin Society in Oxford, England, September, 1959.

cases, but the difficulties are not a good reason to give up the attempt.

On the other hand, if it were possible to outline in advance all the applications of the "golden rule" to the definition of the boundaries between the area of common law and that of legislation, and if, moreover, these applications were to be included in the present book, the whole purpose of my thesis would be simply defeated, since the applications themselves could be considered as constituting the clauses of a code. It would be altogether ridiculous to attack legislation while at the same time presenting the draft of a code of one's own. What one ought always to keep in mind is that, according to the common-law or to the lawyers'-law point of view, the application of rules is an ever-continuing process. Nobody can bring the process to its conclusion by himself and within his own time. I may add that, according to my view, everybody should prevent other people from attempting to do just that.

4. *Who will appoint the judges or lawyers or other* honoratiores *of that kind?* The fourth question—"Who will appoint the judges or lawyers or other *honoratiores* to let them perform the task of defining the law?"—is one that, like the preceding, may have a misleading implication. Once again it seems to be implied that the process of appointing judges and the like, as well as that of defining boundaries between the respective areas of legislation and of common law, is to be performed by certain definite persons at a definite time. In fact, it is rather immaterial to establish in advance who will appoint the judges, for, in a sense, everybody could do so, as happens to a certain extent when people resort to private arbiters to settle their own quarrels. The appointment of judges on the part of the authorities is carried out, by and large, according to the same criteria that would be used by the man in the street. For the appointment of judges is not such a special problem as would be, for example, that of "appointing" physicists or doctors or other kinds of learned and experienced people. The emergence of good professional people in any society is only apparently due to official appointments, if any. It is, in fact, based on a widespread consent on the part of clients, colleagues,

and the public at large—a consent without which no appointment is really effective. Of course, people can be wrong about the true value chosen as being worthy, but these difficulties in their choice are inescapable in any kind of choice. After all, what matters is not who will appoint the judges, but how the judges will work.

I have already pointed out in the introductory chapter the possibility that judiciary law may undergo some deviations the effect of which may be the reintroduction of the legislative process under a judiciary guise. This tends to happen first of all when supreme courts are entitled to have the last word in the resolution of cases that have already been examined by inferior courts and when, moreover, the supreme courts' decisions are taken as binding precedents for any similar decisions on the part of all other judges in the future. Whenever this happens, the position of members of the supreme courts is somewhat similar to that of legislators, although by no means identical.

In fact, the power of supreme courts is usually more important under a common-law system than under other legal systems centered around legislation. The latter try to attain the "consistency of judicial decision" through the binding force of precisely formulated rules. The former usually perform the task of introducing and keeping that consistency through the principle of precedent whenever a common opinion among judges or lawyers would not be likely to emerge. In fact, all common-law systems probably were and are based somehow on the principle of precedent (or of "president," as the English lawyers of the Middle Ages used to say) although this principle is not to be simply confused with that of binding precedent in the common-law systems of the Anglo-Saxon countries at the present time.

Today both the legislators and judges of supreme courts perform the task of keeping the legal system on some kind of rails, and precisely because of this both legislators and judges of supreme courts may be in a position to impose their own personal will upon a great number of dissenters. Now, if we admit that we have to reduce the powers of the legislators in order to restore as much as possible individual freedom, understood as the absence of constraint, and if we agree also that the "consistency of judicial decision" must be reserved for the very purpose of enabling individuals to make their own plans for the future, we cannot help suspecting that the establishment of a legal system that could result in emphasizing in its turn the powers of particular individuals like judges of supreme courts would be a deceptive alternative.

Fortunately, even supreme courts are not at all in the same practical position as legislators. After all, not only the inferior courts, but also the supreme courts may issue decisions only if asked to do so by the parties concerned; and although supreme courts are in this respect in a different position from inferior courts, they are still bound to "interpret" the law instead of promulgating it. True, interpretation may result in legislation, or, to put it better, in a disguised legislation, whenever judges stretch the meaning of existing written rules in order to reach a completely new meaning or when they reverse their own precedents in some abrupt way. But this surely does not warrant the conclusion that supreme courts are in the same position as legislators, who can, as Sir Carleton Kemp Allen would say, "make new law in a sense which is quite precluded to the judge."[6]

On the other hand, under the system of "binding" precedent, supreme courts too may be bound, like the House of Lords in Great Britain, by their own precedents, and while the inferior courts are officially bound by the decisions of the higher courts, "the humblest judicial officer" (as the above-mentioned author rightly says) "has to decide for himself whether he is or is not bound, in the particular circumstances, by any given decision" of the higher courts or even of the supreme courts.[7] Obviously this makes for a considerable difference between judges of supreme courts and legislators as far as the unwelcome imposition of their respective wills on a possibly great number of other dissenting people is concerned. Of course, there may be a great difference between one supreme court and another in this respect. Everybody knows, for instance, that the power of the Supreme Court of the United States is much broader than that of the corresponding supreme court of Great Britain, i.e., the House of

---

[6] Carleton Kemp Allen, *Law in the Making* (5th ed.; Oxford: at the Clarendon Press, 1951), p. 287.

[7] Ibid., p. 269.

Lords. The most obvious difference between the two Anglo-Saxon systems is the existence of a written constitution in the American system, the equivalent of which does not exist in the British system. It has already been pointed out by some American theorists in recent times[8] that the problem of precedent where a written constitution is involved is an entirely different matter from that in case law.

> Added to the problem of ambiguity [i.e., in the words of the Constitution] and the fact that the framers [of it] may have intended a growing instrument, there is the influence of Constitution worship. This influence gives great freedom to the court. It can always abandon what has been said in order to go back to the written document itself. It is a freedom greater than it would have had if no such document existed. . . . Indeed, by admitting appeal to the Constitution, the discretion of the court is increased. . . . The possible result of this in some fields may seem alarming.[9]

In such cases, as the author wisely adds (quoting Justice Frankfurter of the United States Supreme Court), "ultimate protection is to be found in the people themselves."

In fact, a system of checks and balances could easily be developed within the judiciary in this respect, just as a corresponding system has been developed, notably in the United States, among the different functions or "powers" within the political organization. If the position of a supreme court like that of Great Britain, which is bound by its precedents, seems inadequate in meeting with changes and new exigencies, and it is assumed, on the contrary, that a supreme court must be allowed to reverse its precedents or to change its previous interpretation of the written law, i.e., of the written constitution, like the Supreme Court of the United States, special devices could still be introduced to limit the power of supreme courts as far as the binding character of their decisions is concerned. For example, unanimity could be requested for decisions that reverse long-established precedents or that change substantially previous interpretations of the con-

[8] Cf., for example, F. H. Levi, *An Introduction to Legal Reasoning* (4th ed.; University of Chicago Press, 1955), pp. 41 ff.

[9] Ibid., pp. 41–43.

stitution. Other checks could also be devised; it is not my task to suggest them here.

What has been pointed out in regard to the position of supreme courts as compared with that of legislators is even more obviously true in regard to inferior courts and ordinary judges in general. They cannot be considered as legislators, not only because of their psychological attitude towards the law, which they commonly intend to "discover" rather than to "create,"[10] but also and above all because of their fundamental dependence on the parties concerned in their process of "making" the law. No insistence on the interference of personal factors in this process of making the law can make us forget this basic fact. There has been a good deal of agitation on the part of some people over the fact that the private feelings and personal situations of the judges may possibly interfere with their judiciary function. One wonders why these people seem to have paid no attention to the corresponding and much more important fact that private feelings and personal situations can interfere as well with the activity of the legislators and through it, much more profoundly, with the activity of all members of the society concerned. If such interferences cannot be avoided, and if we have a choice, it seems much better to prefer those which are less far-reaching and decisive in their effects.

5. *If we admit that the general trend of present-day society has been more against individual freedom than in favor of it, how could the said* honoratiores *escape the trend?* A reply may be given, in this connection, to the fifth question: How could judges, any better than legislators, escape the contemporary trend against individual freedom?

To give a sensible answer to this question, we should first discriminate between judges of inferior courts and those of a su-

---

[10] As Carleton Kemp Allen would say, judges "make" law only in a secondary sense, as "a man who chops a tree into logs has in a sense *made* the logs. . . . Mankind, with all its resource and inventiveness, is limited in its creative power by the physical material vouchsafed to it. Similarly the creative power of the courts is limited by existing legal material at their command. They find the material and shape it. The legislature may manufacture entirely new material." (Op. cit., p. 288.)

preme court. Moreover, we should distinguish between supreme court judges who are in a position to change the law by reversing their precedents and supreme court judges who are not in that position. It is obvious that whatever may be the personal attitude of a judge toward the above-mentioned trend, judges of inferior courts are limited in the extent to which they are free to follow the trend if this is in contrast with the opinion of superior courts. The judges belonging to superior courts are limited, in their turn, in the extent to which they are free to follow the trend if they cannot at will reverse their precedents or if there is some device, such as the requirement of unanimity, to limit the effects of their decisions upon the whole legal system.

Besides, even if we admit that judges cannot escape the contemporary trend against individual freedom, we must admit that it belongs to the very nature of their position towards the parties concerned to weigh their arguments against one another. Any a priori refusal to admit and weigh arguments, evidence, etc., would be inconceivable according to the usual procedures of all courts, at least in the Western world. Parties are *equal* as regards the judge, in the sense that they are free to produce arguments and evidence. They do not constitute a group in which dissenting minorities give way to triumphant majorities; nor can it be said that all the parties concerned with more or less similar cases decided at different times by different judges constitute a group in which majorities prevail and minorities have to give way. Of course, arguments may be stronger or weaker, just as the buyers or sellers in the market may be stronger or weaker, but the fact that every party can produce them is comparable to the fact that everybody can individually compete with everybody else in the market in order to buy or sell. The whole process implies the basic possibility of an equilibrium in a sense very similar to that of the market, and notably of a market in which prices may be fixed by arbiters freely entitled to do so by the parties concerned. To be sure, there are differences between the latter kind of market and the ordinary one. Since the parties have entitled the arbiter to terminate the bargaining by fixing the prices, they have committed themselves in advance to buy or to sell at those prices, while in an ordinary market there is no commitment until the price has been agreed upon between the parties concerned.

In this respect, the position of the parties before a judge is similar to some extent to that of individuals belonging to a group. Neither the losing party at a trial nor the dissenting minority in a group is in a position to refuse to accept the final decision. On the other hand, however, the commitment of the parties before a judge has very definite limits, not only as far as the final decision is concerned, but also with reference to the process by which that decision is reached. Notwithstanding all formalities and artificial rules of procedure, the underlying principle of a judgment is to determine which of the parties is right and which is wrong, without any automatic discrimination of the kind present in group decisions, such as, for instance, by majority rule.

Once again history has something to teach us in this connection. The compulsory enforcement of judicial decisions is a comparatively late development of the law-making process through judges, lawyers, and people of that kind.

As a matter of fact, the enforcement of a decision reached on a fundamentally theoretical basis (i.e., finding which of the parties is right according to some recognizable standards) was for a long time deemed incompatible with any enforcement of that decision through some kind of coercive intervention against the losing party. This explains why, for instance, in the old Greek judicial procedure, the fulfillment of judicial decisions was left to the parties, who had undertaken on oath to abide by the decision of the judge; and why in the whole classical world kings and other military chiefs used to put aside the emblems of their power when requested by some parties to decide a case.

The same idea of a difference in kind between judicial decisions and other decisions relating to military or political questions underlies the fundamental distinction between governmental power (*gubernaculum*) and the judicial function (*jurisdictio*) which the famous English lawyer of the Middle Ages, Bracton, used to stress so much. Although this distinction was and is now again in danger of being lost through later developments in the constitutional history of England, its importance for the preservation of individual freedom against the power of government in that land and, to a certain extent, in other countries which have imitated England in modern times, cannot be over-emphasized by all those who know that history.[11] Unfortunately, today the overwhelming power of parliaments and of governments tends to obliterate the distinction between the legislative or executive power, on the one hand, and the judicial power, on the other, which has been considered one of the glories of the English constitution since the times of Montesquieu. This distinction, however, is based on an idea that people at present seem to have lost sight of: *Law-making is much more a theoretical process than an act of will, and as a theoretical process it cannot be the result of decisions issued by power groups at the expense of dissenting minorities.*

If the basic importance of this idea is realized again in our time, the judicial function will recover its true significance and legislative assemblies or quasi-legislative committees will lose their hold on the man in the street. On the other hand, no single judge would be so powerful as to distort by his personal attitude the process through which all the arguments of all the parties could compete with one another and to dominate at will a situation similar to that described in Tennyson's lines:

> Where Freedom slowly broadens down
> from precedent to precedent.

---

[11] The most accurate and brilliant treatment of this point that I know of is contained in *Constitutionalism: Ancient and Modern* by Charles Howard McIlwain (Cornell University Press, originally published in 1940 and since re-edited).

THE LAW

AND

POLITICS

This series of lectures under the general heading "The Law as Individual Claim" was given at the Freedom School Phrontistery in Colorado Springs, Colorado, December 2–6, 1963. The Phrontistery (after the Greek word for "a place for thinking") was an experimental six-month program that ran from November 1963 through April 1964. It offered eighteen selected students the opportunity for intensive individual study on questions of human liberty. It was intended to develop material for a curriculum for a proposed Ramparts College liberal arts program.

Eleven distinguished scholars gave lectures at various times throughout the period. In addition to Dr. Leoni, the lecturers included: Drs. G. Warren Nutter, Roger J. Williams, Arthur A. Ekirch, Milton Friedman, Sylvester Petro, Ludwig von Mises, Oscar W. Cooley, James J. Martin, F. A. Harper, and Gordon Tullock.

A version of the first chapter appeared in 1964 in a slightly different form in *Archives for Philosophy of Law and Social Philosophy*, Hermann Luchterhand Verlag, Berlin, Germany.

Chapter 3 was based largely on two earlier articles: "The Economic Approach to Politics," *Il Politico*, Vol. 26, No. 3, 1961, pp. 491–502; and "The Meaning of 'Political' in Political Decisions," *Political Studies*, Vol. 5, No. 3, October 1957, pp. 225–239.

Chapter 4 was based on "Political Decisions and Majority Rule," *Il Politico*, Vol. 25, No. 4, 1960, pp. 724–733.

These lectures were not originally footnoted. Notes have been added for this edition.

1

THE LAW AS
INDIVIDUAL
CLAIM

Contemporary philosophical schools that focus on the analysis of language have probably taught us less than they pretend. Nonetheless, they have reminded us of something that we know well but easily forget. Words are "words," and it isn't possible to deal with them as if they were "things" or, to put it another way, as if they were *objects of sensorial experience* the definitions of which make sense insofar as they refer more or less directly to said experience. The word "law" in particular cannot be dealt with more than others as a "thing"; the less so as it doesn't have a meaning directly or uniquely referrable to a sensorial experience as such.

Any analysis of the "law" presents itself first as a linguistic analysis, that is, as an attempt to overcome the above-mentioned difficulty in finding out the actual meaning of that word in the language. This is not easy because people may use the word *law* from many points of view and with meanings which not only change according to the various kinds of people who use that word, but may also change within the language used by the same kind of people. Even among professors of "law" you may notice that the meaning of the word is not always the same. Long-lasting disputes among international lawyers or constitutional lawyers on the one side and civil lawyers on the other may be quoted in this respect.

This difficulty tends to be tiring and discouraging, the result

189

being that people who start a linguistic analysis about the "law" may be tempted to discontinue it sooner or later in order to adopt one of the following three statements: a) law is what my colleagues X, Y, and Z and I know is "law" and we don't care about other opinions; b) law is what I suggest or I "stipulate" to call in that way without caring very much about other "stipulations" relating to the same word; c) law is everything everybody wants to call in that way whatever that may mean, and it isn't worthwhile carrying on a research that has no end.

While the third statement leads to skepticism, the former two actually generate the most part of the so-called general theories of law. To be honest, tiredness is not, however, the only source of the two former statements. There is also a practical reason for them. Lawyers or teachers of law are not primarily concerned with a theoretical analysis about the meaning of the word "law." They directly or indirectly tend, as any legal operator, to practical results such as convincing a judge and winning a case. Any conventional definition that may lead to their goal is welcome.

Supposing, however, that we have no practical goals and try to avoid skepticism at the same time, I think there is only one escape from the arbitrariness of the two former statements: to take into consideration as far as possible *all* discourses in which the word "law" is involved, in order to see whether we happen to find out a *minimal common meaning of the word "law."* This kind of research is not to be confused with that of the lexicographer who limits himself to register one or more meanings of the same word without necessarily worrying about the connections between all the meanings of the same word. This kind of research is only possible if we accept a postulate: that a *minimal common meaning does exist.* In other words, we must assume that the language of the man in the street, as well as that of the experts on the technicalities of courts, statutes, and precedents, are homogeneous enough to justify the research.[1]

I daresay that this research of the *minimal common meaning of*

---

[1] I have no need to explain at length why I call that a *postulate.* Indeed, no demonstration of said assumption could be supplied until the research is finished and it is obvious that the latter is practically inexhaustible owing to the great number of languages and meanings which should be taken into consideration.

the word "law" is, in the end, the hard destiny of the so-called legal philosopher.

The lack of a preliminary theory of definitions and a satisfactory linguistic approach to the problem of defining the "law" is accountable for the fact that the language adopted in most general theories of law is simply borrowed from the lawyers—or from *some* kinds of lawyers. It is, therefore, transplanted from a field in which people are only seeking in a more or less direct way for *practical* results into a quite different field in which people do not care in the least to reach practical results, but try to work out theoretical conclusions.

One of the usual meanings of the word "law" as borrowed in the general theories from the professional lawyers is that of "legal norm" or generally that of a "system" or "ordering" of norms. Actually this "system" or ordering of norms is the conceptual limit not only of the discourses of professional lawyers but also of legal operators in general; that is, of people who tend to solve some practical problems such as of having a debtor pay his creditor or dissolving a marriage and so on. For these purposes, it is sufficient for them to assume that the law is simply the ordering of *those* norms the "application" of which enables them to reach the above-mentioned ends. Similarly, for economic operators, economy is simply the market or, to put it better, "the market" where they can buy and sell at given prices economic goods or services. People who want to dissolve a marriage or be paid by a debtor need simply to know first the *norms* concerned, just as people who want to buy or sell any commodities on the market need first to know what their prices are. The reasons why each country has certain norms (possibly different from others of other countries, or of the same country in other times) relating to the dissolving of marriages or paying debts are not usually a matter of concern for legal operators unless they are also personally interested in comparative law or in the history of law. In a precisely similar way, the (often remote) reasons why prices are as they are in a certain market at a given moment are not a matter of interest for sellers or buyers, unless they are historians of economy or economists themselves.

Legal operators on the one side or economic operators on the other side are even less concerned with the reasons why there are *norms* in general in the legal field and *prices* in general in the market. Professional lawyers, as well as economic advisors, do not need to know those reasons either, in order to assist their clients. The result is that they all treat norms and, respectively, prices as *ultimate data* from which they move in order to reach their own ends.

It is, however, the task of the economist to reveal the connections between the actions of the economic operators and the prices of the goods they buy or sell. The task of the legal philosopher is to reconstruct the connections between legal operators and the corresponding norms that they may invoke for their purposes. This means that norms are not the ultimate data of the legal process for the legal philosopher, just as prices are not the ultimate data of the economic process for the economist.

Economists have traced back prices as a social phenomenon ultimately to individual choices between scarce goods. It is my suggestion that legal philosophers as well should trace back legal norms as social phenomena to some individual acts or attitudes. These acts reflect themselves in some way in the norms under a legal system, as individual choices among scarce goods reflect themselves in prices on the market under a monetary system.

I suggest also that those individual acts and attitudes be called *demands* or *claims*. Dictionaries define a *claim* as "a demand for something as due." I assume in this connection that *only individuals can make claims, just as only individuals can make choices.* Individuals *do* make claims as well as choices. But while they do not necessarily need to refer to other individuals to make choices, they need to refer to other individuals to make claims.

I know perfectly well that reducing legal norms to individual *claims* may seem paradoxical. It may even shock people who move from commonplace assumptions that are at the basis of most contemporary theories of law. Isn't a norm the expression of a *duty*? Isn't a "legal" norm first of all the expression of a *legal duty*? Are not the legal "rights" (when they exist) the reflection of corresponding *duties* as fixed in the legal norms? Isn't a norm, logically considered, a *prescriptive* sentence? Isn't the nature of *legal duty* as expressed in the norm evidenced by *sanctions* and *coercions* contemplated in the legal norms themselves? These are some of the "obvious" objections that may be raised against my suggestion. My humble reply is that, just as the norms are not the ultimate data of the legal process, the so-called prescriptive or duty nature of the legal norm is not its ultimate nature for the legal philosopher.

At first sight, the analogy between a so-called legal duty and a *moral duty* may be tempting indeed. Moral duties are considered as ultimate data of morals in the Kantian tradition. Why shouldn't we consider legal duties as ultimate data of law as well? Unfortunately, if we do that we get immediately into trouble, as we must first distinguish *moral* duties from *legal* ones, in order to locate conceptually the latter. I don't know of any successful attempt to do that thus far. It is rather common to maintain that legal duties differ from moral ones because the former, at variance with the latter, are presented in connection with some kind of "coercion" or at least with the contemplation of a possible coercion in the formula in which those duties are expressed. I am not very happy with that theory. How can we ignore the fact that many norms which are usually considered as legal (and specifically those which are considered as basic for any legal ordering), lack any coercion, as well as the mention of coercion in the formula in which they are expressed?

Of course, there is a good reason for that, although this reason seems to have escaped many theorists. If abiding with legal norms actually depended in the main on coercion, or even on the mere fear of it, the whole process would be so full of frictions and so difficult that it wouldn't work. It is curious to note how many people are so highly impressed by the peculiar nature of coercion as a purportedly typical ingredient of legal norms that they tend to overlook completely the very *marginal* significance of coercion in any actual legal order as a whole.

Sanctions and coercions do not make the law; they just assist it in a limited number of cases, and besides, as I have already pointed out, they may apply only to some kinds of norms that we would consider as *subordinate* to others. The main norms often do not even mention sanctions or coercions, for the simple reason that no sanction or coercion could assist them in any effective way: such as constitutional norms, in each single nation, or international norms, concerning relationships between nations.

Attempts to distinguish between moral norms and legal norms

on other bases are no more convincing than attempts to distinguish sanctions and coercions as purportedly typical ingredients
of the legal norms. At least I don't know of any attempt that has
been successful thus far.

In its turn, the often tempting analogy between legal rules on
the one hand and technical rules on the other hasn't succeeded
either. Legal rules and technical rules seem to present a similarity because they are both formulated in a "prescriptive" way, and
usually move from some hypothesis. The general formula of both
kinds of rules is approximately reducible to the following: *if you
want A you have to do B.* But once again, what is difficult here is to
locate the area of the so-called legal rules, as distinguishable
from technical rules in general. Any attempt to take into consideration at the same time the purported duty nature of the legal
norms, together with their purported technical nature, simply
complicates the problem even more. Syncretistic theories of the
legal norm are little more than metaphors, and do not explain
too much. This applies to the theories of the late Professor Ale-
sandro Levi, according to which the legal norm should be a kind
of *hinge* connecting economic and moral rules, as well as those of
the late Professor Gurvitch, according to which legal norms
would always present a "dramatic tension" by being an inextrica-
ble mixture of logic, morals, economy, and so on.

No normative theory of the law has succeeded, thus far, in
explaining what a legal norm is, or, to put it another way, what is
accountable for the fact that a norm is "legal," and not, say,
"moral" or "technical" or "social." Nor has the concept of "authority" proved more useful to enable us to distinguish legal
norms from others. People are considered as "legal" authorities
just because there are some "legal" norms that define or pre-
scribe who is to be considered an "authority" in the legal field.
Significantly enough, the top concept of the most celebrated
"normative" theories of the law is not that of authority, but that
of "norm": No real authority in the legal sense creates the fundamental norm of a legal system, according to that theory.

The difficulty of centering a general theory of law on the concept of legal norms, and ultimately on the concept of legal duty,
as expressed in the legal norm, is all but concealed by the undis-
criminating usage of the famous German word *Sollen,* meaning at

the same time the noun "duty" and the verb "to be obliged" or "to have a duty." It isn't sufficient at all to use that verb in the infinitive to make us understand what a *legal duty* is. When I say, "I ought to," it may mean any one of these three things: a) I have the moral duty of . . . ; b) I am forced to . . . if I want to reach the result I wish; c) somebody wants me "legally" to do . . . .

It may well happen that more than one or even all the three meanings mentioned above are present in the expression, "I ought to." But nonetheless, they are three different meanings that should not be confused with each other. Only the third one appears to be the *legal* meaning of the expression. But the difference between this legal meaning and the meanings mentioned above under a) or under b) lies just in the fact that in the former legal meaning I refer to the will of somebody who wants me to do what I ought to do. The meaning under a) refers just to my moral feeling, which may be considered as an ultimate datum in the Kantian way; the meaning of b) refers to the hypothesis that I wish something, which is an effect of a cause I may determine through my action. At variance with both the meanings of a) and b), the meaning of c) refers, ultimately, to a claim on the part of other people relating to myself. If nobody wanted me legally to do something, there would actually be no legal duty on my part, and the expression "I ought to" would have no *legal* meaning at all. Briefly, the expression "I ought to," taken in the legal sense, is not explainable without reducing it to the (legal) claim of somebody else.

Of course, now we should define what a *claim* is and what a *legal* claim is. This means that we have to lift our attention from people who say "I ought to" to people who say, "I have a claim," or "I demand," or "I intend," or "I request." Without those people there is no "law," even if other people are left who do not feel the corresponding way—*even if these people who are left feel moral duties or adopt technical rules.* This doesn't mean, of course, that claims are satisfied if people whose behavior is the object of a claim do not feel the corresponding moral duty of satisfying that claim, or if they do not realize that it is "technically" expedient for them to satisfy said claims. But while the central concept in the meaning under a) is that of *duty,* and the central concept in the meaning under b) is that of *expediency,* the central concept in the meaning under c) turns out to be, in the end, that of a claim on the part of other people.

What does "claiming" mean? Psychologically, claiming is a complex act. First of all, it is obvious that not all demands are *legal* claims, according to the discourses we can take into consideration in this respect. The robber who waits for me in a dark and lonely place "demands" my money. On the other hand, a lender demands my money if I have to give him back a sum. But while the former demand would usually be considered "illegal" in all countries of the world, the latter is usually considered everywhere "legal." It seems to me that the most obvious difference between the two demands is that everybody (including robbers) usually intends not to be robbed by anyone else. Everybody usually intends to get back the money he has lent, including those scoundrels who try to avoid giving back the money they have borrowed from their creditors. The robber or the scoundrel makes a *special* demand, which is in contradiction with the *common* demand, the latter being a demand that they would make themselves towards all other possible robbers or debtors in bad faith.

The supporters of the "normative" theory of the law may object that what enables us to speak of a contradiction between "common" demands and "special" ones is actually the existence of a "norm," and namely, of a legal norm. I wish to counter, however, that it isn't necessary at all to think of a *norm of the legal type* as a criterion to discover the above-mentioned contradiction. The classic notion of "id quod plerumque accidit" (what usually happens) in a given society would be fairly sufficient to enable us to tell "legal" from "illegal" demands. Statistically, the probability that a passer-by transforms himself into a robber when he meets another passer-by in a lonely place is comparatively low, and lower, at any rate, than the contrary at any given time. The same applies to one who borrows money, and the probability that he does not intend to give it back at all. The popular Russian saying—where everybody robs, nobody is a robber—is true. That is, where everybody robs, the very premises are lacking to define the robber, since there is no actually organized community. The demand we have qualified as *special* is statistically *not probable in the community*. It is, so to say, an exception to the rule, and I mean by *rule,* in general, not necessarily a legal norm, but a description of actual events according to a scheme.

What is *implied* in the demand of a creditor when he wants to be paid by his debtor is *the prevision that his debtor will pay.* What is implied in the demand of a passer-by not to be disturbed or robbed by anybody is in its turn a prevision that nobody will disturb him. Probability judgments are at the basis of their respective claims.

On the other hand, what is implied in the attitude of a robber or of a debtor of bad faith when he wants to reach his own ends is the prevision that his demand would simply not be satisfied by his victims under normal circumstances. This is the reason why such a person tries to put himself and/or the victim in a very special situation, in order to increase the usually low probabilities of being satisfied in his *special* demands.

I suggest calling "legal" exactly those demands or claims *that have a good probability of being satisfied* by corresponding people in a given society at any given time, the reasons why they may be satisfied in each single case being variable and based alternatively or jointly on moral or technical rules.

"Illegal demands or claims" on the contrary, are those *that have little or no probability of being satisfied by the corresponding people under normal circumstances."* (As when a robber would demand money on a busy street in broad daylight.)

Clearly "legal" demands on one hand, and clearly "illegal" demands on the other *are located at the opposite ends of a spectrum comprising all demands that people may make in any given society at any given time.* One should not forget, however, the huge intermediate sector of less definable "quasi-legal" or "quasi-illegal" demands whose probabilities of being satisfied are lower than those of clearly "legal" demands, but still higher than those of clearly "illegal" ones.

The position of many, if not all, demands in the spectrum may change and *is actually changing in any society at any given time.* This process, to use Justinian's famous words, "semper in infinitum decurrit" (is always continuing), and we could not grasp it without introducing the time dimension. New demands may appear while old ones fade away, and present demands may change their position in the spectrum. The whole process may be therefore described as *a continuous change of the respective probabilities that all demands have to be satisfied in a given society at any given time.*

Demands or claims, as we saw, are based on *previsions*. They are not, however, reducible to mere previsions. The position of the legal operator is not simply that of an astronomer who foresees an eclipse. It resembles the position of said astronomer if the latter not only foresaw but also *wanted* the eclipse to take place *for some reason of his own and could influence that event through his own action.* No demand is possible without an element of *will*, on the basis of which there is an *interest* of the person concerned. On the other hand, no will of the latter is possible without being based on the above-mentioned prevision. Of course, we must distinguish between several kinds of previsions, relating to the ultimate goal we want to reach when we make a demand. One can foresee, as creditor, that his debtor will pay him, but the creditor also wants his debtor to pay him, and is determined to use some means at his disposal to have the latter pay his debt. This doesn't necessarily mean that he wants or needs to resort to "coercion" of any kind. Maybe the debtor will pay willingly, maybe he will pay just when the creditor reminds him of it, or after a little argument, reproach, and so on. Even while the creditor resorts to the so-called coercion (or the threat of it), this concept is not so relevant in the whole process as it may appear at first sight, for coercion applied to the debtor needs the *cooperation* of the people who have to apply said coercion. These people may, once again, apply coercion willingly or, once again, after a personal intervention of the creditor, without necessarily implying the need for the creditor to resort to other kinds of coercion on the latter people to provoke coercion on his debtor. The relevant concept here is, as before, not coercion but *the will of the creditor to obtain behavior that he foresees as statistically probable, on the part of other people.*[2]

Claims intermingle and may even conflict against each other, "legal" against "illegal," and also "legal" against "legal," and

---

[2] I suggest, in this condition, calling *power* our possibility of being satisfied in our demands regardless of the reasons *why* they are satisfied, and *legal power* our possibility of being satisfied in our legal demands, regardless, once again, of the reasons that induce other people to satisfy them, or to have them satisfied some way or other by the people concerned.

"illegal" against "illegal," their respective success depending on their respective probabilities of being satisfied by the people concerned.

It is interesting to compare the results of the analysis outlined above with some of the main concepts of lawyers and, I might add, of all legal operators. I have already stated that they usually move from the concept of legal norm instead of that of "legal claim." Even those lawyers who tried to theorize the concept of legal claim as a basic concept of the legal language got involved in contradictions whenever they clung to the concept of legal norm as the ultimate one from which to move to develop their theories.

I must now underline some other differences that we can notice in the language and, respectively, in the frame of mind of lawyers and legal operators in general, as compared with the language that I have suggested as typical of the legal philosopher. Not only do lawyers "deduce" legal claims from legal norms, but they also conceive of their deductions as the only possible ones. Claims are legal for lawyers if they are "derivable" from a legal norm, and illegal if they are not. In turn, norms are legal or illegal according to their being or not being accepted by said lawyers and legal operators in general, in order to reach their own practical ends. *Tertium non datum.* The picture of the norms and, respectively, of the claims by legal operators, is always, so to say, black and white. Besides, no time dimension is implied in the picture; the legal operators care for the legal norm of today and *not* for that of yesterday or tomorrow. Finally, they only care for the legal norm they have accepted, as such, in view of their own practical ends, and ignore all others. They have an exclusive view of the legal society. In fact, they only care for *their own* legal society. They may refer as well to other societies, but only insofar as the latter are acceptable or rejectable to them, on the basis of the only norms they have accepted. What legal operators actually need is to make some claims, and their frame of mind as well as their language is adapted to this end. On the contrary, the legal operator doesn't want to make or to support any claim of his own, but just to use existing claims in order to reconstruct their basic connections with each other, and with the legal norms in any given society at any given time.

The legal philosopher not only moves from the concept of claims, but also realizes that claims may be conflicting. Even more, he realizes that claims may be conflicting while all are considered "legal" by different people at the same time. The legal philosopher's picture of the law is, therefore, never black and white, because he has to take into account in his picture a whole sector of claims that the lawyers do not care about. He knows that it is exactly in that sector that things happen which may change the whole picture of the legal operator at any given time. The legal philosopher knows also that there is not one legal society, namely, that accepted by each legal operator, for practical reasons, but also other "legal" societies that may be conflicting with the former, and that other people have accepted in their turn for their own practical reasons. The resulting picture, as given by the legal philosopher, is nuanced and multilateral and unfolding through time, like those Japanese paintings that you can inspect only by unrolling the long roll of paper in which they are contained. In the philosopher's view, the legal norm has not only a different place than in the picture of the legal operator, but it has a different *meaning*. A legal norm is a rule in a statistical sense, while a legal norm in the view of the legal operator is just the description of the claims that he considers as legal, regardless of all other possibly contradictory claims.

The difference between the two points of view is not always so easy to discern. Both the legal operator and the legal philosopher consider in the end as legal claims whose satisfaction they consider as probable. While the legal operator is engaged in the process of influencing that probable event, the legal philosopher is not; he waits to see. Both the legal philosopher and the legal operator consider the legal norm as a sentence expressing claims. While the legal operator invokes the sentence to support his own claims, the legal philosopher studies said sentences as a reflection of claims that are not necessarily his own. As a result, the legal operator does not put in doubt the validity of the sentence just because he doesn't put in doubt the validity of his (corresponding) claims. The legal philosopher is always ready to scrutinize the sentence in order to find out whether it describes accurately "legal" claims in the statistical sense.

From these two different points of view descend two different views of legal norms and of their significance in the whole legal process. The legal operator intends that fixing legal norms, say, by legislation, is the origin of the whole legal process. The legal philosopher, on the other hand, has to consider it as only one of the factors of said process, and not even the decisive one. As a matter of fact, legislation does not necessarily describe the statistically legal claims, although, of course, it may influence the probabilities of their being satisfied at any given time, and in any given society. Indeed, only a few people (the representatives of the people) participate directly in the process of making legislation, and what they do is just describe the claims they make or support, without having them necessarily coincide with claims actually, or going actually to be, satisfied, as a rule, in that society. It is typical that there has been a strong tendency in all times (and this applies especially to our contemporary age) to overrate, if not the accuracy of the description of statistically "legal" claims on the part of legislators, at least the power of the latter to influence the probabilities of the already existing legal claims through legislation.

I would suggest that this tendency is the practical counterpart of the theoretical assumption which puts the "norms" at the beginning of the whole legal process and considers claims only as a logical *consequence* of normative "prescriptions." I suggest that the task of the legal philosopher, besides that of reconstructing the real connections between statistically legal claims and legal norms, is that of reminding all legal operators that fixing legal norms has a limited scope in any legal process.

We may consider legislation as a more or less successful attempt to describe the statistically legal claims, besides "prescribing" them. What legislators describe may be: a) what they think the actual statistically legal norms to be in their own society, or b) what they think the actual statistically legal norms *will* be in that society as a result of their legislation and of the employment of the means they think they have at their disposal (namely, psychological or physical coercion) to produce that result. But once again we must go back at this point to what I noticed before, relating to coercion and its significance in the legal process as a whole. Legislation, in describing a situation that the legislators want in the future, is confronted with the difficulties arising from the marginal significance of coercion in the legal process. Of course, legislation may also describe simply what the present legal situation is, without tending to change it, or even with the very purpose of maintaining it. Legal codes such as those enacted in the last century in Europe are an example in point. Acts and statutes as they are enacted in this century all over the world are mostly an example of legislation that tends to change the already existing situation. In all cases, legislation is both the presentation of claims supported by the legislators themselves and a description of claims that are to be considered as statistically legal in their own society by said legislators. The degree in which each of these two aspects is present in any legislation may vary considerably.

Similar remarks apply to other ways of fixing legal norms besides legislation, such as those performed by judges. The decisions of a judge or the responses of a juris-consult (as in Roman times) are always both presentations of claims that are considered as statistically legal on the one hand, and presentations of claims that are also supported personally, on the other hand, to a certain degree, by their authors. Lawyers and judges, however, are even more conditioned than legislators in their attempt to support their own claims, while describing, at the same time, the statistically legal claims in their own societies at a given time. While the work of the legislator is intended to be, at least by definition, unconditioned, the work of a judge or a juris-consult is by its very definition conditioned by precedents, statutes, and the very claims of the parties concerned. Even more than in the legislator's case, judges and juris-consults are confronted with the marginal significance of coercion and other means to influence the probabilities of existing claims being satisfied by the people concerned.

The legal process always traces back in the end to individual claim. Individuals make the law, insofar as they make successful claims. They not only make previsions and predictions, but try to have these predictions succeed by their own intervention in the process. Judges, juris-consults, and, above all, legislators are just individuals who find themselves in a particular position to influence the whole process through their own intervention. As I have stated, the possibilities of this intervention are limited and should not be overrated. May I add that we should not overrate, on the other hand, the *distortions* that the intervention of those particular individuals and, above all, of the legislators, may provoke in the whole process.

Legal norms, whatever be their origin, decisions of judges, responses of juris-consults, or statutes, almost always influence that process to a point. Even when they simply describe the already existing situation of the legal claims, they tend, at least, to perpetuate that situation by presenting to people a clear-cut picture of what is going on in the already existing legal process. On the other hand, when legal norms describe a future situation that their authors wish to attain by influencing the existing legal process, they may well succeed in preventing people from succeeding in their own claims, even if the authors don't succeed in imposing the satisfaction of other (contrary) claims. To be sure, there is a negative result of legal norms that is more effective than any positive one, since it is easier to prevent people from doing something they want than to force them actually to do something they do not want. Individuals who are in a special position in the legal process may take advantage of it, but not so much as they want or possibly think. Unless I am wrong, this is a teaching that has been more or less obscurely imparted to us by old natural law doctrines; that is, by the doctrine of the rights of man. This teaching should serve those doctrines, although it lacks, or just because it lacks, practical emphasis. It is not so much a claim by a legal operator as a theoretical conclusion of the legal philosopher.

2

LAW AND
ECONOMY IN
THE MAKING

Geneneral studies on the nature of economic science are rather
rare. The same can be said, by and large, of general studies of
legal science. This is probably a good reason why we lack studies
worth mentioning comparing the nature of the law-making process with the nature of the economic process and, specifically,
with the nature of the market process. But this is certainly not the
only reason for that shortage. In our era of specialization, few
economists are also lawyers, and few lawyers are also economists.
We do have a few outstanding examples of economists who are
trained in law, for example, Professor Mises and Professor Hayek.
Some economic or legal advisers of great industries or federations
of industries are lawyers trained in economics. (I could mention,
in this respect, my good friend Arthur Shenfield, who is both a
lawyer and an economist and serves presently as the Chief Economic Adviser for the Federation of British Industries.) People
who are both willing and able to delve into the comparative study
of both processes are extremely rare. I do not pretend to be one
of those persons. Still, being a lawyer by profession, and also being keenly interested in the theory and practice of economics, I
have always considered it very important for lawyers and economists to have a clear idea of what these processes are, of what
their main aspects are as compared with each other, and, finally,
of what the theoretical and practical relationships are between
these two processes.

The importance of an inquiry of this kind is not merely theoretical. Whether politicians feel entitled or not to adopt some policies in view of some ends they try to reach in the economic field depends to a large extent on the ideas they have concerning the respective aspects of each process, and of their reciprocal relationships. Whether the man in the street demands or approves or simply tolerates those policies depends to a great extent on those ideas.

I do not think that politicians and the man in the street are necessarily conditioned by their own political ideologies in their ideas about the relationships between the law-making process and the economic process. On the contrary, I suspect that, in many cases, their own political ideologies may be conditioned by their own more or less clear ideas about the nature and relationships of the law-making process and, respectively, of the economic process.

I shall start from an attempt to describe the main kinds of law-making processes as we know them, at least in the history of the West. We shall see later that all of these kinds of processes may be traced back to a more general, though less apparent way, of producing law, of which I shall speak in the end.

I wish to summarize my argument by saying that *there are three main ways or methods of making law*, which emerge with independent features, though not each independently and to the exclusion of others, all through the history of the West, from the ancient Greeks to the present day. They are: 1) the production of the law through the opinions of a special class of experts called *juris-consults* in Rome, *Turisten* in Germany in the Middle Ages, and *lawyers* in Anglo-Saxon countries. These people produced a kind of law that is called from its origin "lawyers'-law," or as the Germans say, *turistenrecht*. 2) The production of law on the part of another special class of experts called judges. The English expression "judge-made-law" implies exactly what I have in mind concerning this kind of law. 3) The production of the law through the *legislative process*. This is a process that has become so frequent in present days that in many countries the man in the street cannot even imagine another kind of production of what we call the law. Legislation is conceived as the product of the will of some people called legislators, the underlying idea being that what the legislators will is ultimately to be considered as the law of the country.

Legislation differs profoundly from the two preceding ways of "producing law." Lawyers and judges produce law by working on some materials that are considered to be given to them in order to condition their own production. To adopt a happy metaphor of a great contemporary scholar, Sir Carleton Kemp Allen, they "make" law in the same sense that a man who chops a tree into logs has "made" the logs.[1] On the contrary, the ambition of the legislators is to make the law without being conditioned that way. They not only "produce" law, but they also want to produce it by a kind of fiat, regardless of materials and even of contrary wills and opinions of other people. What they mean is not sheer production but, as one of the most famous contemporary theorists and defenders of this process would say, *creation* of the law.[2] The peculiar nature of these features of legislation has been realized for centuries and expressed by the scholars through the contrast between words like *jus* and *lex*, *law* and *will*, *law* and *king*, *law* and *sovereign*, etc. This contrast has been frequently tinged through the ages with metaphysical or religious meanings and implications.

Nonetheless, the contrast is also quite understandable on simply human and worldly terms. If one assumes that the law is a *creation* of a legislator, one must also assume, at least implicitly, that the law is the result of the unconditioned will of some people like kings or sovereigns or so on. Therefore, legislation is traced back, more or less implicitly, to the unconditioned will of a sovereign, whoever he may be. The very idea of legislation encourages the hopes of all those who imagine that legislation, as a result of the unconditioned will of some people, will be able to reach ends that could never be reached by ordinary procedures adopted by ordinary men; that is, by judges and lawyers. The usual phrase by the man in the street today, "There ought to be a

---

[1] Carleton Kemp Allen, *Law in the Making* (5th ed.; Oxford: at the Clarendon Press, 1951), p. 288.

[2] We shall see later precisely what this "creation of the law" means, at least in practice, and what are the limits and the misconceptions related to this idea. It may be said that the law-making process through legislation presents very peculiar features that do not exist or that exist in a much lesser degree in the two other processes of making law.

law" for this or for that, is the naive expression of that faith in legislation. While the processes conducive to lawyers'-law and judge-made-law appear as conditioned ways of producing law, the legislative process appears, or tends to appear, to be *unconditioned* and a pure matter of will.

The very idea that there could be an unconditioned way of producing law has been denied in all times by many eminent scholars. For instance, in Roman times one of the most eminent Roman statesmen, Cato the Censor, the champion of the traditional way of life against the foreign (that is, Greek), used to boast that the superiority of the Roman legal system as compared with the Greek system was due to the fact that the Roman system had been produced piece by piece through a long series of centuries and generations by a great number of people, each of whom had to base his work on experience and on precedents and was always conditioned by the existing situation. Later on, in the Middle Ages, and using a completely different language, owing to his different philosophical and religious background, the celebrated English lawyer Bracton used to say that the King himself was subject to the law, for the law makes the King. "Let the King then attribute to the law what the law attributes to him, namely, domination and power, for there is no King where the will and not the law has dominion." If we translate Bracton's language into more modern words, it boils down to this: Not even the King with all his power can create law; he can only enforce it. There is no unconditioned way of making law at will, not even if we have a great power over other people.

In the eighteenth century another lawyer said the same thing in other words. I am referring to Blackstone, who used to say that the sovereign is not the *fountain* but simply the *reservoir* of the law, from which, through a thousand channels, justice and law are derived for the individual.

The same criticism of the purported possibility of creating the law from nothing on the part of a legislator has been shared by the most famous lawyers in the West. For instance, the greatest German lawyer of the nineteenth century, Savigny, the so-called founder of the Historical School in law, wrote at the beginning of that century that what binds the rules of our behavior (including legal behavior) into one whole "is the common conviction of the people, the kindred consciousness of an inward necessity, excluding all notion of an accidental and arbitrary origin." And another great lawyer, Eugen Ehrlich, whose influence in the United States has become more and more important in recent times through lawyers such as Pound, Timasheff, Cairns, and Julius Stone, stated flatly in our century that, "At the present as well as at any other time, the centre of gravity of legal development lies not in legislation . . . but in society itself." To these critics of the idea of the legislative process as an unconditioned way of producing the law at will, we should add many of the economists, both of the classical and of the neoclassical school. (We shall go back later to legislation and to the idea that underlies all the attempts to substitute legislation for any other kind of law-making process.)

Let us now examine the other two ways of producing law mentioned above. The first one is the way adopted by the lawyers. Probably excepting only ancient Greece, all countries in the West had lawyers as a special class of experts after a certain point in the development of their civilizations. The country in which lawyers seem to have had their highest *status*, however, is ancient Rome. The ancient Roman lawyers "produced" the law through the centuries in a professional, openly recognized, and almost official way. It is true that they themselves were not in general eager to recognize this fact. While working out legal rules they frequently used to refer to old legendary statutes like that of the Twelve Tablets; however, they actually worked out those rules and their fellow citizens accepted them quite willingly, while their government usually did not interfere in that process. Of course, the Romans enacted many statutes during their history, but those statutes related mainly to the functioning of their own government, and extremely rarely to private relationships between individuals. We have records of only about 50 statutes enacted by the Roman legislative powers relating to private relationships among citizens throughout their history—embracing more than 1000 years.

An almost similar status was enjoyed by Italian, French, and German lawyers, both in the Middle Ages and in modern times until the beginning of the last century and, as far as German countries are concerned, until the end of it. The peculiar way of producing law by these lawyers was rather different from the old Roman way. But still they "produced" law of their own in a way that was openly and even officially recognized although submitted to several strictures from time to time until the introduction of the codes on the European continent towards the end of the eighteenth century and at the beginning of the nineteenth. I have already tried to define briefly the nature of the process adopted by Roman lawyers in *Freedom and the Law*. In that attempt, I took advantage of the fascinating studies of some contemporary scholars like the Italians Rotendi and Vincenzo Arangio Ruiz, the Englishman Buckland, and the German Schulz. In this respect I stated:

> The Roman jurist was a sort of scientist: the objects of his research were the solutions to cases that citizens submitted to him for study, just as industrialists might today submit to a physicist or an engineer a technical problem concerning their plants or their production. Hence, private Roman law was something to be described or to be discovered, not something to be enacted—a world of things that were there, forming part of the common heritage of all Roman citizens. Nobody enacted that law; nobody could change it by any exercise of his personal will. This did not mean absence of change, but it certainly meant that nobody went to bed at night making his plans on the basis of a present rule only to get up the next morning and find that the rule had been overturned by a legislative innovation.
>
> The Romans accepted and applied a concept of the certainty of the law that could be described as meaning that the law was never to be subjected to sudden and unpredictable changes. Moreover, the law was never to be submitted, as a rule, to the arbitrary will or to the arbitrary power of any legislative assembly or of any one person, including senators or other prominent magistrates of the state. This is the long-run concept, or, if you prefer, the Roman concept, of the certainty of the law.[3]

I have already pointed out that this concept of law was certainly essential to the freedom that Roman citizens usually enjoyed in business and in all private life. It is very important to note in this connection that the process of making law adopted by Roman lawyers resulted in putting juridical relations among

---

[3] This volume, pp. 83–84.

citizens on a plane very similar to that on which a free market put their economic relations. Law as a whole was no less free from constraint than the market itself. Or to adopt the words of Professor Schulz, the private law in Rome was developed "on a basis of Freedom and Individualism."[4]

I shall take this opportunity to answer one of the reviews devoted to *Freedom and the Law*[5] in which I was accused of being too enthusiastic about the Roman system. I feel I was not. I never said that Roman law provided a "paradise of liberty" and even less that Roman law provided that "paradise" under the rule of the Emperors. Still, I think that there is much to say in favor of the legal system of the Romans, even under the rule of the Emperors, when we compare that system with many others prevailing today. It is true that those Roman rulers who were omnipotent sometimes disposed of the life and property of some citizens at will. But this was always done and considered as an exception and also as an undue exception to the general rule, according to which life and property of the citizens could not be disposed of by the state. Compare that general rule with those prevailing in almost all contemporary states, in which confiscatory practices or other limitations to the free choice of the individuals in the market relate actually, or at least in principle, to all citizens. The comparison between the present legal systems and the old Roman is very flattering for the latter.

A Roman tyrant in the times of the old Republic, like Sulla, could take vengeance against his enemies by trying to put them to death or by confiscating their property. A Roman Emperor in later times could send a murderer to kill some dangerous rival or pretender and issue a decree to confiscate his property. But contemporary rules, even in free countries like this one, have the power in principle, only provided that they abide by some legal formalities, to deprive all citizens of practically all of their property if not their lives.

If we consider the Roman taxation system as compared with

[4] Fritz Schultz, *History of Roman Legal Science* (Oxford: at the Clarendon Press, 1946), p. 84.
[5] Murray N. Rothbard, "On Freedom and the Law," in *New Individualist Review*, Vol. 1, No. 4, Winter 1962, pp. 37–40. Complete edition of *New Individualist Review* reprinted by Liberty Fund, Indianapolis, 1981. Pages 163–166.

many contemporary ones we arrive at similar conclusions. The above-mentioned review of my book has mentioned the purported "crushing taxation" operated by the Romans. We do not know well, unfortunately, the real way in which the fiscal system was operated by the Romans, as there are still several unknown points about it. But it is certain that Roman citizens were not submitted in principle to any real taxation, at least in the classic period. All that their government did was to resort to compulsory borrowing when it was necessary to wage a war. When the war was won, which frequently happened, the money borrowed by the government was given back to the citizens. In their turn, the conquered countries were usually submitted to a taxation (the so-called *vectigal*) that was conceived as a kind of ransom to be paid to the Roman conquerers for the use of the land on the part of the conquered people. But even this taxation never went, as a rule, over 10 percent of the income of the people who had to pay it. If we consider that the taxing power of our contemporary governments, even in free countries such as this one, is practically unlimited and can absorb the quasi-totality of the income of some taxpayers belonging to the so-called high brackets, the comparison with the Roman taxing system is likely to leave us breathless because of its generosity. Contemporary governments in the so-called free countries behave towards their citizens in a way that no Roman government would have behaved, at least as far as fiscal policy is concerned, not only towards its own citizens, but also towards the citizens of conquered countries.

To complete this comparison before reverting to our main argument, I must finally refer to the so-called repressive network of controls and welfare measures purportedly adopted by the Romans, according to my reviewer. Even here, we should sharply distinguish between the classical Roman period and the post-classical period of what we call the decay of the Roman Empire. Controls and welfare measures were practically unknown during the former period. They were occasionally introduced in the later period by some Emperors and reached their peak at the time of Diocletian in the fourth century after Christ, that is, towards the end of the history of the Roman Western Empire. But even if we were to compare the welfare state and planning introduced by Diocletian with the welfare state, nationalization, and planning introduced by our contemporary governments, the comparison would result in favor of the Romans. As a rule, privately owned land was never confiscated in Rome, and the government never imposed itself in the operation of private enterprises. We can make similar considerations about inflation and currency debasement. All that the Roman government could do in this respect was relatively little as compared to the unlimited power of contemporary governments to promote inflation through legal tender laws and similar practices.

But let's go back to our main argument, that is, the "production" of law by lawyers. We shall now try to investigate a little more closely how and from where the Roman lawyers derived their legal rules. Recent studies allow us to conclude that they were probably never clear about their own way of working. However, we can conclude that the ultimate data with which they worked were always the feelings and behavior of their citizens. This was revealed by their habits and customs in making agreements with each other, and in their expectations of other persons' behavior on the basis of those agreements, or even without any explicit agreements. The Roman lawyers included these data within the concept of the "nature of things" and within the other no less important concept of "what most frequently happens." Their own attitude towards those *data* was that of trying to interpret them in order to let their implicit rules emerge. Of course, it wasn't an easy task in many cases, especially when old habits and customs were obviously tapering off, and new and comparatively unprecedented ones were developing.

The task of the lawyers was that of working out a rule that could be considered, as far as possible, as an extension or as an analogue of an already revealed rule, or at least a new rule corresponding to the preceding ones and fitting in with them in a consistent manner. That kind of interpretation of the data, according to those lawyers, was not only possible but also susceptible to a more or less rigorous procedure. In fact, it was always possible, according to them, to make a kind of calculus in order to find out the reasons for the behavior of people in their mutual relationships, and in order to discover their implicit logic. This was what Roman lawyers called, in fact, the *ratio* of these relationships and of their implicit rules. This ratio they used to call *natural*, as it didn't depend on the arbitrary will of anybody concerned, and least of all on the arbitrary will of the lawyers who tried to discover it. It was only when a Roman lawyer was almost completely at a loss, if not in working out a legal rule, at least in giving the reasons for his conclusions on it, that he invoked the authority of another lawyer who had preceded him, and who had come to similar results in similar respects.

Sometimes, in a rather paradoxical way, he resorted to invoking his own authority, although this was rather rare. What is worth noting, relating to this Roman concept of authority, is that resorting to it did not imply, on the part of the lawyers, any mystical implications. Roman lawyers certainly did not refer to any kind of divine revelation for the correct solution of a legal question. What they very probably implied was a kind of hypothesis that their own solution was right, even if they could not prove it for the time being. Even in the history of mathematics you can notice a similar attitude on the part of some great representatives of mathematical thought. There are theorems, like that of Fermat, of which we do not know whether the alleged demonstration actually existed, or whether any demonstration can be discovered in the future. In a similar way, concepts of fundamental importance in modern mathematics, like that of *function*, contrived by the Italian Lagrange, or that of *infinitesimal calculus*, contrived by the German Leibnitz, or the Englishman Newton, were employed at first as provisional results of reasonings that could not be completely justified, because the demonstrations concerned were still to be made.

In other words, what Roman lawyers thought about their own work was that they could always, or almost always, reconstruct completely both the logic of the behavior of their own citizens and the logic of the relationships in that behavior. In a similar way, modern economists who study the so-called economic action of man imply the possibility of reconstructing both the rationale of these actions and that of their relationships with other actions of other operators.

Let's now examine briefly what the work and the attitude of lawyers was in less ancient times. Lawyers on the Continent in the Middle Ages tried to work out legal rules as had their Roman predecessors. Both they and their contemporaries considered

that work as preferable in a logical way, on the basis of a fundamental logic implicit in the data of that work.

There was, however, a main difference between the work of
the latter lawyers and that of the former. Lawyers in the Middle
Ages and in modern times on the Continent, before the introduction of codes, worked out their legal rules by deriving them
from a different kind of data. Instead of considering directly as
their data the behavior of the people, they studied behavior in
an indirect way by looking at them through the screen of a set
of rules already worked out before them by the Romans themselves, and continued in that great legal Bible of the Western
people on the Continent, which was the so-called *Corpus Juris*,
enacted by Emperor Justinian in the first half of the sixth century. Thus, the lawyers in that new era were not interpreting
the behavior of their fellow citizens. Instead they were applying
the words used by the Roman lawyers to interpret the behavior
of their own citizens, and to work out legal rules for them. This
was indeed, on the part of the new lawyers, a rather paradoxical and anachronistic way of working out legal rules for their
contemporaries, but it worked; and this seems to prove that the
rationale of human behavior in what is usually called the legal
field is not so contingent and accidental as to be humanly
bound to a certain historical period or to a certain country of
the world.

It isn't my task here to try to explain the reasons for that
paradoxical procedure on the part of the lawyers of the Middle
Ages and of more modern times in the European countries. I
only want to point out once again that what those lawyers did was
not exactly what they pretended to do. What they actually did
was much more interpreting of the behavior of their contemporaries and its rationale than of the words of their Roman predecessors and their meaning. We have stated, on the other hand,
that their Roman predecessors had, in their turn, pretended to
do something different than they were doing; that is, interpreting words instead of facts—the clauses of a purported written
law (that of the Twelve Tablets) instead of the actual behavior of
living people.

Fundamentally, medieval and modern lawyers on the one
hand, and Roman lawyers on the other hand, have all done the

same thing. They interpret their own fellow citizens' behavior and reconstruct its own rationale and its implicit rules.

Let's now have a look at the category of the law producers I mentioned in the beginning: the judges. The law-making process through judges is probably as old as our Western civilization. When Homer wants to illustrate in the *Odyssey* the barbarous condition of the Cyclops, he says that they even lacked two things: assemblies to make collective decisions on the one hand, and judicial decisions on the other. The Cyclops, as Homer adds, simply lived at home with their families, without having any kind of political or legal system, as we would say now.

Judicial decisions have probably been, in fact, the main way of finding out and rendering explicit many legal rules prevailing in ancient Rome before the era of legislation. Once again, judicial decisions were a usual way of finding out legal rules in ancient Rome through the so-called *Jus honorarium*; that is, through the decisions of the main judicial authority of the Romans, the Praetor. This process of finding out the law through the lawyers and that of finding out the law through the judges co-existed successfully for several centuries in Rome. They were not incompatible; they were even complimentary whenever new legal rules were adopted or required by the citizens. The Praetor pretended not to enter the core of the questions possibly raised by the new rules as far as consistency with the old ones was concerned. He simply pretended to pronounce himself on procedural technicalities, while taking care to reach in this way the goal of accepting and enforcing the new rules. This was a kind of trick, indeed, to which the Praetor was probably induced by his respect both for old customs and for the professional work of the lawyers. Just as the Roman judges had produced law by pretending to deal only with procedural technicalities, the Roman lawyers had produced law in a disguised way by pretending to interpret old words instead of new facts. Greek judges had produced laws more openly, as did English judges in medieval and modern times, although we know that at least the English judges were fond of several kinds of tricks throughout their history. But once again, what judges had in mind in Greece, as in Rome and in England, was the behavior of their own citizens, their rationale, and the rationale of their relationships. They all could and actually did resort to concepts similar to those of the Roman lawyers, like the "nature of things" whose general meaning was that the problems confronting them did not allow solutions to be contrived at their own will, or in an unconditioned way. The Greek judges and orators meant this when they said they were simply following the advice of the Goddess Themis, or that of the Oracle of Delphus. This was implied by the Roman Praetor who pretended to deal only with procedural technicalities, and not with the substance of the law itself. This was meant by English judges who used to speak of the law of the land as something superior to their own arbitrary choice.

We have pointed out thus far a basic similarity between both ways of producing law: that of the lawyers and that of the judges. Let's examine a little more profoundly what the relationships are between the *data* of their work and their work itself. These relationships are not easy to scrutinize, and it is not surprising that the opinions of the scholars about them diverge widely in some respects. Two main conceptions of these relationships have been stated and championed by the theorists.

According to one of these concepts, mainly represented by the above-mentioned Savigny, the interpreters of the law perform a mostly passive and receptive task: They reflect the habits and customs of the people by describing them in their own language, just as a physicist would describe in his own language the relationships between physical forces. According to this theory, there would not be any special reaction on the habits and customs of the people themselves as a result of the work of the professional interpreters. In other words, the latter would not influence, in their turn, customs and habits by their own work. They would just be conduit pipes for a liquid that they did not change. Of course conduit pipes, to be efficient, must be made of good material and built in a proper way. Similarly, the professional interpreters of the law would be learned, clever, and trained, but according to this theory they produce law mainly in the sense that they scrutinize it.

The contrary theory is that customs and habits would just derive from the work of the lawyers and judges. Some scholars like Maine in his famous book, *Ancient Law*, have maintained, for instance, that this happened with the ancient Greeks, whose customs would have been created by the decisions of the judges. Another scholar, the Frenchman Lambert, has insisted on the so-called creative force of jurisprudence, i.e., of judicial decisions, which would be an essential element and one of the most productive agencies in law. An intermediate theory, worked out by Erlich, maintains that we should distinguish clearly between legal rules applied by the courts on the one hand, and legal arrangements existing in society on the other.

Accordingly, the function of the interpreter should be considered as two-fold: On the one hand he should discover the existing legal convictions of the community in order to describe them, and on the other hand he should frame uniform generalizations reflecting those convictions in order to apply them to all cases. This latter operation implies technical aspects that should be considered as different from convictions and consciousness of the people. Just for this latter operation, we should distinguish between lawyers'-law and people's-law, and we should recognize that, although lawyers'-law comes out of the people's-law, it may react on the latter. But all theories, regardless of their emphasis on customs and habits on the one hand and techniques and generalizations of the lawyers on the other hand, recognize in general that there wouldn't be any lawyers'-law or any judge-made-law without the common ground of the people's customs, habits, and convictions. Even Lambert, who was one of the most convinced supporters of the theory that lawyers'-law reacts powerfully on people's habits and customs, admitted that lawyers'-law is, after all, a kind of crystallization in rules of what the Romans and the Canonists of the Roman Catholic Church would have called the common consent of the people concerned (*communis consensus utentium*). Both of these opposite theories can resort to several historical instances to support their own conclusions. If it is not true that custom is something resulting from a long series of judgments in ancient Greece, as Maine maintained, it is true that judgments very probably influenced the custom in the historical period of the Greek civilization before the appearance of the written law. If it is not true that people living in countries based on customary and judge-made-law, as in England, are not simply adapting their own conduct to decisions of the judges by obligatory resignation, as Lambert maintained, it is true that the history of common law in England reveals the decisive influence exercised on it by the outstanding personalities of some lawyers and judges, and even by Acts of Parliament not now to be found on record.

History is never simple and never adapts itself entirely to consistent theories of it. But there is one good reason why we should, I think, take into very serious consideration Savigny's opinion that it is not the lawyers who make the law of the people, but the people who make the lawyers. As a distinguished contemporary scholar remarked in this connection, whatever the importance and the influence of the interpreters may be, not only is there a native law of the community, but the greatest conceivable interpreter can work only with material "which its environment vouchsafes to it, and can express itself only in language and only about things, which are intelligible to contemporary minds." We should also remember in this respect one of the most fascinating comparisons made by Savigny in his famous essay on the vocation of our time for legislation and jurisprudence: the comparison between law and language. Law, he said, like language, is a spontaneous expression of the minds of the people concerned. Grammarians, we should add, may have a great influence on the language, and the rules they work out may well react on the linguistic usage of their country, but grammarians cannot create a language—they are simply given it. People who create languages are usually unsuccessful. Ready-made languages do not work, regardless of their purported utility as simple and possibly universal ways of communication between different people. Only half-learned people can trust the attempts made to introduce Esperanto or similar languages as ready-made universal means of communication. What these purported languages lack is people behind them. In the same way, one could not create a universal or even a particular law if no people were behind it, with their convictions, habits, and feelings. Law, like language, is not a gadget that a man can contrive at will. Of course one can try. But according to the whole experience we have, he can only succeed within very narrow limits or he doesn't succeed at all.

3

THE ECONOMIC
APPROACH TO
THE POLITICAL

I have already stated at the beginning of these lectures that we still lack studies worth mentioning on the nature of the law-making process as compared with the nature of the market process. This statement, however, needs qualification. During recent years, some studies have appeared with the intent of comparing market choice on the one hand and political choice through voting on the other. The law itself may be conceived as an object of choice, i.e., of political choice. To the extent that we identify law with legislation, we can take advantage of the recent studies of political choice as compared with market choice in order to draw a comparison between the market and the law conceived as legislation.

The usual perspective of decision-making or choice-making theories is an individualistic one. It is usually admitted, at least implicitly, that every decision must be someone's decision. But the theorists are also aware of the fact that the decisions of individuals are not only *competitive* (as when individuals are out for themselves) but also *cooperative* (as when individuals try to reach a single decision for a whole group). Some authors call these cooperative decisions "group decisions" and try to work out special systems in order to enable different individuals (by applying independently the standard procedures of the system to a given set of data) to come out with essentially the same inferences and possibly with essentially the same decisions. The same authors recognize, however, that the value of their system is still un-proved, at least for group decisions outside the scientific world. This is a pity (as one of them says) because very few and only questionable mechanisms for other group decisions have so far been invented, for instance, voting procedures (such as majority rule) and *verbal bargaining*. In fact it is admitted that the ballot box "works (only) when decisions are relatively non-technical, and when the group loyalty is strong enough so that minority voters are willing to stay with the group and accept the majority decision."[1] On the other hand, verbal bargaining, which may of course operate in conjunction with voting procedures, is subject to serious limitations.

However, I think that group decision, as the cooperative deci-sion of a number of individuals in accordance with some pro-cedure, is both a useful and an understandable idea for the political scientist—not that we should equate group decision and *political* decision. We probably cannot exclude some individual agents, whose decisions Max Weber would call "monocratic." Nor can we say that all group decisions are political. Boards of directors in trade corporations make group decisions that we should not call political in the ordinary sense. Thus we should be cautious about agreeing with Professor Duncan Black when he thinks of his theory of committee decisions as a political *tout court*.[2]

But it is clear that a great many decisions which are usually called "political," such as decisions of constituencies, of adminis-trative or executive agencies, of legislatures, etc., are really group decisions, or cooperative decisions in the sense indicated by Bross of *single decisions reached by several individuals for a whole group*.

We must note at this point that the individualistic perspective seems to be altered somewhat when we speak of group decisions. The decision of a "whole group" may or may not be the same decision that each individual in the group would make if he were in a position to decide for the whole group. I wonder whether this would be so in the scientific world mentioned by Bross. But

[1] Irwin D. J. Bross, *Design for Decision* (New York: Macmillan, 1953), p. 263.
[2] Duncan Black, "The Unity of Political and Economic Science," *Economic Journal*, Vol. 60, No. 239, September 1950.

it is the case wherever there is no unanimity among the decisions of the several members of a group, and such lack of unanimity in groups is the rule rather than the exception. Group decisions are not usually identical with each single individual decision inside the group.

This fact goes some way toward explaining the appeal of those semi-mystical or semi-philosophical constructions in which the collectivities, such as the state, are conceived as independent entities making decisions as if they were individuals.[3] But there is no need, I think, to cling to any such notion of an "unmeetable person" with whom "one can never converse" (as the late Miss MacDonald would have said) in order to analyze the consequences of lack of unanimity in groups.[4]

But when political decisions are group decisions, then we must take such lack of unanimity into account. And the usual procedure for doing this is voting according to majority principle. A great many political decisions are in fact made this way. They are thus different from individual choices in the market, where voting procedures are not needed in order to buy commodities. Nonetheless, the fact that voting also involves individual choice has led some scholars to compare individual choice in political voting and in the market. It has been said, indeed, that "a substantial part of the analysis will be intuitively familiar to all social scientists, since it serves as a basis for a large part of political theory on the one hand and economic theory on the other hand."[5]

All the features of the process of choosing seem to be present both in the group and in individual decisions—orderings of values, assessments of probabilities, calculations of expectations,

---

[3] One of the recent attempts to revive this kind of assumption, it seems to me, is the idea that a "social welfare function" or a "rational social choice" can be obtained by means of mathematical tricks such as those analyzed in Kenneth Arrow's famous essay *Social Choice and Individual Values* (New York: John Wiley and Sons, Inc., 1951). In such a view, computing machines become the modern substitute for the *Volksgeist* or the *Verhunft*.

[4] Margaret MacDonald, "The Language of Political Theory," *Logic and Language (First Series)*, ed. Antony Flew (Oxford: Basil Blackwell, 1955), pp. 167–186.

[5] James M. Buchanan, "Individual Choices in Voting and the Market," *Journal of Political Economy*, LXII, 1954, p. 334. The essay is reprinted in *Fiscal Theory and Political Economy: Selected Essays* (Chapel Hill: University of North Carolina Press, 1960).

choices of strategies, etc. Voting is held to resemble market choice, and the market itself is thought of (not very consistently) as a big decision group where everyone votes by buying or selling commodities, services, etc. On these analogies Duncan Black has been led to consider his theory of committees a "general theory of economic and political choice." Conceived as theories of committee decisions, both sciences "really form two branches of the same subject." "Each relates to choosing of some kind," makes "use of the same language, the same mode of abstraction, the same instruments of thought, and the same methods of reasoning." In other words, in both sciences the individual is represented by his scale of preferences, and both properly leave technological facts outside. Although there is a difference in the degree of knowledge of the outcome of the various lines of action that might be chosen, this knowledge often being greater in economics than in politics, there would be no difference in principle "between the economic and political estimates which people can make."

Moreover, (according to Black) the same instrument is common to both sciences—*the concept of equilibrium.*[6]

According to Black, in economics "although the conception has been differently treated by different authors" the underlying idea has always been that equilibrium results from equality of supply and demand. "In political science, the motions before a committee stand in some definite order on the scales of preferences of the members. Equilibrium will be reached through one motion being selected as the decision of the committee by means of voting. The impelling force towards having one particular motion selected will be the degree to which the members' schedules, taken as a group, rank it higher than the others. . . . " Black recognizes that there are obstacles in the way of this process and

[6] Here Black seems to echo an idea implied by Pigou in two articles published, if I remember correctly, in the *Economic Journal* in 1901 and 1906, where Pigou pointed to an analogy between supply and demand in the market in relation to goods, and supply and demand in the political field in relation to laws and orders. One is also reminded of the ideas in Arthur F. Bentley's *The Process of Government* (Bloomington: The Principia Press, 1935 [first published in 1908]) and of the American theorists whose ideas have been rather severely examined in David Easton's *The Political System: An Inquiry into the State of Political Science* (New York: Alfred Knopf, 1953).

that one of them is the particular form of committee procedure in use because it can be shown that with a given group of schedules, "one procedure will select one motion, while another procedure will select another." This fact does not prevent Black from concluding that although each science uses a different definition of equilibrium, "the underlying conceptions are the same in kind." If the definition of equilibrium relates to equality of demand and supply, the phenomena will be economic in nature; if it relates to equilibrium being attained by means of voting, they will be political, and in both sciences the most general type of theory of equilibrium "would be formulated in terms of mathematics." The pure theory would enable us to work out the effects of any given change in political circumstances. The initial state of equilibrium, before the change was introduced, would be examined; and when the data had altered so as to incorporate the given change, the new state of equilibrium would give the effects of the assumed political change. "The method by which the effects of such political change would be traced is that familiar in economics as the method of comparative statics."

I dealt with Black's theories in my lectures on the "Theory of the State" at Pavia in 1953–1954, and I was later surprised and pleased to see that several criticisms I had made had been worked out independently by Buchanan in his article published in 1954 on "Individual Choices in Voting and the Market." Buchanan was concerned at that time with the general problem of comparing market choices and political voting, not in the usual terms of the relative efficiency of centralized and decentralized decision-making, but in terms of a more complete understanding of the individual behavior involved in the two processes. Although he did not quote Black's theory, and may not have been acquainted with it at that time, Buchanan managed to prove that very important differences exist between market choice and voting choice, and that the analogy of the popular saying "one dollar, one vote" is only partially appropriate. In the market choice the individual is the choosing entity as well as the entity for which the choices are made; whereas in voting (at least in what we usually call political voting) while the individual is the acting or choosing entity, the collectivity of all the other individuals is the entity for which the choices are made. Moreover, the act of choosing in the market and the consequences of choosing stand in one-to-one correspondence. On the other hand, the voter can never predict with certainty which of the alternatives present will be chosen.

Buchanan indicated other fundamental differences between the two processes. The individual choosing in the market "tends to act as if all the social variables were determined outside of his behavior, while the individual in the polling place, by contrast, recognizes that his vote is influential in determining the final collective choice." On the other hand, "since voting implies collective choice, the responsibility for making any social or collective decision is necessarily divided, and there is no tangible benefit or cost directly imputable to the chooser in the polling place in connection with his personal choice." The result is probably a less precise and less objective consideration of alternative costs than takes place in the minds of individuals choosing in the market. A further and most important distinction has been emphasized by Buchanan in much the same way as it was emphasized by me in the lectures I mentioned before: "Alternatives of market choice normally conflict only in the sense that the law of diminishing returns is operative. . . . If an individual desires more of a particular commodity or service, the market normally requires only that he take less of another." By contrast, "alternatives of voting choice are more exclusive," that is, the selection of one precludes the selection of another. Group choices, so far as the individuals belonging to the group are concerned, tend to be "mutually exclusive by the very nature of the alternatives" which are regularly (as Buchanan admitted in 1954) of the "all or none variety." This feature arises not only because of the poverty of the schemes usually adopted and adoptable for the distribution of voting strength, but also because (as both Buchanan and I maintained in 1954) many alternatives that we usually call political do not allow these combinations or composite solutions which render market choices so articulate in comparison with political choices. An important consequence is that in the market the dollar vote is never overruled. As illustrated by Mises, the individual is never placed in the position of a dissenting minority: " . . . on the market no vote is cast in vain,"[7] at least so far as the

---

[7] Ludwig von Mises, *Human Action* (New Haven: Yale University Press, 1949), p. 271.

existing or potential alternatives of the market are concerned. To put the point the other way around, there is a possible coercion in voting that does not occur in the market. The voter chooses only between potential alternatives: "He may lose his vote and be compelled to accept [to quote Buchanan again] a result contrary to his expressed preference."

We can see that between the choices of individual voters and resulting group decisions there is no consistency (in the sense previously assumed) whenever voters are on the losing side. The voter who loses initially makes one choice but eventually has to accept another that he has previously rejected. His individual decision-making process has been overthrown. It is true that on the winning side consistency may be discerned between individual choices and group decisions; but we can scarcely speak of a consistency of the whole process of group decisions in the same way we can speak of consistency in an individual process of decision making. And perhaps we can go further and doubt whether there is any sense whatever in speaking of a rationality in this voting process, unless we refer simply to conformity with the rules set for decision procedures. In other words, we had probably better speak here not of process but of procedure. A consistent procedure may well be the second best when a consistent process of choice cannot be traced. A real comparison between these two kinds of consistency has appeared to some scholars as just as devoid of sense as trying to find out "whether a pig is fatter than a giraffe is tall."[8]

Another conclusion to be drawn from what we have said before is that the concept of equilibrium can be used only in different ways in economics and in politics. In economics equilibrium is defined as equality of supply and demand, an equality understandable when the individual chooser can so articulate his choice as to let each single dollar vote successfully. But what kind of equality between supply and demand for laws and orders can be assumed in politics—where the individual may lose his vote; where he can ask for bread and be given a stone?

There is still, however, the possibility of using the term "equi-

---

[8] Robert A. Dahl and Charles E. Lindblom, *Politics, Economics and Welfare* (New York: Harper and Brothers, 1953), p. 241.

librium" in politics whenever you can imagine that all the individuals belonging to a group are unanimous in taking some
decision. As Rousseau once said, a community is to be conceived
as "unanimous" at least as far as its members agree to submit to
majority rule. This means that whenever a group decision takes
place, the individual members of the group are unanimously
convinced that a bad decision is better than none, or, to put it
more properly, that a collective decision which a member of the
group considers bad is better than none. Unanimous agreement
does not require any special procedure in order to make the
decision that has been considered as adoptable by the members
of the group. A group decision, when unanimously agreed upon,
may be considered as consistent as any other taken by the individual chooser in the market. Thus it seems that we are here
confronted with the same kind of pig as in economics, and it
makes sense to ask whether this "political" pig is fatter than the
"economic" one. The latter considerations may lead, and in fact
did lead, independently in the article I quoted above, in lectures
I delivered in Claremont, California, in 1958 (which became
Freedom and the Law), and in Professor Buchanan's recent work
(published in collaboration with Gordon Tullock) *The Calculus of
Consent*,[9] to emphasize again rather strongly some possible similarities between the economic and the political decisions.

If a community is to be considered as "unanimous," at least as
far as its members agree to submit to some kind of majority or,
to say that more generally, to some kind of less than unanimous
rule, the similarity between those unanimous political decisions
and economic decisions re-emerges at a higher level. People do
not yet decide any particular political issue, but first decide what
rules they are to adopt for all kinds of political decisions—that is,
for the political game.

In fact, the choice of the rules for the political game may
be due to a process as rational and as free as that resulting in
any other choice in the market. At this higher level, people may
compare costs and benefits relating to any rule to be chosen for

---

[9] James M. Buchanan and Gordon Tullock, *The Calculus of Consent* (Ann Arbor: University
of Michigan Press, 1962). Comments in this and the following lecture are based on an
earlier mimeographed edition produced for limited circulation.

making political decisions. They may decide, for instance, that in some cases some rules will be more adoptable than others, and specifically that unanimity rules or qualified majority rules will be more suitable than others to protect potentially dissenting individuals from possibly harmful effects of the coercive action of deciding majorities.

The comparison between the political and the economic action in this respect is not limited, however, to the level of the choice of the general rules for making decisions. It is an undoubted merit of Tullock and Buchanan to have recently extended the analysis to ordinary political decisions, also under the assumption that the latter are taken in accordance with procedural rules (they call them "constitutional" rules) unanimously agreed upon by the members of the political group concerned. A typical trait of this analysis is the recognition of the fact that vote trading (or logrolling) takes place very frequently in the actual political process, and the corresponding recognition that vote trading, under certain conditions, should be considered beneficial to all the members of the political group, just as trade of ordinary goods and services has been considered beneficial, by the founders of economics, to all the members of the community in which the market system has been adopted. Moreover, the conditions under which the vote trading may be beneficial to all the members of the political community are similar to the conditions under which the usual trading of commodities and services is beneficial, that is, to the conditions under which no monopoly and no conspiracy can be established by one or more members of the community in order to exploit the others.

By "trading" their votes through a long-run and continuous process of bargaining until a unanimous agreement is reached among them, all the members of a political group are confronted with many possible alternatives and are able to prevent any coalition of members of the group from making decisions that may be harmful to the others. The resulting situation should be a general agreement similar to that which renders a competitive market possible and efficient. This theory is presented as descriptive as well as normative, according to the usual type of modern theories of choice.

One must ask, however, how far such an analysis can go in

assimilating political decisions to economic decisions from this point of view. I propose to examine here the limits of a conception which admits vote trading in politics by assuming simply that voting means merely a way of securing some utilities for the individual concerned, according to some privately accepted set of values.

To begin with, I wish to suggest a reconsideration of a probable weak point in this otherwise clever and interesting analysis of the possible similarities between political and economic decisions. It seems to me that this analysis, in the form adopted by the authors at the present stage of their work, reveals some lack of preliminary and precise definitions relating to some basic concepts of the analysis itself. "Political" or "collective" choice on the one hand is distinguished from "private" or "voluntary" choice on the other. According to the theory, private choices may be individualistic as well as cooperative. In their turn, cooperative choices on the one hand and collective choices on the other are always, quite correctly, considered as different in kind, even when they seem to be similar. But unless I am wrong, a "collective" action is never defined satisfactorily or explicitly in this theory. The reason for this weakness in an otherwise accurate and penetrating analysis is probably a psychological one. The whole theory is based on an individualistic point of view on which I agree quite cordially. But the more the authors try to emphasize the role that voluntary consent has in a political community both at the "constitutional" and at the ordinary level, the less they seem to be inclined to recognize openly, although they admit it implicitly, that what makes a "collective" decision "collective" and not simply "cooperative" at the individualistic level is the fact that the former is always, in the last analysis, susceptible to being enforced upon all the members of the group—regardless of the particular individual attitude towards that decision at any given time. Decisions that can be enforced are, in the last analysis, coercive decisions. While coercion is something that economists never need to take into consideration when they are concerned with goods and services being voluntarily supplied or demanded in the market, it is also something that one cannot help taking into consideration when one moves from the market to the political scene.

In connection with their hesitancy to openly recognize the importance of the concept of "coercion" (whatever this may mean) in their own analysis of politics, the authors of the theory explicitly reject any power-approach to the problems they are confronted with in dealing with political decisions. They assume that that approach is irremediably contradictory to the economic one. They adopt the argument that while you can simultaneously maximize, through the economic exchange, the utilities of the seller and the buyer in the market, the result being a net gain for both, you cannot do the same if you try to maximize individual power. You cannot have at the same time maximized powers both for the man who wins and the man who loses in a struggle for power.

I have already suggested on another occasion that this comparison, although accepted as a matter of course by several economists, is not presented in a proper way. I would not compare power with utility. Power, like the commodities or services taken into consideration by the economists, has its own utility for the individual concerned. But this is not the only similarity between power and commodities or services. There is a sense in which you can exchange power as well as you can exchange commodities or services. And the exchange of power may also result in maximizing utilities for the individuals who participate in the exchange. If I grant you the power to prevent me from hurting you, provided that you grant me a similar power to prevent you from hurting me, we are both better off after this exchange, and we are precisely better off in terms of utilities. In other words, we have both maximized the utility of our respective power. (A similar maximization obviously occurs when two or more individuals agree to join their powers in order to prevent other people from doing something harmful to them.)

May I suggest that a political community starts precisely when this exchange of powers takes place—an exchange that is preliminary to any other, of commodities or of services. As a matter of fact, the power approach is not a recent device of political scientists. You find it in the classic political literature and the whole Aristotelian theory of politics may be considered as based to a great extent on that approach, since Aristotle recognized at the very beginning of his treatise on politics that there are men who are destined by nature to have power over others (*arkoi*) and men who are destined by nature to be subject to the power of others (*arkomenoi*). There is in the Aristotelian theory an explicit recognition of the profit that both *arkoi* and *arkomenoi* derive from cooperating, although Aristotle fails to see clearly that any collaboration between the *arkoi* and the *arkomenoi* always implies the existence of some minimum powers (at least of some negative ones) guaranteed to the *arkomenoi* as a kind of consideration for the more obvious and positive powers granted to the *arkoi*.

This way of considering the question would not at all exclude the economic approach. It would reconcile it with an approach (i.e., the power approach) that seems to be increasingly adopted by political scientists today.

But unless I am wrong there are several limits for a conception which admits vote trading in politics by explicitly assuming that voting simply means a way of securing some utilities for the individuals concerned, and implies that those utilities are similar in kind to those dealt with by individuals in the market.

1) We have seen that the authors of this theory do not assume that vote trading would be beneficial in all cases. They insist on the conditions, according to Pareto's rules under which such trading could be really beneficial to all members of the community concerned, that is the conditions under which no monopoly and no conspiracy can be established by one or more members of the community concerned in order to satisfy their "sinister interests" at the expense of some or all of the other members.

These limiting conditions are, however, not the only ones that we should take into account. To begin with, there is a stage in which no vote trading would make any sense, i.e., the constitutional stage. According to the authors of the theory, this is the point for deciding what kind of rules are the most suitable in order to successfully make any sort of decisions including those to be reached through some bargaining of the kind that results in vote trading. The reason vote trading would not make any sense at this stage is not only because we do not yet have any procedural rule according to which we may vote. There is a still more important reason. The process of finding out the rules is a theoretical one. There are, of course, useful ways of finding such rules, but you cannot exchange their utilities, as if they were yours only, with the utilities of other ways of finding the same rules, as if the latter utilities belonged only to other people. There is no sense in bargaining when it is a question of knowing what is the sum of $2 + 2$ or what is the square of the hypotenuse of a right triangle in Euclidian geometry.

To put it in more general terms, there is no rationality in bargaining or in trading whenever it is a question of omitting a truth judgment relating to any subject whatsoever. The arguments leading to a correct conclusion are not for sale.

While the authors of the theory assume, at least implicitly, that no vote trading could reasonably take place at the constitutional stage, they seem to neglect the possibility that, at a lower stage than the constitutional, voting could be a process through which the members of a political community are supposed to emit truth judgments regardless of their personal interest in the matter concerned. If this is the case, bargaining and vote trading would be as irrational as they were at the constitutional stage.

We can conceive of several issues on which the voters may be requested to emit truth judgments regardless of their own personal interests in the issue. If we assume, for instance, that a jury is a political institution, and that consequently its members emit, by voting, a political decision, nobody would maintain that they would act rationally if they traded their votes with other members of the jury, according to some consideration of their personal utilities. Of course we can conceive of corrupted members of a jury who might be bribed by people interested in their decision. We could call their vote trading "rational" though very objectionable from an ethical point of view. But this is not the case as long as we assume that members of a jury are not going to be bribed by anybody. Vote trading in the latter case would appear simply irrational from all points of view. Similar considerations apply to any other kind of truth judgments to be emitted by the members of a political community through the process of voting.

Indeed, the authors of the theory may counter by saying, quite correctly, that voting is not the right procedure to follow in order to reach sound conclusions relating to some objective truth, and that therefore the attempts to do that on the political scene risk being sheer illusion. Still, there are cases in which truth judgments on the part of the voters are useful in order to know their opinions—if any—concerning a given political issue. In those cases the voting procedure may be the most appropriate way of finding out precisely what those opinions are regardless of the fact that these opinions may be true or false according to some scientific tests. It is obvious that there would be no vote trading in the latter cases.

2) It is probably reasonable to suspect that the applicability of the vote-trading model is limited whenever differences emerge between the individual choice in the polling place and in the competitive market—which are conspicuous enough to force us to neglect the existing similarities. For instance, a) the fact, already stated above, that there is more uncertainty and in general less knowledge of the costs and the benefits involved in the process of choosing through voting than in the process of buying or of selling in the market renders it much more difficult to trade votes than to trade commodities and services in the market. Moreover, b) vote trading seems to be irremediably less beneficial than regular trading in the market because the voter takes much less responsibility for his choice than any operator in the market. While unsuccessful operators are pushed out of the market and better ones step in, nothing of that kind happens on the political stage where unsuccessful voters never go out, and new possibly successful voters are not allowed to step in as successful operators do in the market. It may be countered that in the political process unsuccessful voters may be forced to abandon the political scene qua voters whenever they allow a tyrant to end the democracy. This fact, however, far from being acceptable evidence in favor of the similarities between unsuccessful voters on the one hand and unsuccessful operators in the market on the other, forces us to recognize important differences between the former and the latter. In the case of unsuccessful voters taken over by a tyrant, each and all of the voters must go out of the political scene qua voters, including the potentially successful ones—the resulting situation being not a selection of the best voters but the final ruin of a political community based on the voting system. c) A similar limitation to the applicability of the vote-trading model seems to emerge where alternative issues in

politics are more exclusive than those offered to the individuals in the market. Vote trading in the presence of two mutually exclusive issues will be comparable to the trading of commodities and services in a situation in which oligopoly or oligopsony dominates the market, that is, in a situation in which market prices are less likely to emerge than in a situation in which a more regular competition takes place. Finally, d) it should be noticed that while the inconveniences we have underlined take place under any minority or majority rule, the relationship between collective action taken under the rule of unanimity on the one hand, and purely voluntary action, such as occurs in the market, on the other hand is not as close as it probably appears to the authors of the theory. Under unanimity, a voter whose consent is necessary to all the other voters to make a group decision is only to a certain extent comparable to an individual whose consent is necessary to other people who wish to buy from him or to sell to him services or commodities in the market. Neither the former nor the latter is forced to accept other people's decisions without his own consent. This consent, however, is certainly a necessary although not a sufficient condition for the existence of a competitive market.

In fact, the voter under unanimity rule is in a position which may be closely related to that of a discriminating monopolist who can realize the whole benefit of the exchange of the commodities or of the services he is able to sell, and can therefore acquire the whole, or almost the whole, of the so-called consumer's surplus. This fact, which has been sometimes rather improperly termed as a possible "blackmail" on the part of a dissenting voter under unanimity rule, should not be neglected in a theory that tries to secure in politics the conditions of a competitive market. Whenever out of a group of 100 voters, 99 are in favor of a given decision and 1 opposes it, the attempt of the latter to not only be compensated for giving up his opposition, but more than compensated by his 99 fellow voters with a net gain for himself is perfectly rational from the point of view of the very theory we are discussing. If this happens, the Pareto rule may be respected, but we cannot compare the position of the voters to that of the individuals in a competitive market. It may be countered that any voter under unanimity rule may be interested in giving his consent to the other 99 for a small benefit, rather than risking the loss of that benefit if the other 99 voters think that the price requested by the last one for his consent is too high. But this fact does not prevent the dissenting voter from bargaining in a much better condition than the other 99 voters—a condition comparable to that of a discriminating monopolist. Of course, discriminating monopolies may occur in the market as well as in political decisions. But while they tend to be reduced in the market at least in the long run, until costs are equalizing prices, there is no hope of a similar result for group decisions under unanimity rule.

The authors themselves admit that their theory may supply only a partial explanation of the actual process of voting in politics. The corresponding normative value of the theory is limited accordingly. Unless we are wrong, more accurate inquiry about the limits of the applicability of this interesting economic approach to politics would probably be useful both to economists and political scientists in order to reach a deeper understanding of their respective subjects.

4

VOTING VERSUS
THE MARKET

We have seen in the preceding lecture that notwithstanding many similarities that may exist between voters on the one hand and market operators on the other, the actions of the two are far from actually being similar. No procedural rule seems able to allow voters to act in the same flexible, independent, consistent, and efficient way as operators employing individual choice in the market. While it is true that both voting and operating in the market are individual actions, we are compelled, however, to conclude that voting is a kind of individual action that almost inevitably undergoes a kind of distortion in its use.

Legislation considered as a result of a collective decision by a group—even if consisting of all citizens concerned as in the direct democracies of ancient times or in some small democratic communities in medieval and modern times—appears to be a law-making process that is far from being identifiable with the market process. Only voters ranking in winning majorities (if for instance the voting rule is by majority) are comparable to people who operate on the market. Those people ranking in losing minorities are not comparable with even the weakest operators on the market, who at least under the divisibility of goods (which is the most frequent case) can always find something to choose and to get, provided that they pay its price. Legislation is a result of an all-or-none decision. Either you win and get exactly what you want, or you lose and get exactly nothing. Even worse, you get something that you do not want and you have to pay for it just as if you had wanted it. In this sense winners and losers in voting are like winners and losers in the field. Voting appears to be not so much a reproduction of the market operation as a symbolization of a battle in the field. If we consider it well, there is nothing "rational" in voting that can be compared with rationality in the market. Of course voting may be preceded by argument and bargaining, which may be rational in the same sense as any operation on the market. But whenever you finally come to vote, you don't argue or bargain any longer. You are on another plane. You accumulate ballots as you would accumulate stones or shells—the implication being that you do not win because you have more reasons than others, but merely because you have more ballots to pile up. In this operation you have neither partners nor interlocutors but only allies and enemies. Of course your own action may still be considered rational as well as that of your allies and enemies, but the final result is not something that can be simply explained as a scrutiny or a combination of your reasons and of those of people who vote against them. The political language reflects quite naturally this aspect of voting: Politicians speak willingly of *campaigns* to be started, of *battles* to be won, of *enemies* to be fought, and so on. This language does not usually occur in the market. There is an obvious reason for that: *While in the market supply and demand are not only compatible but also complementary, in the political field, in which legislation belongs, the choice of winners on the one hand and losers on the other are neither complementary nor even compatible.* It is surprising to see how this simple—and I would say obvious—consideration of the nature of group decisions (and particularly of voting, which is the usual procedural device used to make them) is overlooked by both the theorists and the man in the street. Voting, and particularly voting by majority rule, is often considered a *rational* procedure not only in the sense that it renders it possible to reach decisions when the members of the group are not unanimous, but also in the sense that it seems to be the most logical one under the circumstances.

It is true that people usually admit that a unanimous decision would be ideal. But owing to the fact that unanimity in group decisions is rare, they feel entitled to conclude that the second best is making decisions by majority vote—the implication being that these decisions are not only more expedient but also more logical than any others.

On another occasion I have dealt with a defense of this position by Dr. Anthony Downs.[1] I think it is worthwhile to reconsider Downs's argument, which has the merit of summarizing in a short way all of the main reasons presented in favor of majority rule in the political literature that I know.

According to Dr. Downs,

> the basic arguments in favor of simple majority rule rest upon the premise that every voter should have equal weight with every other voter. Hence, if disagreement occurs but action cannot be postponed until unanimity is reached, *it is better for more voters to tell fewer what to do than vice versa.* The only practical arrangement to accomplish this is simple majority rule. Any rule requiring more than a simple majority for a passage of an act allows a minority to prevent action by the majority thus giving the vote of each member of the minority *more weight* than the vote of each member of the majority.[2]

To continue our favorite comparison between voting and operating on the market: This argument seems to be the same as saying that we must give a one dollar bill to everybody in order to give each one the same purchasing power. But when we consider the analogy at closer quarters, we realize that in assuming that 51 voters out of 100 are "politically" equal to 100 voters, and that the remaining 49 (contrary) voters are "politically" equal to zero (which is exactly what happens when a group decision is made according to majority rule) we give much more "weight" to each voter ranking on the side of the winning 51 than to each voter ranking on the side of the losing 49. It would be more appropriate to compare this situation with that resulting in the market if 51 people having one dollar each combine in buying a gadget which costs 51 dollars, while another 49 people with 1 dollar each have to do without it because there is only one gadget for sale. The fact that we cannot possibly foresee who will belong to the majority does not change the picture much.

---

[1] See Bruno Leoni, "Political Decisions and Majority Rule," *Il Politico,* Vol. XXV, No. 4, 1960, pp. 724–733.

[2] Anthony Downs, *In Defense of Majority Voting* (Chicago: University of Chicago, 1960). (A mimeographed essay, it was written as a general critique of a paper by Gordon Tullock, "Some Problems of Majority Voting." This latter paper was an early version of Chapter 10 in *The Calculus of Consent.)*

Some historical reasons obviously played a very important role in preventing people from reflecting on the contradictions of a doctrine that claimed to support equality of opportunities for everybody in politics and simultaneously denied that very equality through the application of the majority rule. The supporters of majority rule used to conceive of it as the only possible means of opposing the unrestricted power of oligarchies or tyrants over the large masses of people. The "weight" given to the will or to the "ideal vote" of tyrants in the political societies that they dominated appeared so disproportionately overwhelming in comparison to the weight left to the will of all of the other individuals in those societies that the application of majority rule seemed to be the only suitable way to restore the equality of "weights" for the wills of all the individuals concerned. Very few people bothered to inquire whether the political scale was not going to become unbalanced on the opposite side. That common attitude is poignantly expressed, for instance, in a letter that Thomas Jefferson wrote to Alexander von Humbolt on June 13, 1817:

> The first principle of republicanism is that the *lex majoris partie* is the fundamental law of every society of individuals of equal rights: to consider the will of the society enounced by the majority of a single vote as sacred as if unanimous is the first of all lessons in importance, yet the last which is thoroughly learnt. This law once disregarded, no other remains but that of force, which ends necessarily in military despotism. This has been the history of the French revolution; and I wish [so Jefferson added in some prophetic mood] the understanding of our Southern brethern may be sufficiently enlarged and firm to see that their fate depends on its sacred observance.[3]

Only later in the last century did several prominent scholars and statesmen start to realize that there was no more magic in the number 51 than in the number 49. For instance the French *garantistes* as well as some famous English thinkers had no hesitancy in declaring their dislike for the unconditional application of majority rule in political decisions, and for the underlying

---

[3] *The Writings of Thomas Jefferson*, vol. 15, Editor in Chief, Andrew A. Lipscomb (Washington, D.C.: The Thomas Jefferson Memorial Association of the United States, 1904), p. 127.

assumption that Herbert Spencer was to brand in 1884 as the superstition of "the divine right of majorities."[4]

But let us repeat Dr. Downs's summary of the main arguments in favor of majority rule. "If disagreement occurs but action cannot be postponed until unanimity is reached, it is better for more voters to tell fewer what to do than vice versa. The only practical arrangement to accomplish this is simply majority rule."

We may admit that the circumstances hypothesized by Downs, *urgency of a decision* and *lack of unanimity,* may occur more or less frequently in all political societies. The fact, however, is that both urgency of decision and lack of unanimity may be, so to speak, *artificially* created by people who are in a position to compel all the other members of a political community to make any group decision whatsoever instead of making none. I propose to go back to this question. I only wish to point out here that even if we assume that both urgency and lack of unanimity are the existing conditions of the decision concerned, to state flatly, as Dr. Downs does, that therefore "it is better for more voters to tell fewer what to do than vice versa" is a simple nonsequitur. Indeed, we can easily imagine situations in which only a few people have the necessary amount of knowledge required to make the corresponding decision, and that therefore it would be much less reasonable in these cases for more voters to tell fewer what to do than vice versa.

Of course the enthusiastic supporters of unconditional majority rule may counter that they derive their conclusion not so much from the hypotheses of urgency and lack of unanimity as from the implicit hypotheses of equal knowledge, or even of equal ignorance, on the part of the voters of the issues at stake. This last hypothesis, however, is rather unrealistic, particularly in contemporary highly differentiated societies. The same author admits in another connection, "specialization creates minority groups with objective interests [and, I would add, with corresponding kinds of knowledge] which differ widely from each other." Thus, the real basis of the conclusion is still the famous

---

[4] See "The Great Political Superstition," *The Man Versus the State,* Herbert Spencer (Indianapolis: Liberty Fund, Inc., 1981), p. 129.

concept of "equal weight" of voters or, to say it more properly, the amphibious use of this slippery concept.

There is one more point of the summation presented by Downs to be examined. "Any rule," he says, "requiring more than a simple majority for passage of an act allows a minority to prevent action by the majority, thus giving the vote of each member of the minority *more weight* than the vote of each member of the majority."

Let us concentrate first on the last part of this statement. It seems to be indubitable that if the rule adopted is a qualified majority rule, the number comprising the winning majority out of 100 voters would be, say, 60 or 70, instead of 51, and the corresponding number comprising the losing minority would be 40 or 30 instead of 49. But this does not mean that the vote of each member of the minority is now given "more weight" than the vote of each member of the majority. The fact is that once again out of a total or set of 100 voters, the winning voters ranking in the subset of 60 or 70 are still each given, according to the new rule, more weight than is given to each of the voters ranking in the subset whose sum is 40 or 30. The 60 or 70 voters are considered in this new example as "politically" equal to 100, while the other 40 or 30 are considered as "politically" equal to 0.

The only difference we can notice in this example is that each voter, when the "magic" number is 60 or 70, has—*in abstracto*—a lesser probability of ranking in the losing subset than he had in the previous example where the magic number was 51. But it would be wrong to derive from this statement the conclusion that "therefore" each voter ranking in the losing subset in the latter example is given more weight than each voter ranking in the winning one.

We must now examine the first part of Mr. Downs's statement whose last part we have just considered.

As we saw, Downs refers to any rule requiring more than a simple majority for making a political decision as one allowing a minority to prevent action by a majority, and he seems to imply that this possible prevention should always be rejected according to his principle of the equal weight of the voters.

It is obvious, however, that there are several kinds of "prevention" and a more careful analysis of this concept is probably indispensable before drawing conclusions.

It may be useful to remember in this connection an example presented at the beginning of this century in this country by a distinguished scholar (whose name is probably unduly forgotten in our time: Lawrence Lowell) in his stimulating book, *Public Opinion and Popular Government.*[5] I have quoted this example on another occasion but it seems to me so good that I would like to repeat it. Bands of robbers, said Lawrence Lowell, do not constitute a "majority" when after having waited for a foot traveler in a lonely place they deprive him of his purse. Nor can the latter be called a "minority." There are constitutional protections and, of course, criminal legislation in the United States as well as in other countries, tending to prevent the formation of such "majorities." I must admit that several "majorities" in our times have often much in common with the peculiar "majority" described by Lawrence Lowell. Notwithstanding this, it is still possible and, I would say, very important to distinguish between the paradoxical "majorities" of the Lowell type and "majorities" in a more orthodox sense. Majorities of the Lowell type are not allowed in any efficiently organized society of this world for the simple reason that practically every member of these societies wants to be given the possibility of preventing at least some actions by any majority. Downs's argument that in those cases each voter of the minority is given more weight than each voter of the majority would not be considered very impressive by anybody, even if we assumed that argument were correct.

Would we then maintain that those cases in which each individual wants to preserve his power to prevent majorities, regardless of their size, from taking actions like robbing or murdering are perfectly similar to other cases in which a capricious or wicked dissenter would be able to prevent his fellow citizens from reaching some innocent and useful ends of their own? It seems obvious that the word *prevention* has a different meaning in each case, and that it would be advisable to distinguish between these cases before assuming any general conclusion about the applicability

---

[5] A. Lawrence Lowell, *Public Opinion and Popular Government* (New York: Longmans, Green, & Co., 1913).

of the majority rule. In other words, even if we admitted the correctness of the "equal weight" argument, we should recognize the necessity of some important qualifications that would reveal the insurmountable limits of the argument itself.

There is one more argument that we have to consider among those presented in favor of simple majority rule. As we saw, Downs not only objected to the application of other rules as contrasted to the principle of "equal weights," but stated rather flatly that "the only practical arrangement" in order to let more voters tell fewer what to do was "simply majority rule." The idea is that if we adopt any other (qualified) majority rule, a minority would be able to prevent a majority from telling the former what to do. Or, to put it in another way, a minority would tell a majority what not to tell. Unfortunately for the supporters of unconditional majority rule, this argument in favor of simple majority rule is no more correct than the preceding ones.

The adoption of simple majority rule does not prevent strongly organized minorities from telling all the other members of the political community what to do. The Italian theory of elites presented by Mosca, Pareto, and to a certain extent by Roberto Michels has always strongly emphasized this possibility. In their recent essay, *The Calculus of Consent,* John Buchanan and Gordon Tullock, while trying to reject the elite point of view, have rather unconsciously adopted it in their analysis of vote trading as a real phenomenon taking place in representative democracies of our times.

Unless I am wrong, Buchanan and Tullock managed to demonstrate in a probably irrefutable way that whenever a minority is well organized and determined to bribe as many voters as necessary in order to have a majority ready to pass a desired decision, the majority rule works much more in favor of such minorities than is commonly supposed. If for instance only ten voters out of a hundred gain the whole benefit of 100 dollars from a group decision whose costs of 100 dollars are to be charged equally to each member of the group, those ten voters may be interested in bribing 41 more people—at least by refunding to each of them his individual cost for the decision, that is, 1 dollar each. In the end, 41 people belonging to the majority will then break even, 40 belonging to the official minority will pay 1 dollar each without getting any benefit from the decision, and each of the real gainers will get 10 dollars benefit against 5.10 dollars cost from the decision taken by the group.

Of course the rule may also work in an opposite way when the losing 40 manage to organize themselves the next time and bribe at least two members of the majority in order to transform the latter into a minority and leave the ten shrewd fellows with empty hands. But it is obvious that simple majority rule may actually work in favor of a minority in both cases.

True, one cannot say that simple majority rule is the only one besides minority rules susceptible to working in favor of minorities. All other majority rules may work in favor of some minorities when the benefits resulting from the group decision are concentrated and its costs are distributed enough to encourage shrewd minorities to bribe as many voters as necessary to form the majority prescribed by the existing rule. The costs of that bribing, however, increase according to the number of voters prescribed for the formation of a valid majority. It may well happen that the costs involved in the process of bribing an increasing number of voters will discourage any shrewd minority from attempting to maximize their utilities at the expense of their fellow voters or of a part of them. The conclusion seems to be that simple majority rule is to be less discouraging for said minorities than other possible qualified majority rules. This sounds rather different from the statement we have been considering so far. That is, that simple majority rule would be the "only practical arrangement" in order to let "more voters tell fewer what to do."

One of the interesting possibilities also pointed out in the analysis made by Buchanan and Tullock of the way in which simple majority rule may work is the continuous attempt on the part of new minorities of maximizers to bribe other voters originally indifferent to the issue concerned in order to create new ephemeral majorities at the expense of the less informed, less shrewd, or less careful minorities. Another interesting possible result pointed out by the same authors is that the disproportion between benefits and costs for the maximizing minorities induces them to neglect the possibility of minimizing the total costs of the group decision they are promoting in their own behalf.

The general situation may be termed, as I termed it in another connection, a legal war of all against all or, to adopt the famous expression used by the eminent French economist and political scientist Frederic Bastiat, the great fiction of the state "by which everyone seeks to live at the expense of everyone else."[6]

A continuous overinvestment through group decisions tends to take place in a political community whenever the decision-making rules are such as to encourage minorities of shrewd maximizers to get something for nothing by letting minorities of less shrewd victims foot the bill. Dr. Downs has tried, however, to defend simple majority rule against the accusation of favoring the initiatives of maximizing minorities at the expense of other members of the group. In his essay devoted to the analysis of an article of Tullock's that has been substantially reproduced in the new book by Tullock and Buchanan, Downs makes the already mentioned remark that all kinds of qualified majority rules may work in approximately the same way as simple majority rule in order to encourage shrewd minorities to maximize their own profits at the expense of other voters. In fact, Downs is forced to admit that simple majority rule is not exempt from the above-mentioned criticism. But he seems to completely neglect the fact, now stressed by Tullock and Buchanan, that qualified majority rules appear to be more discouraging than simple majority rule for all kinds of shrewd maximizing minorities.

Downs also tries to defend simple majority rule as well as other (qualified) majority rules from the accusation that they would tend to produce overinvestment through a series of group decisions passed by ephemeral and changing majorities. He admits that "logrolling" takes place in the real world, but he assumes that if the costs actually tended to exceed the benefits in the decisions adopted by political communities based on representatives elected by the people, these representatives would be obliged to reveal the bad results of the vote trading at the end of their legislature. Then the electors would get disgusted and punish them by appointing other representatives.

However, this argument does not seem very convincing. One

---

[6] Frederic Bastiat, *Selected Essays on Political Economy* (New York: D. Van Nostrand Co., 1964), p. 144.

trait of the political game is that in contemporary political societies logrolling starts earlier than in the Chambers of the representatives. It actually starts in the constituencies when the
constituents accept some (for them) disadvantageous items of a
political program in order to get some benefit from other items
that are advantageous for them. They may consider among the
disadvantageous items of the program the possibility that the
logrolling their representative is going to start at the Chamber
will result in some net losses for them at a given moment. This
moment may or may not coincide with the moment at which
their representative will present himself to his electors at the end
of the legislature. But even if it coincides, their representative
will be able to argue that, if he were to be returned to office, he
would have new opportunities for improving the present situation through a more beneficial series of logrolling on behalf of
his electors. Because the political game is never finished, there is
no reason for the electors to fire a representative who can always
state that at a given moment, or in a series of given moments, the
results of his logrolling were beneficial for his electors, and who
can further argue that analogous or even higher benefits would
result from his continuation of the same logrolling in the next
legislature.

Downs tries, however, to adopt another argument in favor of
his thesis. He concedes that if voters are ignorant of some of the
costs resulting from a series of group decisions they may vote for
a program containing a government budget which is really too
large. But, he says, if we admit ignorance into the picture, voters
may also be ignorant of some of the benefits they receive, and if
this is the situation ignorance may produce a government budget
that is too small as well as one that is too large.

It seems to me that this argument is even less convincing than
the preceding one. We moved from the rather realistic assumption that shrewd minorities know better than their fellow voters
what costs and benefits will emerge for them from a decision that
they try to have passed by the group, notwithstanding the possible overinvestment that this decision implies for the group. If
such a decision is to pass, it is precisely because other voters are
to foot the bill, which means that they are careless or less organized or ignorant of the real consequences for them emerging

from the decision. Ignorance may be, therefore, one of the reasons overinvestment occurs, although it is not the only one. But let us assume that ignorance (on the part of the losing voters) *is* the only reason. Downs counters that ignorance may also produce a government budget which is "too small." But this is a completely different case which has very little to do with the case of overinvestment that we have just considered. Downs's argument would be acceptable only if we could assume that merely because of the ignorance of the voters who are footing the bill for a decision promoted by a shrewd minority, the benefits of that decision for the group may not only be less but also greater than the costs. But this would imply that investment is a form of gambling in which rational and well-informed operators are no more likely to succeed than irrational or ignorant ones. If ignorance could randomly produce the same beneficial effects as information, economic activities would obviously be very different from what they are now. In the world in which we live, the assumption that ignorance may pay as well as information seems to be rather inappropriate to explain human action—not only in the economic field but in the other fields as well. On the other hand, it is reasonable to assume that minorities who promote a group decision for their own benefit know what they are doing better than the other voters. They have a precise idea of what they want and of the possible results for them of the corresponding group decision. They may know equally well that the benefits of the decision for the other members of the group will be less than the costs for those same members. But they can disregard this fact. The final result will very probably be an investment that will cost much more than it would have cost under different conditions.

We have seen that simple majority rule is not the only rule that may cause these effects. *Any other kind of (qualified) majority rule may have similar results.* We have also seen, however, that qualified majority rules may work better than simple majority rule to discourage maximizing minorities from imposing their will on the whole group through the well-known procedure of logrolling. It would seem at this point that the more you increase the majority necessary for making a group decision, the more you protect the dissenting minorities from being exploited by well-organized elites of maximizers. However, this is not the case. As Buchanan and Tullock have shown in their work, the costs of reaching an agreement among the voters of a group tend to increase rather sharply when the qualified majority rule approximates the unanimity rule. In other words, any voter tends to consider his consent as very precious when he knows that the number of voters needed for a valid decision is very high. If the other voters want his consent he may be tempted to act in the same way as a discriminating monopolist in order to obtain the full advantage of the bargain.

A situation which is to a certain extent analogous to that occurring with shrewd minorities under simple majority rule tends to emerge under highly qualified majority rules or under unanimity rule. New minorities of maximizers may emerge, not in order to buy other people's votes at the cheapest price, but merely to sell their own votes at the highest price to those voters who want to have a decision passed under the existing rule, i.e., a highly qualified majority rule. Unanimity rule would simply exacerbate this tendency, and this is the reason unanimity rule is very rarely adopted because of the high or even prohibitive costs that it may imply for all those who want to have a decision passed under that rule.

If we now go back to the concept of "equal weight" of the voters, *we must conclude that no rule for decision making is really apt to give equal weights in the sense of equal possibilities to each and all of the voters.* However, it may be presumed that some qualified majority rules tend to put all of the voters in a position of a fair equilibrium, while minority rules, simple majority rules, highly qualified majority rules, and finally unanimity rules inevitably result in disequilibrium for the voters concerned.

This conclusion reminds us of some insurmountable differences which we must assume exist between the process of voting and that of trading in the market under conditions of competition.

Political competition appears to be much more restricted by its very nature than economic competition, particularly if the rules of the political game tend to create and maintain disequilibria rather than work in the opposite direction.

We must conclude that there is little sense in praising the simple majority rule as the best possible rule for the political game. There is much more sense in adopting several kinds of rules according to the ends we want to reach, e.g., adopting qualified majority rules when the issues at stake are rather important for each member of the community, or adopting the unanimity rule when the issue is absolutely vital for each of them. I believe almost all of these points have been brilliantly stressed in the recent analyses based on the economic approach.

But we must bear in mind that none of the rules adopted or adoptable in political decisions can produce a situation which is really similar to that of the market under conditions of competition. No vote trading could be sufficient to put each individual in the same situation as the operators who freely buy and sell goods and services in a competitive market.

When we consider law as legislation it can be clearly shown that the law and the market can in no way be considered similar from the point of view of the individual and his decisions.

In fact, the market process and the legislative process are inescapably at variance. While the market allows individuals to make free choices provided only that they are prepared to pay for them, legislation does not allow this.

What we should now ask and try to answer is: Can we make a more successful comparison between the market and *nonlegislative* forms of law?

INDEX

The typeface for the text of this book is *Baskerville*. Its creator, John Baskerville (1706–1775), broke with tradition to reflect in his type the rounder, yet more sharply cut lettering of eighteenth-century stone inscriptions and copy books. The type foreshadows modern design in such novel characterisitcs as the increase in contrast between thick and thin strokes and the shifting of stress from the diagonal to the vertical strokes. Realizing that his new style of letter would be most effective if cleanly printed on smooth paper with genuinely black ink, he built his own presses, developed a method of hot-pressing the printed sheet to a smooth, glossy finish, and experimented with special inks. However, Baskerville did not enter into general commercial use in England until 1923.

Editorial services and index by Custom Editorial
Productions, Inc., Cincinnati, Ohio
Book design by Hermann Strohbach, New York, New York
Typography by Shepard Poorman Communications Corporation,
Indianapolis, Indiana
Printed and bound by Worzalla Publishing Company
Stevens Point, Wisconsin